IVY
LEAGUE
AUTUMNS

IVY

LEAGUE

AUTUMNS

AN ILLUSTRATED HISTORY OF COLLEGE
FOOTBALL'S GRAND OLD RIVALRIES

RICHARD GOLDSTEIN

ST. MARTIN'S PRESS ⋈ NEW YORK

Book design by Gretchen Achilles

Library of Congress Cataloging-in-Publication Data

Goldstein, Richard.
    Ivy League autumns: an illustrated history of college football's grand old rivalries / by Richard Goldstein
       p. cm.
    Includes bibliographical references and index.
    ISBN 0-312-14629-9
    1. Ivy League (Football conference)—History. I. Title
GV958.5.I9G65 1996
796.332'63'0974—dc20   96-19586
                                                           CIP

First Edition: September 1996

10 9 8 7 6 5 4 3 2 1

FOR NANCY

CONTENTS

ACKNOWLEDGMENTS

I'M GRATEFUL TO the men of Ivy football who provided recollections of Saturdays past. For some, there are even memories of distant New Year's Days when the Ivies ruled the Rose Bowl.

A special word of thanks to Herster Barres, Ralph Horween (at age 99, he could still see himself scrambling in crimson for a blocked kick at Pasadena on January 1, 1920), Levi Jackson, Ken Keuffel, Gil Lea, Walt Matuszak, Anthony (Skip) Minisi, Cliff Montgomery, Endicott (Chub) Peabody, Ernie Ransome, Jerry Roscoe, Gene Rossides, George Savitsky, Homer Smith, and Charlie Yeager.

For making their schools' photo files and football archives available, a thank-you to Chris Humm of Brown, Cheryl Hart of Centre College, Todd Kennedy of Columbia, Dave Wohlhueter and Elli Harkness of Cornell, Kathy Slattery of Dartmouth, John Veneziano and Mike Jackman of Harvard, Chuck Yrigoyen of the Ivy League office, Michael Yates of Massachusetts Institute of Technology, Gail Zachary of Penn, Jerry Price of Princeton, and Steve Conn and Geoff Zonder of Yale.

I appreciate the enthusiasm and backing of my editor, Shawn Coyne of St. Martin's Press, a Harvard man who cheerfully allowed me to recall even some great days for Yale.

Once again, Stuart Krichevsky very ably represented me.

My wife, Nancy, was there with her love and support on every third-and-long.

INTRODUCTION

THE GENTLEMAN FROM Missouri felt compelled to bring a matter of some delicacy to the attention of his fellow senators.

The Foreign Relations Committee was considering the nomination of Archibald MacLeish to be an assistant secretary of state one day during the World War II years when Senator Bennett Champ Clark interrupted the proceedings.

Mr. Clark thumbed through a small book whose contents were far afield from the world of power politics—a collection of poetry. Moreover, the theme was love. Its author, the nominee at the witness table.

The senator wished to know whether someone inclined to pen such sentimentality possessed the fortitude for tough decisions in a turbulent world.

MacLeish would recall how "I could think of no wholly responsive answer." Just then, Senator A. B. (Happy) Chandler of Kentucky came to his rescue.

"I also have a question for Mr. MacLeish if the senator should yield. I should like to ask him if he did not play football at Yale."

"The chairman rose," remembered Archibald MacLeish—once a "substitute on a series of Yale teams which never beat Harvard" when he wasn't founding a campus literary society with Thornton Wilder—and "that, so far as I am aware, was all the answer Bennett Champ Clark of Missouri ever got."

The nominee was confirmed.

The neo-Gothic towers of Yale conjure up images of an intellectual and cultural elite. Yet the Yalies and their brethren of the Ivy League pioneered the most rugged of American team sports. They have been wallowing in the football muds since the presidency of U. S. Grant.

On a November Saturday in 1869, Princeton and Rutgers played the first football game (it was really more like soccer). The following autumn, Columbia fielded a team, and in 1875 the game that would become The Game was born when Harvard faced Yale on a racetrack oval in New Haven.

An 1870s Yale man named Walter Camp essentially invented college football, devising most of its major elements with the exception of instant replay. Yale would dominate the nineteenth-century game, its reputation so revered that Gilbert Patten, the creator of Frank Merriwell, had his dime-store-novel hero perform his derring-do in Eli blue and white.

The eight Ivy schools—Brown, Columbia, Cornell, Dartmouth, Harvard, Penn, Princeton, and Yale—supplied the all-Americans of football's formative years and their alumni spread the game's gospel by filling coaching posts throughout America.

When the twentieth century was young, the sports pages hailed the Ivy athletes from old-stock America: the likes of Hobart Amory Hare Baker—Princeton's version of Frank Merriwell—a gentleman-sportsman who never once punctuated a touchdown run with an end zone tango.

By the 1920s, the Ivy football teams were drawing huge crowds and basking in the sportswriters' hyperbole. Two years before Grantland Rice glanced into a blue-gray October sky and discerned "The Four Horsemen" of Notre Dame, he had anointed Princeton's unbeaten squad of 1922 as "The Team of Destiny."

The Depression years were brightened on Morningside Heights when Columbia rose up to shut out Stanford in the 1934 Rose Bowl. And the Lions weren't the first Ivy team to play in Pasadena on New Year's Day. Brown, Penn, and Harvard had been there before.

While the schools of the Eastern establishment have a long and proud football history, the "Ivy" designation is not so hoary. It dates back only to the late 1930s, when Cas Adams of the *New York Herald Tribune*, much taken with the ivy climbing the walls at those stone campus temples, bestowed the sobriquet.

And the Ivy League is one of the younger athletic conferences. Chagrined by scandals plaguing big-time college sports, the presidents of the Ivy schools moved in the early 1950s to bring their athletic programs wholly under academic control. Their vehicle was a formal conference—celebrating its 40th anniversary this autumn—with round-robin football competition that scrapped any lingering ambitions for a Top 20 ranking. (The official name of the Ivy League happens to be the Council of Ivy Group Presidents.)

Ivy students had, at any rate, traveled a considerable emotional distance from the days when a Princeton player could tell his teammates "A Team That Won't Be Beat Can't Be Beat" and expect to be taken seriously. (John Prentiss Poe Jr., a turn-of-the-century descendant of an even more renowned poet, is credited with that inspirational credo.)

By the 1950s, a defeat by an ancient rival no longer brought despair. The *Harvard Crimson*, for instance, seemed almost mirthful in previewing a matchup with an unbeaten 1950 Princeton team featuring the spectacular tailback Dick Kazmaier and a pair of talented platoons. "Two powerful elevens will take the field in Princeton's Palmer Stadium this afternoon," the newspaper observed. "In a few minutes they will be joined by Harvard's football players."

Around that time, students in Harvard's so-called cheering section greeted a succession of quick Yale touchdowns with a banner declaring "Who Gives a Damn?"

While Ivy teams of the nineteenth century exemplified "muscular Christianity"—in the vernacular of the age—today they co-exist uneasily with football's bluster.

As D. Keith Mano, a writer and longtime Columbia football fanatic, has observed: "There is the peculiar Ivy attitude toward football: half bitter, ancient partisan zeal, half ironic distance. No fan at Penn's Franklin Field would wear hogsnout headgear or yell, 'Hook 'em Quaker.' Your typical Ivy band won't play a tribute to Marvin Hamlisch while blinded by thigh glare from six semi-nude baton flippers. One Columbia band member plays the rigatoni box; another (I think) plays his apartment radiator."

Only in the Ivy League could a mascot suffer the indignity befalling the furry Brown undergrad who arrived at Yale Bowl a few autumns ago dressed in his Bruno the Bear ensemble. A turnstile attendant refused to let Bruno pass because he didn't have a ticket.

But the Ivy football players still go at it hard each Saturday, and some even make the pros. (Not without twin burdens. As Pat McInally, a star receiver at Harvard in the 1970s, remarked after concluding a career with the Cincinnati Bengals: "At Harvard they labeled me a jock. When I went to the pros, they considered me an intellectual.")

Amid de-emphasis, traditions endure—the waving of a tattered little crimson flag held aloft by some honored Harvard alumnus at every Yale game since the 1880s; the white handkerchiefs when the Elis prevail at Yale Bowl; the Dartmouth bonfire.

The Ivy League, meanwhile, is very much attuned to the new age of marketing. In the fall of 1995, Yale unveiled a sleek logo starring Handsome Dan the bulldog. Designed by Starter, a New Haven–based national marketer of licensed sports apparel, it featured stripes from the back of the dog's head giving the effect of motion. It was a look that, in the words of the Elis' athletic director, Tom Beckett, underlined how Yale was "an exciting place to be." More pointedly, Wayne Dean, the director of marketing for Yale athletics, observed how "Yale, like any athletic department, is looking for new streams of revenue."

Eight decades after a Yalie named Cole Porter saluted the football team with his "Bulldog, Bulldog, Bow, Wow, Wow," the venerable Ivy League is determined to be modern. As Cole Porter did not put it—everything old is new again.

PART

ONE

"YOU YOUNG MEN WILL COME TO NO CHRISTIAN END"

LONG BEFORE "Monday Night Football," there was "Bloody Monday."

As far back as the 1820s, the meadows at Cambridge and New Haven were scenes of semi-organized mayhem for college men. On the first Monday of the school term at Harvard and Yale, the sophomores would battle the freshmen in games that ostensibly involved kicking a round canvas ball, but seemed mostly directed at kicking the opponent.

The dubious joys of this autumnal rite eventually gained notoriety beyond the campuses. By the 1850s, New York newspapers became curious enough to dispatch correspondents.

A reporter at one Bloody Monday match had quite a tale for his readers:

"The history of this annual contest, if told without a shade of exaggeration, would make nearly the same impression on the public mind as a Spanish bull-fight. The contending classes prepared for the game in the spirit of the ring. Boys and young men...knocked each other down, tore off the clothing, and, after the contest was over, eyes were bunged, faces blackened and bloody, shirts and coats torn to rags and shins broken."

The Yalies' intramural afternoon of kicking, pushing, and charging had been dubbed "one-old-cat," then came to be called the "annual rush."

The Yale administration called it barbaric—and in 1857 it abolished the Monday bashing. Harvard's faculty banned the bloody game in 1860.

Soon, the sons of America's elite would face far tougher tests of their emerging manhood, leaving behind the ball fields and classrooms for the battlefields of Gettysburg, Antietam, and Shiloh.

When soldiers had free moments in their Civil War encampments, they would sometimes kick around a ball. But by the time the college men came back to the campuses, they presumably had seen enough of violence—at least there would be no resumption of Bloody Monday.

The formal arrival of what would come to be college football was, however, not far off.

On the morning of Saturday, November 6, 1869, a group of young men from Princeton journeyed on a branch-line railroad to the nearby college town of New Brunswick. The contingent received an enthusiastic greeting from the Rutgers student body, and then a bit of sightseeing was at hand. The hosts took the visitors on a quick trip around town—broken up by a cultural timeout at a billiards parlor—and then everyone sat down for lunch.

Finally came the business at hand. At three o'clock, on a chilly, windy afternoon, some 25 students from each school assembled at a commons between College Avenue and Sicard Street. They were to play a game that would give Rutgers a chance to restore lost honor.

A Rutgers student named William Leggett had challenged Princeton to a series of three games, evidently seeking belated vengeance for Rutgers's 40–2 loss to Princeton in a baseball game back on May 2, 1866.

What was played this day resembled soccer, but tradition would stamp the afternoon's affair as the first college football game.

The idea was to drive a round ball through goalposts set 25 feet apart (with no crossbar) at opposite ends of a field that measured more than 100 yards long and about 60 yards wide. The ball could be advanced by kicking, dribbling, or batting it with the hands while it was in the air—running with it or throwing it was forbidden. There was no time limit—the first team to score six goals would be the winner.

Some 100 spectators gathered, perching atop a fence, stretching out on the sidelines, or watching from buckboard seats (evidently the first luxury boxes). The players cast formality aside when they lined up, draping their jackets, vests, and hats on the fence. The only semblance of a uniform belonged to Rutgers, its players wearing red bandannas tied like turbans.

Princeton's Class of 1869 would adopt orange as its colors in honor of William of Orange, Prince of the House of Nassau, for whom the school's first building, Nassau Hall, was named. But on this day, the Princeton players settled for romping in their street clothes.

The Princeton rooters did provide some color with the college "yell," a variation of the chants voiced by New York City's Seventh Regiment when it marched through Princeton en route to Washington during the Civil War. Eventually known as the "locomotive" cheer, since its cadence resembled that of a steam train starting to move, it would develop into "Rah, Rah, Rah—Tiger, Tiger, Tiger—Sis, Boom, Bah—Princeton."

Princeton's players took up the yell during the Rutgers match, evidently hoping to intimidate their opponents. But the bellowing merely left the Princeton side out of breath.

Princeton and Rutgers competing on November 6, 1869, at New Brunswick, New Jersey, in an artist's rendition of the first college football game—actually a match resembling soccer. (PRINCETON UNIVERSITY)

The game was less than five minutes old when Rutgers got the first goal, scored after a series of short, dribbling kicks. Then Princeton turned to brawn to combat the Rutgers finesse. A husky blond Princetonian named Jacob Michael—better known as Big Mike—began to charge into the Rutgers team, frightening smaller players and creating loose balls.

With Rutgers leading by 4 goals to 2, college football had its first smashup. As Big Mike and Rutgers's George Large pursued a ball kicked toward the sideline, they collided, sending the fence crashing down, the fans with it. But nobody was injured and the game continued.

Then came a near blunder. A Rutgers player, whose name has escaped into the mists of history, headed toward his own goalposts and was about to score a goal that would be credited to Princeton. A teammate managed, however, to block his kick.

That apparently sent the whole Rutgers team into a frazzle because Princeton came back with a pair of goals to tie things. Then Rutgers's Leggett—the man who had handed out the invitations—proved a rude host. He noticed that the Princeton players, taller than the Rutgers men, were reaching above them to bat the ball to each other. So he told his teammates to kick the ball along the ground. The strategy worked. Rutgers scored another two goals and emerged with a 6–4 victory.

The following Saturday, the schools met again, this time on Conover's Field at Princeton. The home field edge held up once more, Princeton evening matters with an 8–0 victory.

Among the spectators was a Princeton professor's son named Henry Duffield. Long afterward, he would recall the frustration faced by the players at football's dawn:

"The ball was not an oval but was supposed to be completely round. It never was, though—it was too hard to blow up right.

The game was stopped several times that day while the teams called for a little key from the sidelines. They used it to unlock the small nozzle which was tucked into the ball, and then took turns blowing it up. The last man generally got tired and they put it back in play somewhat lopsided."

The third game of the challenge series was never played. College football was only a week old, but a cry for "de-emphasis" was already being voiced. Faculty members canceled the finale, complaining that the games were taking too much time from studies.

Legend has it that a Rutgers professor, pedaling his bicycle on the fringes of the playing field during that first game, momentarily silenced the crowd by pointing his umbrella toward the frivolity and shouting, "You young men will come to no Christian end."

But this latter-day Nostradamus was sorely mistaken. Rutgers's William Leggett became a clergyman in the Dutch Reformed Church. William Gummere, the Princeton captain, would serve as chief justice of the New Jersey Supreme Court for three decades. Jacob Michael, Princeton's "Big Mike," would become dean of faculty at the University of Maryland, and George Large, the Rutgers player who crashed into the fence with him, would be elected as a New Jersey state senator.

Princeton and Rutgers were back at it in 1870 when Princeton, playing at home, won a belated third game by 6 goals to 2.

Rutgers introduced Columbia to football (still, basically soccer) that autumn and came away with a 6-goals-to-3 victory.

Stuyvesant Fish, Columbia's first football captain, leader of the 1870 team.
(COLUMBIA UNIVERSITY)

Columbia hadn't inaugurated its football program with distinction, but its captain carried a noteworthy name. He was Stuyvesant Fish, a son of the original Hamilton Fish, a Columbia grad (Class of 1827) who served as a United States congressman, senator, New York governor, and secretary of state.

Stuyvesant's breeding did not spawn a genteel style on the field, to hear a Rutgers player named James Van Rensselaer Weston tell it years later:

"While rolling and prostrate on the ground I saw Stuyvesant Fish, the Columbia giant, trying to jump over me. He landed with his No. 14's just grazing my cheek. As he was nearly as large and raw-boned as Abe Lincoln, I had a narrow escape."

(There would be two schools of Fishes so far as the Ivies went. Stuyvesant's uncle Petrus; his brother Hamilton, a congressman and speaker of the New York State Assembly; another brother, Nicholas, and Nicholas's son, the third Hamilton Fish, were also Columbia men. But the fourth Hamilton Fish would be an all-America tackle for Harvard in 1908 and 1909 before turning to a political career in which he bedeviled his fellow Harvard alumnus Franklin D. Roosevelt.)

Everybody took a break from football in 1871, but in November 1872, Yale issued a challenge to Columbia and came away with a 3-goals-to-0 victory at the Hamilton Park racetrack oval in New Haven. Columbia played Rutgers twice, a scoreless tie and then a 7–5 defeat.

In October 1873, things began to get organized. A convention was held at New York City's Fifth Avenue Hotel out of which sprang the Intercollegiate Football Association, comprising Yale, Columbia, Princeton, and Rutgers.

Harvard had also been invited but stayed away. A different sort of football was stirring in Cambridge, and Harvard did not want to be enmeshed in soccer-style competition. Known as "the Boston game," and introduced by students who had played it in prep school, the Harvard version resembled English rugby—a player could run with the ball or throw it, and tackling was allowed.

So the four members of the new association went ahead with their soccer-accented football in the fall of 1873 without Harvard. The first international game was played that season, Yale scoring a 2–1 victory over England's Eton Players team.

But Harvard soon found an opponent for its rugby-style game. McGill University of Montreal issued a challenge, and the schools met at Jarvis Field in Cambridge on May 14 and 15, 1874, blending somewhat different rules. Harvard won the first match by 3–0 and the second one ended in a scoreless tie. The following autumn they played in Montreal, and Harvard was victorious again, this time by 10–0.

In the fall of 1969, college football would celebrate its formal centennial, and the Princeton-Rutgers "first game" would be reenacted before the schools met in their season opener. But when the 1874 season got under way, Harvard would claim that the real centennial year had arrived, maintaining that its games with McGill marked the true birth of American college football.

There's merit in the argument. For the four schools who started out playing soccer style would soon come around to Harvard's version, which in turn evolved into today's game.

While Harvard was snubbing the rest of the minuscule college football world, the game stirred in upstate New York. The boys at Cornell had taken up the sport, and just about everybody wanted to join in. One day in 1870, eighty freshmen battled eighty sophomores all afternoon, resting only when the referee called timeout to resuscitate a continually deflating football. In October, an intramural game was played for the benefit of Thomas Hughes, a visiting member of the British Parliament.

It was a case of mass confusion, so far as the Britisher could fathom.

"All who cared to play collected into two irregular crowds, unorganized and leaderless, and stood facing one another. Most, but not all, of the players took their coats off. Then a big, oddly-shaped ball arrived, somebody started it with a kick-off, and away went both sides in chase, wildly jostling one another, kicking, catching, throwing, or hitting the ball, according to fancy, all thoughts more bent, seemingly, upon the pure delight of the struggle than upon any particular goal.

"'Are there any goals, and if so, where?' we asked, toiling after the ball, which appeared to be visiting all sides of the field with strict impartiality and equal satisfaction to the players.

"'Oh, yes, anywhere between those trees'—two great elms, standing perhaps thirty feet apart. Occasionally the ball got wedged in a dense 'scrummage' of the contending parties, and while some went in boldly to extricate it, many more would stand round looking on and naïvely clap their hands for joy."

Joining the students in the fun that day was Cornell's vice president, William Russel. He may have loved the game, but his boss—Cornell President Andrew D. White—regarded football as a lot of nonsense. In 1873, when Cornell players sought permission to go to Cleveland for a game with the University of Michigan, White turned them down. "I will not permit 30 men to travel 400 miles to agitate a bag of wind," he huffed.

Cornell went its own way in the 1870s and 1880s, combining soccer, rugby, and a free-for-all. Since no other school could fathom this version of football, it was confined to intramurals. The first intercollegiate game for Cornell would not come until 1887, when it was beaten, 24–10, by Union College at Ithaca.

By the mid-1870s, there was talk of a game between Harvard and Yale, which had faced each other in rowing as far back as 1852 and already had a rivalry going in baseball. But a major problem remained: whose rules would they play by?

Delegates from the schools met at Springfield, Massachusetts, on October 16, 1875, and came away with something called "concessionary" rules—a blending of their contrasting styles. But Harvard really won the argument. When the teams met on Saturday, November 13, at New Haven, they would be playing mostly by rugby-like regulations.

The Harvard squad, accompanied by 150 fellow students, was met at the New Haven train station by the Yalies, who showed their opponents the campus, highlighted by a visit to the new boathouse.

The game that would be known as The Game got under way at Hamilton Park at 2:30 P.M. on a slightly overcast, windless day, the 2,000 spectators paying 50 cents apiece. The Yale players wore dark trousers, blue shirts, and yellow caps. Harvard's men

The Harvard team of 1875, winner of the first Harvard-Yale game by 4 goals to 0.
(HARVARD UNIVERSITY)

chose crimson shirts and stockings, their more colorful attire supposedly making it easier to pick out a teammate in the mob of players.

The fans who came down from Cambridge displayed splendid sportsmanship, according to *The Crimson* newspaper, which told how "the Harvard students formed in a group and encouraged the players, lavishing their applause on Yale or Harvard, as the occasion required it."

Bewildered by having to play mainly under Harvard's rules, Yale got off to a dismal start. The *New Haven Register* would note how "the first two goals were scored by Harvard with an ease almost ludicrous, the Yale men, from their utter ignorance of the game, doing very little, except to look on."

Tossing the ball skillfully while Yale relied on a kicking game that did little good under the rugby-like rules, Harvard went on to a 4-goals-to-0 victory.

Afterward, everybody gathered for a festive supper, followed by singing in the college yard. But later that evening, when some Harvard men roamed beyond the Yale campus, things got out of hand. Seven Harvard students were arrested for "hooting and singing in the public streets." They were each fined $5.29.

Harvard's effective use of the rugby style that day bolstered its case for how football should be played. Two observers from Princeton were so impressed that the school decided to switch from the soccer to the rugby style, and soon it proposed another rules convention.

Representatives of Harvard, Yale, Princeton, and Columbia met at Springfield on November 26, 1876, to form a second Intercollegiate Football Association. This time they adopted a format similar to that of rugby, and the shape of college football was emerging.

The University of Pennsylvania made its football debut that fall, facing Princeton at the Germantown Cricket Club in Philadelphia on November 11. The Princeton team needed an incentive to bother with the fledgling Penn squad. It came via Penn's payment of $50 in traveling expenses.

Penn held Princeton scoreless for 47 minutes, but lost by 6 goals to 0. Two weeks later, Penn visited Princeton and fell by the same score, but was hardly vexed.

"Our reception by the Princeton men was simply royal," Penn's *University Magazine* reported. "They insisted on our taking of a delightful lunch some time before the

Brown's first team, the 1878 squad, which lost to Amherst in its only game of the season. (BROWN UNIVERSITY)

game and after it invited us to a supper that sent delight to every heart."

Brown began play in 1878, losing at Amherst by 4 goals to 0 in its only game of the season, and Dartmouth got under way in 1881 with a victory and then a tie against Amherst.

Although Harvard and its rugby-like style sent college football on the road it would follow, Yale emerged as the game's most influential force. That was largely because of one man—a New Haven native, or "townie," named Walter Camp.

The son of a school principal, Camp prepped at Hopkins Grammar School and enrolled in Yale as a 17-year-old in 1876. Standing 6 feet tall and weighing 157 pounds, he was a sports whirlwind. He joined the baseball team and was said to have been one of the first curveballers. He ran hurdles, rowed, swam, and played tennis.

But his heart was in football. He was swift, strong, a long-distance punter, and a fine placekicker and dropkicker.

Camp made the Yale team as a freshman halfback, and in his seven years as a player (he remained on the varsity during an abortive stint in medical school) Yale emerged as the nation's first football power, winning 30 games, tying 6, and losing only once.

In the game's early years, there were no full-time, paid coaches—the captain took charge. Serving as Yale's captain for three seasons, Camp held strategy sessions at his room in Durfee Hall and became something of an autocrat—a stickler for discipline.

He may also have been a sore loser, blaming shenanigans by four upperclassmen for the only losing game he played in, a 1–0 defeat by Princeton at Hoboken, New Jersey, in 1878. "The Blue went back to New Haven with a very salutary lesson on the evil of neglecting the laws of training," he remarked.

Camp would go on to coach at Yale, but would have an impact far beyond New Haven—he became the game's foremost rule-maker, the man who essentially invented college football.

The influence of Camp and the dominance of the Yale teams in football's first decades lent a special aura to the school.

Many years later, Harry Mehre, the coach at Georgia, would regard Yale as sacrosanct, remarking how "I would rather beat any team in the country than Yale. For me and most of us, Yale means American football."

Knute Rockne, asked once to reveal where his famous Notre Dame "shift" came from, responded: "Where everything else in football came from. Yale."

In 1878, still in his teens, Camp attended a rules meeting at Springfield, and from then until his death in 1925 he was a member of every rules committee, "the father of American football."

Soon everybody would be playing by the same regulations, thanks to the leadership of Camp.

Yale, which had been pushing for 11 players as the required lineup ever since it faced Eton, which used that number, eventually got its wish. In 1880, at Camp's urging, the alignment was set as seven linemen, a quarterback, two halfbacks, and a fullback.

(After winning its second matchup against Harvard, Yale had refused to play the Crimson in 1877 because of an argument over manpower—Yale wanted 11 to a side while Harvard insisted on its customary 15.)

Camp also altered the way the football was put into play, replacing the rugby scrum with the center snap in 1880.

The 1882 season brought another major change. Up to then, a team could hold the football until it punted to gain field advantage or fumbled it away.

That brought boring fiascos like the Princeton-Yale game of 1881, in which Princeton kept the ball without scoring for the entire first half, then Yale did likewise in the second half.

Camp proposed a solution. Now, if a team did not advance the ball 5 yards or lose 10 yards in three plays, it would lose possession. That was the beginning of the "downs" system, and it changed the look of the field as well. White lines were painted to denote 5-yard intervals, giving rise to the term "gridiron." (Ten yards would be required for a first down beginning in 1906, and teams would get four downs rather than three starting in 1912.)

Camp also pioneered audible signal-calling and developed a point-scoring system to take the place of "goals scored" representing kicks between the goalposts. Carrying the ball over the opponent's goal line for a touchdown would become the prime object as the kicking game began to assume lesser importance.

But Camp wasn't at the scene of every football first. Harvard staked a claim, too.

When it played Tufts in June 1875, the players wore white shirts and pants with crimson trimming and hose, supposedly the first football garb. There were no helmets in the early days—long hair served as the only protection for the scalp.

By 1877, Princeton was sporting what were probably the first full uniforms—black jerseys with an orange P, a tight canvas jacket, black knee pants, and stockings. (The orange stripes, bringing the Tiger nickname, came along in 1880.) The canvas jackets, called smo cks to honor their designer, a Princeton football player named L. P. Smock, had a practical value. Opposing players couldn't hang on to them to bring a Princeton man down. Harvard sharply protested use of the jackets when it met Princeton for the first time in 1877, and play was stopped for a while to argue the point. But the Crimson were soothed by the time the afternoon ended since they won the game.

In 1878, Princeton showed off its uniforms before college football's first significant crowd, some 4,000 spectators turning up at Hoboken in a rainstorm for that stunning triumph over Yale that sent Camp to his only defeat as a player. The teams shelled out the exorbitant sum of $300 to rent the field.

The fall of 1881 saw the beginning of intersectional play when Michigan visited Harvard, Yale, and Princeton—eventually known as the Big Three—and lost to all of them.

But the biggest matchups of the nineteenth century were the annual Yale-

Yale and Princeton groping their way to a scoreless tie at the St. George's Cricket Grounds in Hoboken, New Jersey, on November 27, 1879. (YALE UNIVERSITY)

Princeton games, grand social occasions as well as battles between powerful teams.

The 1885 game at New Haven was especially memorable.

The teams came in with hard feelings, a dispute between them in 1884 having caused Referee William Appleton of Harvard—the sole official—to declare that matchup "no game."

His decision evidently pleased no one, because he was not invited back in 1885. After a long deadlock, the teams agreed to replace him with none other than Walter Camp. He was a Yale man, but his integrity was unquestioned.

Yale may, in fact, have regretted the selection of Camp since he did nothing to favor his alma mater. In the first half, Yale's Harry Beecher returned a punt 65 yards for

an apparent touchdown, but Camp said it was no score—Beecher had stepped out of bounds.

Yale's George Watkinson kicked a field goal—then worth 5 points—to give the Elis a 5–0 lead, and the score stayed that way until only a few minutes remained. Then came one of the most celebrated plays of the nineteenth century.

Yale had kept the ball for much of the second half and could have tried to run out the clock. But the Yale captain, Frank Peters, realizing that the game had become exceedingly dull, went over to the sidelines and asked Ray Tompkins, one of the coaches, if the squad could consider kicking the ball away. "Oh, kick it and have some fun," Tompkins supposedly said.

Watkinson sent a punt downfield, and Henry Lamar—better known as "Tillie"—grabbed it on the bound at his 15-yard line after another Princeton back had muffed it. Lamar headed down the left sideline. Watkinson and Beecher converged on him but collided with each other, and Lamar raced between them and into the Yale end zone. Yale demanded that the score be nullified, claiming that Lamar had stepped out of bounds in the encounter with Beecher and Watkinson. But Camp said he had not, his second ruling against Yale on a sideline play.

Lamar's score made it Yale 5, Princeton 4, a touchdown counting for 4 points. While the Princeton players celebrated, their quarterback, Dick Hodge, practiced holding the ball for a dropkick that would be worth a game-winning 2 points. When the excitement died down, he kicked the ball through the uprights. Captain Peters of Yale threw himself to the ground in anguish as Princeton emerged with a 6–5 victory.

But Yale, having suffered its first loss since 1878, would pick itself right back up. A Yale team would not lose another game until a defeat by Princeton in 1889's final game. By the time that season arrived, college football had undergone vast and controversial changes that would eventually threaten its very existence.

Harvard students arriving in style for an 1887 game. (HARVARD UNIVERSITY)

"BLOODBATH AT HAMPDEN PARK"

THE PARISHIONERS AT Brooklyn's Plymouth Church on the Heights were presumably expecting a traditional sermon when they gathered one Sunday in the late autumn of 1883.

But the Reverend Henry Ward Beecher—one of the nation's most prominent clergymen—would depart from the Bible that particular morning in order to deliver a sports update.

Beecher described watching Yale beat Princeton, 6–0, on a muddy Polo Grounds field the afternoon before. Then he tempered the passion of a sports partisan with his admiration for strength of character.

"I always did hate Princeton, but I took notice there was not a coward on either side, although I thank God that Yale beat [them]," Beecher told his flock.

The football played by Yale, Princeton, and their fellow Ivy-to-be schools was viewed by society's best elements as a sterling example of manliness, of "muscular Christianity" in the nineteenth-century vernacular. Opinion-makers applauded the brawn—the renewal of heroic virtues once exemplified by the Civil War soldier—that complemented the brains at the nation's elite colleges.

The sport was championed by artists and by writers.

Frederic Remington, remembered today for his depictions of cowboys on the Great Plains, illustrated the rugged Eastern college football for *Harper's* magazine. He knew whereof he drew, having played for Yale in 1879 and 1880, once dipping his jersey in blood at a New Haven slaughterhouse before a Harvard game to appear "more businesslike."

The renowned war correspondent Richard Harding Davis, who had played football at Lehigh, wrote of the sport's glorious combat.

On Thanksgiving Day 1893, Remington and Davis, respectively managing editor and a roving reporter for *Harper's*, teamed up for illustrated coverage of the Yale-Williams game.

Davis didn't have much drama to work with since Yale romped by 82–0, but he provided a vivid account of the rumble-and-tumble football players of the era.

"They all limped. The majority of them I discovered, when it was time to rub them down, were only held together by yards of rubber bandages. They were covered with porous plasters and sticking-plasters, and they were painted in fine stencil-like effects with iodine, and the bodies of most of them resembled envelopes that have passed through the Dead-letter Office, and have been stamped and canceled and crossed and recrossed with directions.

"There is nothing so marvelous in surgery as the rapidity with which a Yale football player can recover from breakages and sprains that would send any other man to bed for a month."

The football of the late 1880s and 1890s was very different from the game that Walter Camp had fashioned. In good part, that was because of Camp himself.

The game played by his beloved Yale had been a wide-open affair, the linemen spaced far apart from each other, and the backs spread out as well, ready to receive long lateral passes when they weren't running with the ball.

Bringing down an open-field runner was no easy task. So when the rule-makers gathered for their annual convention in March 1888, Camp proposed yet another wrinkle, this one aimed at giving a break to the defense. Up to then, a player could be tackled only at the waist or above. Now Camp suggested letting tacklers go as low as the knees.

The change was adopted—but it worked only too well. Even the most elusive runners could no longer gain consistent yardage in the open field.

So the coaches devised new methods of attack. The offensive line was contracted, the linemen now standing shoulder to shoulder. The backs were drawn in and placed close behind them. Instead of open-field running, there would be a series of maneuvers aimed at overwhelming, rather than outmaneuvering, the defense. Out of this came Harvard's flying wedge, a variation on the V wedge first developed by Princeton, and other power formations. And out of that came numerous deaths, broken bones, and calls for reforming or even abolishing the game.

The autumn of 1888—when the new tackling rules went into effect—saw the emergence of an extraordinary Yale team as Walter Camp became the school's first formal (though unpaid) coach. Actually, he was co-coach. On weekdays he worked for the New Haven Clock Company, so his new wife, Alice Graham Sumner, the sister of the prominent Yale economics and sociology professor William Graham Sumner, attended practices, taking notes as she roamed the sideline.

Pudge Heffelfinger of Yale, considered by many the greatest guard in college football history. (YALE UNIVERSITY)

The formula worked. Yale went 13-0 and outscored its opponents by 698 to 0.

The best-remembered player from that team was a man with a wonderful football name—Pudge Heffelfinger.

His real first name was William, but he'd picked up the nickname while playing sandlot football in Minneapolis at age 15. Pudge wasn't really pudgy. He was large for the players of that era—his teammates averaged about 170 pounds—but even in his senior year he weighed only 200.

Playing left guard, Heffelfinger was extremely quick, powerful, intelligent, and fearless. He pounced on opponents while playing defense and led the line charge on offense, springing from a semi-erect stance.

He would still be flinging his body around decades later. In 1922, at the age of 54, Heffelfinger played in a charity game at Columbus between Ohio State grads and a team of former collegians from around the country. At age 65, he saw action in a game at Minneapolis benefiting disabled World War I veterans.

Heffelfinger's specialty was moving to the right, then turning in to lead interference for a Tennessean named Thomas (Bum) McClung, Yale's star halfback.

McClung ran with an elusive hip-shift scissors stride and became a master at using the straight-arm. He would later be successful in public life as well, serving as treasurer of the United States.

In the middle of Yale's 1888 line was William (Pa) Corbin, the captain, 24 years old but seemingly a football elder statesman, his long face and handlebar mustache lending an imposing aura.

The right guard was a tough guy named George Woodruff, a hammer thrower in track and field who broke Yale's strength-test records. And he looked the part. Born in Pennsylvania, he had been taken by his parents to Nebraska via covered wagon as a child, and when he arrived at New Haven he sported a coonskin cap.

At right end was a 27-year-old who had

Yale's 1888 team, which rolled to 13-0 and outscored its opponents by 698–0. In front row, *left to right*, **Thomas (Bum) McClung, William Wurtenberg, William (Pa) Corbin, the captain, and William Graves. In back row,** *left to right*, **Amos Alonzo Stagg, William Rhodes, George Woodruff, Pudge Heffelfinger, Charles Gill, Fred (Kid) Wallace, and William Bull.** (YALE UNIVERSITY)

started his football career late but would long outlast his contemporaries—Amos Alonzo Stagg, 157 pounds of grit.

Stagg had been an outstanding pitcher for Yale, then agreed to go out for football as well because the team was short of ends.

As Pa Corbin remembered him, "His legs were so short that he had to take about two strides to every one of Kid Wallace, the other end."

To develop stamina, Stagg ran two miles from the practice field after the day's workouts while his teammates returned in a horse-drawn omnibus.

He would do graduate work in Yale's divinity school while playing football but hardly turned the other cheek. In the after-

math of the 1889 game against Harvard, a woodcut caricature depicted Stagg delivering a stiff chop to the head. The caption read, "Stagg's Ministerial Uppercut."

After two seasons at Yale, Stagg took a coaching job at the International YMCA College in Springfield, Massachusetts. He went on to coach for 57 years, 40 of them at the University of Chicago, which he built into a national power.

The toughest challenge for Yale's 1888 team came in the season finale against undefeated Princeton. (The Elis may have been overconfident, having beaten Wesleyan by 105–0 the previous Saturday.) Yale completed an unbeaten, unscored-upon season with a 10–0 victory on two field-goal dropkicks by Billy Bull, the fullback, the first coming with blood streaming down his face from a head cut, the second from a sharp angle on the 37-yard line with a minute left in the game.

These talented players hardly needed a good-luck charm, but got one nonetheless in 1889 with the debut of the Yale bulldog. Handsome Dan I was purchased from a New Haven blacksmith for $65 by Andrew Graves, a football tackle and member of the Yale crew. The *Philadelphia Press* would report how "a favorite trick was to tell him to 'Speak to Harvard.' He would bark ferociously and work himself into physical contortions of rage never before dreamed of by a dog."

Yale came into the 1889 season-ender against Princeton unbeaten in 48 games and seeking its fourth straight undefeated season. But Heffelfinger and Handsome Dan couldn't do it all. Princeton, led by running back Knowlton (Snake) Ames, who would slither his way to 62 career touchdowns, sprang a 10–0 upset on a rain-swept Berkeley Oval in Manhattan.

Handsome Dan I patrolled the sidelines until his death in 1898. He would inspire future Yale teams from his place of honor at Payne Whitney Gymnasium, where he was stuffed and placed in a glass case.

On the next-to-last Saturday of the

The 1890 Harvard team, which went 11-0. The captain, Arthur Cumnock, an end on the first all-America squad the previous season, holds a football reading "Harvard 12, Yale 6," the Crimson's first victory over Yale since their inaugural game of 1875. (HARVARD UNIVERSITY)

Frederic Remington's oil painting of the Yale-Princeton game on Thanksgiving Day 1890 at Eastern Park in Brooklyn. (YALE UNIVERSITY)

1890 season, the Yale-Harvard game provided a matchup of unbeatens. Harvard's big star was lineman Marshall (Ma) Newell, 166 pounds of aggression on the field but evidently a sweetheart off it. (He supposedly got the nickname for "mothering" lonely freshmen.) But the man of the moment would be Harvard's unsung quarterback, Dudley Dean, who scored the clinching touchdown in the Crimson's 12–6 victory on a daring play. Lining up in the defensive secondary, Dean squeezed through the center of the Yale line, stole the ball from quarterback Frank Barbour, and raced 50 yards for a score.

Yale ended its season by walloping Princeton, 32–0, at Brooklyn's Eastern Park on Thanksgiving Day before a crowd of 25,000 as Bum McClung ran for four touchdowns.

By then the Yale-Princeton games had been moved off the campuses, rotating at New York area sites—the old Polo Grounds, Berkeley Oval just north of Central Park, Manhattan Field, or Eastern Park. Clearly, the affair was becoming big business.

Each year on the morning of the game a parade moved up Fifth Avenue past fine restaurants and department stores flying the schools' banners. Carriages carrying

Yale students and their dates were decorated in blue, the men wearing scarves and ties with their school colors, the women bedecked in violets, all chanting "Bulldog! Bulldog!" The Princeton carriages were trimmed in orange and black, the ladies wearing chrysanthemums and cheering for "Old Nassau" or letting loose with the "Siss Boom Bah" locomotive yell.

When the fans arrived at the field, it was time for the horseless-carriage version of a tailgate party. Restaurants and gourmet caterers provided large wicker baskets with luncheon delights, and there was plenty of liquid refreshment. After the game, there would be partying through the night.

The 1890 game at Eastern Park embodied the raucousness and color that made Princeton-Yale a premier rivalry of the nineteenth century.

The demand for tickets was so great that a portable grandstand was brought in from Philadelphia and reassembled. Several hours before the game got under way, some 2,000 fans were already in those seats. Then came a mini-disaster when the stands collapsed, sending the fans tumbling to the ground and injuring 50, several seriously.

An investigation by the Brooklyn Buildings Department found that stakes driven into soft ground had given way. But the newspapers charged that the stands were constructed with flimsy lumber. George Linton, a member of the Eastern Park management, had another view. He blamed "a crowd of Princeton enthusiasts who persisted in dancing and stomping on the seats to keep time with their unearthly yells."

(But management later offered cash settlements to the injured.)

Chaos reigned on the field as well. Several hundred people without tickets—many of them well-connected politicians—crowded the sidelines, blocking the view of paying fans. "The Brooklyn policemen were incompetent," reported the *New York Times*. "They stood around like so many dummies and made no effort to prevent the invasion of the imposters. They watched the game to the neglect of everything else."

Meanwhile, banners waved, horns blared, whistles shrieked, and the rival fans drowned each other out with school yells.

That evening the fun continued in Manhattan, Yale fans descending upon the Fifth Avenue Hotel while Princeton rooters crowded the Hoffman House. The Yale backers then collected on their bets, pocketing perhaps $50,000 in winnings.

Some 500 Yale students later marched up Broadway and mobbed the Casino Theatre, where Lillian Russell was starring in the opera *Poor Jonathan*. They sang their school songs as they took their seats, blasted away on tin horns and hung blue banners from the theater boxes.

During a tender love scene, one Yale man shouted to the embracing couple to "Break away." Miss Russell protested that she could not continue amid the heckling. That simply brought more horn-blowing and another round of Yale school yells, but the show went on. A bit later, the students made amends by tossing bouquets to Miss Russell, who scooped them up to another round of cheers.

In 1891, Yale produced another team

that was unbeaten and unscored-upon, this time rolling up 13 victories and 488 points.

Now Yale boasted an intimidating force at end in freshman Frank Hinkey, who would become a four-time all-American. Wherever the runner was, Hinkey would appear, whipping him to the ground.

"When Frank tackled the ball carrier, it was like an exploding bomb," Walter Camp would marvel. "I called him the disembodied spirit. He moved like a ghost."

Frank Butterworth, a star Yale fullback, would remember how Hinkey was a master at "jerking both legs of the runner out from under him, bringing him down with a slam and a thud that the runner long remembered."

Hinkey, a native of Tonawanda, New York, who had prepped at Phillips Academy in Andover, Massachusetts, hardly seemed football material. He stood only 5 feet 8, weighing perhaps 145 pounds, his complexion pale, his lungs continually troubling him. But he had large hands, seemingly oversized for his torso, and his slender frame was all muscle.

Shy and moody, he had few friends. He lived only for football—and violent encounters—suffering from depression once the season ended.

George Foster Sanford, the center on the 1891 Yale team, would recall how he once broke into a hotel room to rescue a man who had gotten into a scrap with Hinkey. Sanford, a 200-pounder, pulled the pair apart and hurled Hinkey into a corner.

For a moment, Hinkey lay stunned. Then he looked up and said, "Sanford, that

Frank Hinkey, a slender but ferocious Yale end who was named an all-American four times. (YALE UNIVERSITY)

was the greatest sensation I've ever experienced—try it again."

The autumn of 1891 was Pudge Heffelfinger's last season at Yale, and he made all-American for the third year in a row.

He hadn't been selected four times simply because the idea for an all-America team wasn't hatched until his sophomore season. It's not clear whether Walter Camp or Caspar Whitney, editor of the publication *The Week's Sport*, thought up the concept, but it seems they worked together in 1889 to name the first squad. It was an all-Ivy group—five players from Princeton and three each from Harvard and Yale.

As the game moved into the 1890s, a new wrinkle was added to the wedge formation developed by Princeton in the mid-1880s.

Momentum was added to mass when Harvard developed a flying wedge in 1892. It was devised not by a coach but a fan named Lorin Deland, a Boston business-man who became fascinated by football after reading a book called *The Game of War*. He applied combat tactics to sport: mass your greatest strength against the enemy's greatest weakness, and at an unexpected moment.

The flying wedge was unveiled in the Yale game at Springfield on November 19—one of the great surprise plays in football history. At the start of the second half, the Harvard players split up into two groups well behind the scrimmage line. After Bernie Trafford, the Harvard captain and quarter-back, signaled by waving his arms, the two groups raced forward and converged. The fullback, Charlie Brewer, took the football and the Harvard players, already under full steam, chugged on as a wedge protecting him. The play gained 30 yards.

Yale won, 6–0, but the new play took hold. By 1893 many teams were using it, transforming football into an even more brutal game.

Wedge plays were soon curbed by the rule-makers, but ingenious coaches devised formations to skirt the restrictions. There would continue to be an alarming number of deaths and injuries, bringing cries for reform or even abolition of college football.

Controversy raged in the highest Ivy circles.

Harvard's president, Charles Eliot, charged that win-at-all-cost coaches had transformed players into "powerful ani-mals," providing commercial spectacles rather than amateur sport. Universities, he said, seemed to be "places of mere physical sport and not of intellectual training."

But Brown's president, William H. P. Faunce, maintained that collegiate rowdi-ness was nothing new. He said that critics had forgotten "the old drinking and carous-ing of a generation ago, the smashing of window panes and destruction of property."

A political science professor at Prince-ton named Woodrow Wilson—a former student football manager—also defended the sport. His wife, Ellen, said that her husband was so depressed over the school's first-ever loss to Penn (by 6–4 in 1892) that only fellow Democrat Grover Cleveland's presidential election victory that week lift-ed his spirits. "Really, I think Woodrow would have had some sort of collapse if we had lost in politics, too," she said.

Two years later, football's enemies had fresh ammunition—a confrontation that would be known as "the bloodbath at Ham-pden Park."

Yale's 12–4 victory over Harvard in November 1894 before a presumably shocked crowd of 25,000 at Springfield left the *New York Times* straining for metaphors.

"An ordinary rebellion in the South American or Central American states is as child's play compared with the destructive-ness of a day's game," said the *Times*, "and the record of French duels for the last dozen years fails to show such a list of casu-alties as this one game of football produced."

The notorious affair even found its way

into the German press. The newspaper *Münchener Nachrichten* related a horrific tale.

"The football tournament between the teams of Harvard and Yale, held recently in America, had terrible results. It turned into an awful butchery. Of twenty-two participants, seven were so severely injured that they had to be carried from the field in a dying condition. One player had his back broken, another lost an eye, and a third lost a leg. Both teams appeared upon the field with a crowd of ambulances, surgeons and nurses. Many ladies fainted at the awful cries of the injured players. The indignation of the spectators was powerful, but they were so terrorized that they were afraid to leave the field."

Nobody came close to dying, but the casualty list was indeed impressive. On the Harvard side, Charles Brewer suffered a broken leg, Edgar Wrightington a broken collarbone, and Bob Hallowell a broken nose. As for Yale, Fred Murphy, Frank Butterworth, and Al Jerrens incurred head injuries. And there were assorted black eyes and bloody shins.

Rumor had it that Murphy, Yale's big right tackle, had died at a Springfield hospital.

A youngster named Jack Doyle worked at that game as a messenger for the newspapermen, relaying their copy to couriers—there was no telegraph wire at Springfield. Years afterward, he recalled what happened to Murphy.

"I remember when they carried him out of the game. They just dumped him in a pile of blankets, covered him up and then turned to look at the game again. A bit later just out of curiosity, I went over and lifted the blankets apart and looked in. There he was still unconscious—and nobody was paying any attention to him. They were all wrapped up in the game. So I covered him up again and went to have another look at the game myself."

Soon afterward, Butterworth's father charged that a Harvard player had deliberately kicked his son in the eye, and a newspaper report claimed that Yale's Frank Hinkey had purposely kneed Wrightington.

Everybody denied playing dirty, but the uproar brought cancellation of the Harvard-Yale game for the next two seasons.

In a nice contrast to the bickering between Harvard and Yale, the future looked bright indeed at the University of Pennsylvania.

A new stadium known as Franklin Field opened in 1895—across from the Pennsylvania Railroad's South Street Station—for the first running of the Penn Relays. Built at a cost of $100,000, it boasted a covered, double-decker grandstand seating 5,000 and open grandstands holding another 5,000. There were hopes that someday temporary seating could accommodate an additional 25,000 fans. (That vision proved modest indeed. The first incarnation of Franklin Field was replaced by a horseshoe structure in 1903, and the current double-decker stands were built in the 1920s. Turnouts at Franklin Field often reached 80,000 in the 1940s as Penn repeatedly led the nation in home attendance.)

Penn turned out a series of terrific teams in the 1890s at its new field. It won 55 of 56

George Woodruff, a former star lineman for Yale who coached the powerful Penn teams of the 1890s. (UNIVERSITY OF PENNSYLVANIA)

opposing linemen ahead of the running backs.

An advertisement in the game program placed by the J. A. Warren smoked meats company of Princeton read: "No Pennsylvania interference or momentum plays can break through a line fed on Warren's beef."

Woodruff's innovation proved otherwise—Penn won by 12–0.

Victors in all 12 games, Penn's 1894 team featured one of football's greatest backfields and a novel tactic to go with the guards back formation. It was the "quarterback kick," the forerunner of the "quick kick." Carl Williams, a kicking specialist, could place the football long or short. In those days, a backfield man on the kicking team could recover a punt before it got to the defender. Williams often delivered a short kick, and then one of his backfield mates sprinted downfield and recovered the football. "Pass the ball with your foot," commanded Woodruff in this era before the forward pass.

Arthur Knipe, the left halfback, was a fast and powerful man on off-tackle plays, and George Brooke, the fullback, concentrated on plunging into the line. Charley Gelbert, an end and halfback, made all-American three times.

But one man would be viewed in particularly heroic terms with the passing of years, probably as much for the fate he met beyond the football scene as his feats on it.

He was Winchester Osgood, a star halfback at Cornell for four seasons who played at Penn in 1893 and 1894 while studying civil engineering.

Decades later, John Minds, a Penn team-

games from 1894 to 1897, then rolled over 10 more opponents—nine via shutouts—in 1898 before falling to Harvard.

The mastermind behind Penn's success was George Woodruff, the former Yale lineman who took over the coaching in 1892.

Woodruff devised a mass-momentum variation called the "guards back" play, unveiled against Princeton on November 10, 1894, at the Trenton Fair Grounds. Two guards lined up in the backfield. Sometimes they ran with the ball but were usually extra blockers, churning into the

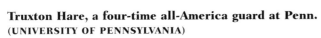

Winchester Osgood, a star runner at Cornell and Penn whose thirst for combat would later take him to the battlefields of Cuba.
(UNIVERSITY OF PENNSYLVANIA)

mate, remembered Osgood as "the greatest broken-field runner that I have ever seen, and I don't except Red Grange."

Broad-shouldered with a thick chest on his 180-pound frame that made him seem almost muscle-bound, Osgood was a boxer, wrestler, cyclist, gymnast, rower, track man, and baseball player when he wasn't on the football field. He ran with a smooth and balanced stride, evading tacklers with a slight twist of the torso.

After graduating from Penn, Osgood sought a new challenge on a different field of battle. The son of an army officer, he joined the Cuban insurrection against Spain and became a major in the artillery. In October 1895, he participated in the siege at Guiamaro.

A correspondent for the *New York Herald* described what happened:

"On the second day of the siege, as Major Osgood, under heavy fire from the Spaniards, was training one of his pieces on the forts, a Mauser bullet struck him in the forehead. He uttered the word, Well! and, bending forward on his cannon, hugged it and breathed his last in behalf of Cuban liberty."

Legend would have it that Osgood was riding his horse toward a Spanish block-house when a bullet hit him in the forehead and that he remained upright in the saddle even after dying. The truth was somewhat more prosaic, but, according to the *Herald's* account, dramatic enough.

Penn went undefeated for a second straight season in 1895, lost only to Lafayette (6–4) in 1896, then rolled to a 15-0 record in 1897.

The 1897 season saw the arrival of two superb linemen at Penn—Truxton Hare and John Outland.

A Philadelphia native, Hare would be considered by many the equal of Pudge Heffelfinger at guard. And his powerful legs served him well on offense when he carried the ball in the guards back for-

Truxton Hare, a four-time all-America guard at Penn.
(UNIVERSITY OF PENNSYLVANIA)

John Outland, the Penn player for whom the Outland Trophy, awarded to the nation's top lineman, is named. (UNIVERSITY OF PENNSYLVANIA)

mation, often dragging as many as five tacklers with him. He made all-American every year he played, one of only four men selected by Walter Camp four successive seasons. (The others were Frank Hinkey and Gordon Brown of Yale and Ma Newell of Harvard.) Hare capped his career by running 65 yards for a touchdown against Cornell on Thanksgiving Day 1900.

Outland, a Kansas farmboy, transferred to Penn to complete medical studies after playing two seasons at the University of Kansas. He was an all-American twice at Penn, as a tackle in 1897 and a back the following season. Outland would become a surgeon, but his interest in athletics endured. Contending that guards and tackles never received the recognition they deserved, he pushed for an annual award to the nation's top lineman. The idea was picked up by the Football Writers Association of America, which inaugurated the Outland Trophy in 1946.

While Penn was thriving, one of its chief rivals in years to come—Cornell—was just beginning to build a football program.

When Winchester Osgood arrived at Ithaca back in 1888, Cornell was only in its second year of play. The team had a 4-2 record that season, but the outlook was murky.

"The football team has been both weak in its play and strong in its tendency to noise and profanity during the games," Robert Thurston, a school administrator, complained in November 1888. "It looks as if a movement may be made to quash them."

But the following season, Cornell football not only remained alive, it had a real home. The first games had been played on whatever open land was available. But in 1889, a nine-acre athletic complex named Percy Field (the father of Percy Hagerman, a Cornell athlete, had contributed $9,000 for the project) was erected.

And Cornell now had a president who welcomed football. The program had mostly been confined to intramurals ever since President Andrew White refused to allow "30 men to travel 400 miles to agitate a bag of wind" back in 1873 when he vetoed that game with Michigan. But Charles Kendall Adams, who succeeded White in 1885, saw football as a publicity tool.

Encouraged by Adams, the team celebrated the opening of Percy Field by walloping Rochester, 124–0, and it went on to a 7-2 season that included a 66–0 romp at

Glenn (Pop) Warner, a Cornell guard of the 1890s who would become one of college football's most renowned coaches. (CORNELL UNIVERSITY)

age of 21, he instantly became known as "Pop."

Warner played two seasons for Cornell, but that was just a launching for a coaching career that would bring 319 victories in 44 seasons (five more than the former Yale man Amos Alonzo Stagg achieved).

After practicing law and coaching at Georgia, Warner returned to Cornell as head coach in 1897 and 1898, leading the school to a 10-2 record in his second season.

Warner borrowed a trick play in his first year at Cornell and used it with great success. His Georgia team had been victimized by the hidden-ball stunt Coach John Heisman introduced at Auburn. So when Cornell met Penn State, Warner tried it himself.

A strong strip of elastic bound the bottom of the jerseys in those days, the shirts being worn outside the pants. When the hidden-ball play was called, the quarterback would shove the football up the back of a teammate's shirt.

"I would go between opponents close enough to almost

Ann Arbor in a much-belated encounter with Michigan. The only two defeats were to mighty Yale, 56–6 and 70–0.

Four years later, Cornell and Penn began what would be an enduring rivalry, often a Thanksgiving Day matchup. That 1893 inaugural was a disaster for Cornell, which suffered a 50–0 drubbing to conclude a 2-5-1 season.

Winchester Osgood had moved on to Penn that autumn but there was a new man at Ithaca with quite a football career ahead of him, a 200-pound guard (also the school's heavyweight boxing champion) named Glenn Warner. Having entered Cornell in 1892 as a law student at the ripe old

Clint Wyckoff of Cornell, a quarterback who in 1895 became the school's first all-American. (CORNELL UNIVERSITY)

The Princeton squad of 1896, which romped to a 10-0-1 record and proclaimed, "We're No. 1."
(**PRINCETON UNIVERSITY**)

touch them, and they would stand open-eyed, wondering where the ball was," Cornell running back Allen Whiting would remember. "Generally, we would go straight for a touchdown."

In 1899, Warner left Cornell to coach at the Carlisle Indian Industrial School in southeastern Pennsylvania, established in the late 1870s to educate the young children of Indian tribes forced by the army to relocate.

He was replaced at Cornell by Percy Haughton, who coached there for just two seasons, a prep for his years of renown at Harvard.

Warner pulled his hidden-ball stunt once again in 1903, this time for Carlisle against Harvard in the last game at Soldiers Field before the opening of Harvard Stadium.

"Neither the Indian boys nor myself considered the hidden ball play to be strictly legitimate," Warner would acknowledge. "We did, however, know that the play would work against Harvard and, at least, prove to be a good joke on the arrogant Crimson players."

The play was sprung when Carlisle, leading by 5–0, received the second-half kickoff. Carlisle's Jimmy Johnson caught the ball around the goal line and then the team gathered in a huddle-like formation with everyone facing outward. Johnson, in the midst of the huddle, slipped the ball under the back of Charlie Dillon's jersey and shouted "Go." The Carlisle players spread out as they headed downfield, but

Dillon took a direct path to the Harvard goal.

When Dillon, a guard, ran toward Harvard's deepest defender, Carl Marshall, the Carlisle player swung his arms as if preparing to block. Marshall stepped aside and Dillon sauntered into the end zone.

Harvard had been outfoxed. But the "arrogant Crimson" came back for a 12–11 victory.

Warner returned to the Cornell coaching job the following season and stayed through 1906. But he wouldn't be pulling

The Poe brothers of Princeton. *Left to right,* **Arthur, Class of 1900, whose run in 1898 and field goal in 1899 won games against Yale; S. Johnson, 1884; Neilson, 1897; Edgar Allan, 1891; Gresham, 1902; John Prentiss Jr., 1895.**
(PRINCETON UNIVERSITY)

the hidden-ball stunt again. It was barred after a protest by Harvard.

At the turn of the century, a man carrying a distinguished name in the literary world produced heroics on the football field for Princeton. He was Arthur Poe, a son of John Prentiss Poe, who in turn was a nephew of the poet Edgar Allan Poe.

John Prentiss, who graduated from Princeton in 1854 and served for many years as attorney general of Maryland, fathered six sons who played football at his alma mater—S. Johnson (Class of 1884), a half-back; Edgar Allan (1891), a quarterback; John Prentiss Jr. (1895), a fullback; Neilson (1897), a halfback; Arthur (1900), a left end; and Gresham (1902), a right end.

The second Edgar Allan Poe was the quarterback on the first all-America team in 1889 and the Princeton captain in his junior and senior years. Like his father, he would serve as Maryland's attorney general.

But the best football player among the brothers was Arthur, a 5-foot-6-inch, 145-pounder who would be named to the College Football Hall of Fame.

Arthur's first spectacular performance came in the 1898 Yale game when he picked up a fumble by Al (Dusty) Durston and raced virtually the length of the field, then 110 yards, for the only touchdown of a 6–0 victory. He also had an 80-yard run against Navy and a 40-yard run against Brown that season.

Poe sank Yale again in 1899 with another dramatic blow. With Princeton trailing by 10–6 late in the game, Yale's Malcolm McBride fumbled. The Princeton left end, Bill Roper (a future Princeton coach of considerable repute), recovered at the Elis' 45. With about a minute to play, the Tigers moved to the 21-yard line, and Poe, who had never attempted a dropkick before, came on for a field goal. Yale was convinced a fake was in store, that Poe would run with the ball. But he booted it from the 35 and it sailed squarely between the goalposts for a 5-point field goal giving Princeton an 11–10 victory. Teammates hugged Poe, kissed him, then broke away for an improvised war dance as orange and black flags waved frantically in the stands at the old Yale Field.

Arthur's brother John Prentiss Poe Jr. was a phrase-maker of some note in an era when pep talks could charge up college boys. He told his mates that "a team that won't be beat can't be beat." The slogan (later falsely attributed to Coach Bill Roper) might not rank with "Win one for the Gipper," but presumably inspired many a Princeton man.

John Prentiss's zest for combat did not leave him when he departed Princeton. He sought action in the Spanish-American War, but his unit, the Fifth Maryland, never got to Cuba. Then he enlisted in the regular army and served in the Philippines during the 1899 insurrection. In 1907, he went to Central America when a war erupted between Honduras and Nicaragua. He intended to join the Nicaraguan army, but his boat stopped first in Honduras so he joined up on that side. Soon he would be known as "El Capitán Poey." He was later captured in Nicaragua and held as a Hon-

The 1899 Columbia team, led by a pair of all-America running backs, Harold Weekes (*front left*) and Bill Morley, beside him. (COLUMBIA UNIVERSITY)

duran spy, but supposedly was rescued by a United States gunboat that happened to be named *Princeton*. In 1914, he found a much grander stage on which to test his manhood, joining Britain's famed Black Watch. War, he once said, was "the greatest game on earth." John Prentiss's great adventure ended the following year when he was killed in action around the Loos coal fields.

Neilson Poe also served in World War I, volunteering for officer candidate school at age 41, and would suffer shrapnel wounds in the second battle of the Marne and receive the Distinguished Service Cross. In

1942, he came back to Princeton as an assistant football coach.

For Columbia, the 1890s was mostly a missing decade—the school dropped varsity football after the 1891 season and didn't restore it until 1899. But when football returned, two star runners—Harold Weekes and Bill Morley—spiced things up.

Weekes, a 210-pounder—huge for a running back in those days—specialized in a "flying hurdle." He got the ball 5 yards behind his linemen, who were bunched together, then sprang forward and used the shoulders of Morley and other teammates as a springboard to hurdle the opposing line. The idea was to land on his feet and keep going.

Morley had unlikely origins for a New York collegian, hailing from the New Mexico Territory. He was easy to pick out heading to practices at South Field, 116th Street and Broadway, since he was the only fellow on Morningside Heights sporting a ten-gallon hat. All this earned him the nickname "Wild Bill."

Weekes and Morley played key roles in a huge upset, Columbia's 5–0 victory at Manhattan Field over a Yale team that had shut out its first five opponents.

Weekes ran 50 yards for a touchdown, sprung by a block from Morley. Then Morley scored what seemed to be another touchdown, but the officials called the play back on a penalty.

In a page-one story, the *New York Times* called the game "one of the most disastrous defeats Yale has ever experienced," a match in which Columbia "outplayed, both offensively and defensively, the arrogant sons of Eli."

From then on, sportswriters dubbed Weekes and Morley the "chain-lightning backs." Both would be all-Americans, though Weekes received more publicity, Morley doing much of the blocking for him.

In the autumn of 1900, a Yale team that had beaten its first seven opponents without yielding a point faced Columbia again, this time at the old Polo Grounds. The weather had been dry, so Yale arrived with cleats designed for a hard field. But Columbia's coach, the old Yale lineman George Foster Sanford, had prevailed on firemen to let loose their hoses, turning the turf to mud, after he had supplied his players with wooden cleats to cut through the muck.

The Yale coach, Malcolm McBride, was no dummy. He got ahold of two dozen pairs of shoes and found a carpenter willing to nail wooden mud-suckers into them while the first half was being played. Columbia built a 5–0 lead as Weekes ran 50 yards for a score, duplicating his feat of the previous fall against Yale. But Yale's shoes arrived at halftime and McBride's men rallied for a pair of touchdowns and a 12–5 victory. Yale went on to a 12-0 season, scoring 336 points and yielding just 10.

Morley, meanwhile, wasn't thrilled to see Weekes getting the Lions' share—so to speak—of the glory, and nagged Sanford to let him try the catapult play. During a scrimmage one day, the coach told Morley that he'd finally get his chance. But Sanford persuaded a big end named Slocovich to punch Morley in the jaw as he came flying over the line. Morley did a double somersault, presumably curing him of his hurdling ambitions. (In 1902, Morley got a chance to play his own pranks when he succeeded Sanford as coach. In four seasons his teams would go 26-11-3 for a .688 percentage, the highest of any coach in Columbia history.)

Yale continued to roll in 1901 and went into the Harvard game unbeaten in 24 straight matches. The Crimson came in with an 11-0 record and closed out a perfect season with a 22–0 victory.

But Yale dominated again in 1902 behind an "Irish line" led by end Tom Shevlin, a boastful character who could back up his words with deeds, and tackle Jim Hogan, the inspiration for the fight song "Down the Field."

The 1903 season brought the opening of Harvard Stadium, the world's first massive reinforced-concrete structure and the first large, permanent arena for athletic contests in the United States.

Modeled on Greek and Roman architecture—semicircular at one end, open at the other—the stadium was a gift of the Class of 1879 and was built in four and a half months at a cost of $310,000. It was dedicated on November 14, but Dartmouth spoiled the party with an 11–0 victory.

Some scholarly types had misgivings about the grand stadium. The June 1904 issue of the *Harvard Engineering Journal* reported that "many friends of the university have been made uneasy at the thought of giving outdoor sports a more permanent form and one which seemed to offer to the public an annual spectacle out of proportion to their importance in a great seat of learning."

Harvard had the stadium, but Princeton and Yale boasted the dominant teams in 1903. Their matchup at New Haven on November 12 was the game of the year, Princeton having shut out all its opponents, and Yale, also unbeaten, having yielded only 15 points.

Yale got off to a 6–0 lead and was driving for another score when it was stopped on the Princeton 26. Ledyard Mitchell dropped back for a field goal, but Princeton's captain and star lineman, John DeWitt, smashed through the line as the ball was snapped and grabbed it. He raced 70 yards for a touchdown, then dropkicked the extra point to tie the game (touchdowns, like field goals, were then worth 5 points). With time running out, DeWitt struck again, booting a 53-yard field goal on a dropkick. Princeton had an 11–6 victory and the national championship.

Pennsylvania was on top in 1904, winning all 12 games and being scored upon only by Swarthmore in a 6–4 victory. The team was led by Bob Torrey, the center, who on defense was a forerunner of the modern roaming linebacker. The quarterback, Vincent Stevenson, emulated Columbia's Weekes by flying high when he was about to be tackled. Weekes, however, did it on called plays while Stevenson was adept at the maneuver in open-field running. Penn went unbeaten again in 1905, but was tied once, a 6–6 game with Lehigh that broke a 21-game winning streak.

As for other Ivies-to-be, Dartmouth and Brown never approached national championship caliber in the late nineteenth century.

The closest Dartmouth came to an all-American was quarterback Walter McCormack, who made Caspar Whitney's third team in 1896. But Dartmouth had outstanding squads just after the turn of the century, losing only five games from 1901 to 1905, with McCormack the coach the first two seasons in that span.

Brown had an all-America halfback in

Dave Fultz, who went on to play major league baseball for seven seasons. The 1896 Brown team that Fultz played on had a student manager who would soon find far more lucrative callings—John D. Rockefeller Jr.

A Brown man who had played informal football at the school would be remembered every December long after his death.

In the fall of 1887, a 17-year-old from Titusville, Pennsylvania, named John Heisman arrived for his freshman year. The day he stepped off the train at Providence would long remain vivid.

"Was I impressed with the Ivy-clad halls? Ah, no. I gave but a fleeting glance to the buildings, for there at my feet on campus a game of football was in progress. On one side were freshmen. Opposed to them were town boys.

"Soon my joys knew no bounds when I was asked to join the game, all 144 pounds of me. When the game ended I had one roughly black eye and a freely bleeding nose. But I was happy. I had played football."

To Heisman's chagrin, Brown had no varsity team that autumn. After having played mini-schedules in 1878, 1880, and 1886, the school suspended intercollegiate play once more.

Heisman settled for club football in his two years at Brown, then transferred to Penn to pursue a law degree. He played varsity football there as a center, tackle, and end.

His true calling would not be the law. During a game between Penn and Prince-ton at Madison Square Garden (the 1890s version of the domed stadium) the galvanic lighting system injured Heisman's eyes. The team physician told him to avoid eye strain for the next two years, so instead of joining a law firm in the fall of 1892 he became the first football coach at Oberlin College in Ohio. Heisman would coach college football for 36 seasons, including a stint at Penn from 1920 to 1922, and would rank among the game's major innovators. But he is remembered today mostly for the trophy that bears his name, awarded in December to the top college football player in the nation (or at least the one with the best campus publicity apparatus).

Another Brown man with a football connection who would remain in the public eye long after his years at Providence was Theodore Francis Green, Class of 1887, a future United States senator from Rhode Island.

In reminiscing on his college days, Green would recall having been annoyed at Brown's inability to find a suitable mascot.

"Sometimes when a cartoon called for something to set against the bulldog of Yale or the tiger of Princeton, a despairing artist would display some colonial Puritan and let it go at that."

Looking for a symbol embodying the qualities of Brown men—which he saw as "strength, independence and courage"— Green hit on the perfect mascot: a Brown Bear.

A member of the building committee for the school's Rockefeller Hall, Green somehow secured the head of a real bear,

and when the building opened on January 20, 1904, he had it placed over the great arch of the trophy room—the central point of student life.

"So that, I suppose, is the Bear's birthday," Green would proudly note.

The following fall, students brought a live bear to the Dartmouth game at Springfield. A bronze Bruno was later placed outside Marvel Gymnasium, and each autumn the Brown football captain would be photographed alongside it.

Green would liken the bear to a collegiate football player. "It is intelligent and capable of being educated (if caught young enough!)," he would observe. "Remember, an athlete can make Phi Beta Kappa."

John Heisman, the man behind the trophy, played on club teams at Brown and then on varsity squads at Penn, where he later coached.
(UNIVERSITY OF PENNSYLVANIA)

"BULLDOG, BULLDOG, BOW, WOW, WOW"

TEDDY ROOSEVELT—ADVOCATE of the strenuous life, champion of American muscle in international affairs ("Speak softly and carry a big stick"), Rough Rider extraordinaire—was hardly a softy.

And he believed that football, with all its viciousness, had lessons to teach. In an article in the children's magazine *St. Nicholas,* he once hailed "in-sports manliness" as a substitute for frontier life and had used football as a metaphor.

"In life, as in a football game, the principle to follow is: Hit the line hard; don't foul and don't shirk, but hit the line hard."

While New York City police commissioner in 1896, he was said to have helped get Harvard, his alma mater, and Yale to resume a rivalry suspended by the "bloodbath" of 1894.

But even Teddy Roosevelt became disgusted with the continuing brutality of the game played by Harvard and the other Ivy schools.

Despite rule changes aimed at curbing mass-momentum plays, coaches were finding ways to muster brute force. The *Chicago Tribune* counted 18 football deaths and 159 serious injuries around the nation in 1904.

Roosevelt almost certainly read an article in *McClure's* magazine by a close friend, a journalist named Henry Beach Needham, who told of how a star player for Dartmouth—a black man—had been knocked out of action early in a game with Princeton with a broken collarbone.

The Princeton quarterback, accused of deliberately injuring the player because of his race, denied he had any such motive.

"We didn't put him out because he is a black man," responded the quarterback. "We're coached to pick out the most dangerous man on the opposing side and put him out in the first five minutes of play."

Soon after the article appeared, Roosevelt attacked the blatant disregard for the rules when he spoke at a Harvard commencement.

By the fall of 1905, Roosevelt had developed a personal stake in college football: his son Ted Jr. was playing for the Harvard freshman team. Roosevelt was worried that the school's president, Charles Eliot, who viewed football as an unseemly commercial spectacle and a spur to illegal betting, would use concerns over violence as a reason to abolish it.

Now Roosevelt tried to save football. He summoned officials of the Big Three schools—Harvard, Yale, and Princeton—along with Walter Camp, still a rules committee member and a longtime acquaintance, to a White House conference on October 9 to demand reform.

At Roosevelt's request, the Big Three drew up a statement condemning brutality. But the 1905 season brought more mayhem.

A melee erupted during Columbia's scoreless tie with Wesleyan at the New York Yankees' ballpark in Washington Heights.

Henderson Van Surdam, who played in that game for Wesleyan, would long remember the day.

"On one of their wide end runs, I simply ran the back out of bounds and marked the spot where he went out. To my amazement he ran back on the field and started for the goal line. He was tackled by one of our halfbacks. He then started crawling, and the fullback ran up and jumped on him, knocking

him cold. And then a riot started with coaches and players slugging it out against each other until the police quieted the ruckus."

Later in the season it was Yale's turn to be angry with Columbia. Though ripping the Lions, 53–0, Yale charged that a Columbia player had intentionally twisted the ankle of its quarterback, Tad Jones.

In yet another incident, Harvard nearly walked off the field during the Yale game when no penalty was called after a Crimson player had been flattened while calling for a fair catch. In the Harvard-Yale freshman game, Theodore Roosevelt Jr. was roughed up amid rumors he was singled out for punishment.

Columbia's coach, the former all-American Bill Morley, insisted that nothing was amiss with the college game. The death rate, Morley said, was "wonderfully small." But Professor Herbert Lord, chairman of Columbia's Committee on Student Organization, denounced football as "an obsession" that "has become as hindersome to the great mass of students as it has proved itself harmful to academic standards and dangerous to human life." His view prevailed over Morley's—Columbia abolished football after the 1905 season and did not restore it until 1915.

But most other schools looked toward reform instead of abolition. As an outgrowth of the White House meeting, a new rules committee was created, and it sought ways to open up the game.

Walter Camp pushed the idea of widening the field by as much as 40 feet. But the closeness of the new Harvard Stadium's

The captain of Yale's 1907 team, Bill Knox, works with Walter Camp on mastering the forward pass, legalized only the season before. (YALE UNIVERSITY)

stands to the sidelines would have required major structural changes.

That problem boosted the cause of those advocating the forward pass, among them John Heisman, the old Brown and Penn man and now a coach, who predicted that passing would "scatter the mob."

The pass was legalized for the 1906 season, but with many restrictions. The ball had to be thrown from at least 5 yards behind the line of scrimmage, and an incompletion drew a 15-yard penalty and loss of down. Passing would, however, help cut down on violent encounters.

So far as Eastern football was concerned, one of the first passes came on October 3, 1906, when Sammy Moore of Wesleyan threw to Irvin Van Tassell for a gain of 18 yards against Yale. One of the season's most spectacular pass plays came in the Yale-Harvard game, when Paul Veeder of Yale threw a 30-yard pass to Robert Forbes, who was downed on Harvard's 3-yard line. Howard Roome then carried the ball in for the game's only touchdown.

Yale was nationally dominant again, going unbeaten from 1905 to 1907.

The 1905 team, which went 10-0 and yielded only a single field goal, was led by lineman Tom Shevlin and the Jones brothers, Tad and Howard, who had played together in the backfield at Middletown High School in Ohio, then prepped at Exeter. Tad starred at quarterback and Howard at end.

Yale won nine games in each of the following two seasons while playing a pair of scoreless ties, with Princeton in 1906 and Army in 1907.

Princeton almost beat Yale in 1907, but the Elis pulled the game out, 12–10, after trailing by 10 points at halftime, thanks to a pair of touchdowns by fullback Ted Coy.

A powerful runner at 6 feet and 195 pounds, an excellent punter and dropkicker, the handsome Coy epitomized the college football hero.

In his career at Yale, from 1907 to 1909, he would taste defeat only once, a 4–0 loss to Harvard in 1908.

"Coy was a terrific line smasher," John Reed Kilpatrick, his old teammate and later president of Madison Square Garden, would recall. "He was a great athlete who could play any position, and he was a remarkable kicker. He ran over people, hitting low, with his knees working like pistons and leaving a stream of tacklers behind him on the field."

Percy Haughton, who coached a string of powerful Harvard teams in the pre–World War I years, showing his form as a Crimson player at the turn of the century. (HARVARD UNIVERSITY)

Yale's 1909 team shut out all ten opponents, ran up 209 points, and allowed no one inside the 20-yard line. By now the Jones boys had become coaches, Howard taking over at Yale and Tad coaching Syracuse. The brothers faced each other that season with Yale winning by 15–0. (In 1922, the Joneses were opponents again. This time Howard was at Iowa and Tad had become the Yale coach. Howard prevailed once more, by 6–0.)

The 1909 Yale-Harvard game at Cambridge was the matchup of the year, both teams coming in undefeated. Coy had been operated on for appendicitis before the season and was below par, but kicked two field goals for an 8–0 victory.

Harvard may have suffered a setback, but a golden era had begun—the Percy Haughton years.

Haughton had been an outstanding punter at Harvard in the late 1890s, then coached at Cornell in 1899 and 1900, succeeding Pop Warner. He took over the coaching job at Harvard in 1908 and produced a 9-0-1 team while leading the Crimson to a victory over Yale after six straight shutout defeats. In Haughton's years at Cambridge, Harvard would post a 5-2-2 record against Yale that included two routs—36–0 in 1914 and 41–0 in 1915. His teams would win 71 games, lose only 7, and play 5 ties.

Harvard stars (*left to right*) Charlie Brickley, Tack Hardwick, Eddie Mahan, and Mal Logan.
(HARVARD UNIVERSITY)

Haughton coached a host of all-Americans, including running backs Percy Wendell, Charlie Brickley, Eddie Mahan, and Eddie Casey and linemen Hamilton Fish, Stan Pennock, Tack Hardwick, and Bob Fisher.

Mahan was adept at kicking and passing as well as running. Out of Natick, Massachusetts, the town that also produced Casey, Mahan often disdained the help of blockers, preferring instead to sidestep tacklers. "I simply give them the foot, right or left, and then take it away," he once said.

Hardwick, like Haughton a product of Groton prep school, was a fierce blocker and, wearing leather wristbands, loved to rabbit-punch opposing linemen. He had been earmarked as a running back, but—the story goes—was shifted to the rougher life of an end when Haughton was impressed by his combative skills in the intrateam fight the coach liked to stage in midseason.

One of Haughton's players was a man who would receive little notice on the football field but become a prominent figure in Massachusetts political life—Leverett Saltonstall, a future governor and senator.

In his freshman season, 1910, Saltonstall was a backup tackle, playing behind another politician-to-be, Tudor Gardiner, a future governor of Maine. The next year, Saltonstall joined the varsity as a substitute end.

Upon going on to Harvard Law School, he coached the freshman team, and one of his protégés was Eddie Casey. "I only succeeded in having him hurt his shoulder when tackling the dummy as I had directed," Saltonstall would recall.

Haughton was a master at organization, a perfectionist who spent long hours on game plans, then used color-coded dominoes to show his assistant coaches what each man was supposed to do.

He was also creative. On offense, he emphasized clever ball handling and deception, especially the "mouse trap" play in which defensive linemen were allowed to break through, then were cut down from the side.

And he was a formidable disciplinarian. "He was all iron," as Tack Hardwick once put it.

"Haughton was born an aristocrat, yet he could be very rough," Mahan, captain of the 1915 team, would recall. "During the first six weeks of the season he was a tyrant and drove, cursed, and manhandled players. After this period of rugged work was over, he would turn around and become very affable and seem to be everyone's best friend."

Lothrop Withington, the Harvard captain in 1910 and later a coach under Haughton, would remember him as generally "aloof" from his players.

"He believed it was necessary to maintain a military discipline and that the slightest letdown would result in a breakdown of discipline."

Haughton's coolness even extended to former Harvard athletes. At Yale, old stars would always be hanging around the practices, giving advice, but Haughton would have none of that. Grantland Rice would recall how one afternoon Charlie Brickley, famed for beating Yale with five dropkick field goals in 1913, and a couple of other former players dropped by. As the coach left for the workout, they began to trail along. "I'll see you fellows back here," said Haughton. "There's no room on the practice field."

The 1908 season saw a battle of wits between Haughton and Pop Warner.

Back in 1903, Warner's Carlisle Indian team had fooled Harvard with his hidden-ball trick. Now he had another scheme. In an early-season victory over Syracuse, Warner had directed the sewing of football-shaped pads on the jersey elbows of his halfbacks and ends. The Syracuse players were continually tackling men who seemed to have the football, but did not.

Carlisle showed up at Cambridge with those simulated footballs, but the Crimson were ready with a trick of their own. When Carlisle appeared for pregame practice, Haughton walked over with a bag of footballs and invited Warner to select one as the game ball. The Carlisle manager, Dick Eggelston, pulled out three balls—all dyed crimson, matching the Harvard jerseys. Warner got the point and removed the leather footballs from the Carlisle jerseys. Then Harvard handed the Indians their only loss of the season, 17–0.

Haughton is best remembered today for a gruesome and often-repeated story.

The tale surfaced during World War II, when a Liberty Ship named *Percy D. Haughton* was to be launched in South Portland, Maine, and christened by the coach's daughter, Alison Haughton Derby. Just before the ceremony, a column appeared in a Boston newspaper questioning whether Haughton deserved such an honor. The columnist reported that Haughton had climaxed his pep talk before the 1908 Yale game by bringing a bulldog into the locker room, then choking it to death and tossing it at his players' feet.

The account was certainly graphic, but untrue, and the Boston sportswriter recanted following numerous protest letters. But Haughton had indeed displayed theatrics at the expense of the Yale mascot. The day before that game, while his team was being led on a hike by trainer Pooch Donovan outside its headquarters at the Elm Tree Inn in Farmington, Connecticut, Haughton drove by. Tied to the rear of his car was a long rope fastened to the neck of a papier-mâché bulldog dressed in a blue blanket with two large block *Y*s.

Not long after that, the Yale bulldog saw better days—he was saluted in a school fight song.

Back in 1904, a Yale student named Caleb O'Connor wrote "Down the Field," praising the prowess of tackle Jim Hogan.

By 1910, Hogan was long gone, so the *Yale Daily News* sponsored a competition for a new song.

A sophomore from Peru, Indiana, won the contest with "Bingo, Eli Yale."

Bingo! Bingo!
Bingo! Bingo! Bingo!
That's the lingo.
Eli is bound to win.

It became a campus hit and was published by Remick, a top New York sheet music outfit.

The following year there was another songwriting competition at Yale, and this time the student produced a more enduring lyric.

Bull Dog! Bull Dog!
Bow, wow, wow!
Eli Yale!

Bull Dog! Bull Dog!
Bow, wow, wow!
Our team can never fail.

So began the songwriting career of Cole Porter, only 5 feet 6 inches and averse to physical exertion but a booster of Yale's football team. He would become a Yale cheerleader and produce a host of other football songs—"A Football King," "Beware of Yale," and "Eli"—among the more than 300 lyrics he turned out while a student.

Where did Porter get his inspiration? A profile in the *New Haven Register* in November 1911 stated that "some of the peculiar and distinctive features of his work have been explained by the fact that he spent several years in the mountains of Rumania, and heard many strange birds while up there."

He had, of course, been nowhere near

Rumania. That little touch was evidently supplied by Porter himself to create an air of worldliness around him.

At Harvard, football spirit was buoyed by a student who would later find a much larger stage for his cheerleading: John Reed, Class of 1910, whose enthusiastic eyewitness account of the Bolshevik Revolution—*Ten Days That Shook the World*— would bring him burial in the Kremlin Wall (and portrayal by Warren Beatty in the movie *Reds*). While at Harvard, Reed wrote a song imploring the Crimson to "twist the bull-dog's tail" and "call up the hearse for dear old Yale."

Walter Lippmann, a classmate of Reed, would remember how he "proved himself to be the most inspired song and cheer leader that the football crowd had had for many days."

"At first there was nothing to recommend him but his cheek," noted Lippmann. "That was supreme. He would stand up alone before a few thousand undergraduates and demonstrate without a quiver of self-consciousness how a cheer should be given. If he didn't like the way his instructions were followed he cursed at the crowd, he bullied it, sneered at it. But he always captured it. It was a sensational triumph for Jack Reed but wasn't altogether good form at college."

Cole Porter's Yale and John Reed's Harvard weren't the only dominant teams among the Ivies in the century's first decade. The 1908 Penn squad went 11-0-1 behind Bill Hollenback, a superb fullback who had played on the 1904 team that was 12-0.

Jim Thorpe, whose Carlisle Indians tied Penn to keep it from a perfect 1908 season, remembered Hollenback as the toughest man he ever faced.

"Every time we had the ball and I tried to break through the line, Bill was there to stop me," said Thorpe. "I did the same to him when he carried the ball. He stood 6 feet 3 inches and weighed 210 and was a hard man to bring down. Our personal duel lasted 60 minutes. The final score ended 6–6 and we both spent a week in the hospital recuperating."

Penn remained strong even after Hollenback departed, losing only one game in both 1909 and 1910.

In the autumn of 1909, college football experienced a dark moment, a reminder that all those reform efforts aimed at curbing the game's brutality could still fall short. Percy Haughton's second Harvard team went 8-1, but the success was overshadowed by one play in the Army game.

Hamilton Fish, Harvard's all-America tackle and captain, had been playing opposite Icy Byrne, Army's acting captain. Fish would remember how Byrne was exhausted yet insisted on staying in because a player could not return once he had been removed.

"Our line went into a shift," Fish recalled. "I was lined up about four yards away from Icy when—bam—our 200-pound fullback smashed over my tackle position and straight into Byrne. Icy stiffened, held his ground, but the impact was too much. His neck was broken, the game was immediately stopped. He died in the hospital later that evening."

Hamilton Fish, an all-America tackle and captain of the 1909 Harvard team, later a longtime congressman from New York's Hudson Valley area. (HARVARD UNIVERSITY)

Some would blame Fish for Byrne's death because it was assumed he had blocked the Army player, having lined up face-to-face with him earlier. But there evidently were no such feelings at West Point. In 1912 and 1913, Fish, then living in Garrison, New York, across the Hudson River from the military academy, was invited to coach the Army tackles. Among the Cadet players was Dwight D. Eisenhower.

Fish went on to a long career as a congressman, becoming a leader of the isolationist bloc before World War II. At a football dinner 50 years after his stint at Army, he had a chat with Eisenhower. Ike told Fish how he remembered his wearing a coonskin coat back in his coaching days at West Point. Fish had no such recollection, but would note how "I had a new respect for Eisenhower as a politician after that. Any man who could remember me in a coonskin coat back in 1913 had a great political gift."

The 1909 season saw a spectacular player emerge at Brown in Bill Sprackling, a 5-foot-9-inch, 150-pounder who was a speedy runner and a fine passer and kicker. And he played with abandon, shunning a helmet, shoulder pads, or hip pads.

Sprackling's most electrifying moment came at the old Polo Grounds when he returned a kickoff 110 yards in a 21–8 upset over Carlisle and Jim Thorpe. The following season, when the teams met at Providence, Sprackling again showed he was a match for Thorpe as Brown won by 15–6.

Three weeks before the second victory over Carlisle, Sprackling was a one-man gang when Brown defeated Yale, 21–0, its first victory over the Elis in 18 games going back 30 years. Sprackling kicked three field goals (a fourth was nullified by a penalty), threw for a touchdown, and accounted for 456 of Brown's 608 yards via running from scrimmage, passing, punt, and kickoff returns.

He would be the only three-time all-American in Brown history.

Down at Princeton, a young man who would come to personify the gentleman-athlete donned the orange and black in the autumn of 1911.

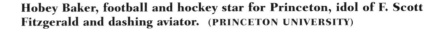

Hobey Baker, football and hockey star for Princeton, idol of F. Scott Fitzgerald and dashing aviator. (PRINCETON UNIVERSITY)

The son of a socially prominent Philadelphia Main Line family and a sports star at the elite St. Paul's School of Concord, New Hampshire, where he played hockey as well as football, Hobart Amory Hare Baker came to Princeton with every advantage enjoyed by the old-stock Eastern establishment.

Hobey Baker had wavy blond hair (easily noticed since he refused to don a helmet) and blue-gray eyes, and his 5-foot-9-inch, 160-pound frame was the picture of grace as he ran with the ball.

He was considered modest, generous, and a devotee of teamwork.

F. Scott Fitzgerald, who entered Princeton in the fall of Hobey's senior year, saw him as "an ideal worthy of everything in my enthusiastic admiration."

The protagonist in *This Side of Paradise*, Fitzgerald's first novel, is Amory Blaine. But Hobey is another character, named Allenby. As Amory sits on the steps of his rooming house, a group of Princeton students, singing and clad in white, march by. "There at the head of the white platoon marched Allenby, the football captain, slim and defiant, as if aware that this year the hopes of the college rested on him, that his hundred-and-sixty pounds were expected to dodge to victory through the heavy blue and crimson lines."

In an era when kicking still played a major role—teams punted numerous times, hoping for better field advantage or a fumble on the return—Baker was adept at catching kicks on the run, then springing for long gains.

Against Yale in 1912, he ran a punt back 88 yards, and the 92 points he scored that year would stand as a Princeton record until 1974.

After graduation, Baker worked on Wall Street and took flying lessons. In 1916, he "buzzed" the Princeton-Yale game at the recently opened Palmer Stadium. But after that, grander adventures beckoned.

Baker was one of the first American aviation officers in France with the Lafayette Escadrille, serving as commander of the 141st Squadron—its symbol a Princeton Tiger. In December 1918, a month after the armistice, he took a Spad biplane up for a test on a rainy night. The plane's carburetor had failed only a few days before. Now the engine quit again, and the plane crashed nose down a few hundred yards from the hangar. Moments after being pulled from the wreckage, Hobey Baker died. He was 26.

Also a hockey star at Princeton, Baker became the only athlete elected to both the

College Football Hall of Fame and the Hockey Hall of Fame. (The Hobey Baker Award is given annually to the top American college hockey player, the sport's version of the Heisman Trophy.)

And he would be enshrined at Princeton. The hockey arena would be named the Hobart A. H. Baker Memorial Rink (he is depicted there in his airman's uniform) and his photograph would be hung in the Nassau Inn between pictures of two latter-day Princeton heroes—Bill Bradley and Dick Kazmaier.

But Hobey Baker's rise coincided with the eclipse of upper-class dominance in collegiate football. The 1913 season was the first one in which Yale, Harvard, Princeton, and Penn players did not comprise a majority of the first-team all-America squad. Except for 1914, when Harvard had five all-Americans, the four schools would never constitute a majority again.

There were grand plans afoot nonetheless on the Ivy campuses.

The autumn after Baker graduated from Princeton, Palmer Stadium opened. The first game, played on October 24, 1914, was a success in one way but a disappointment in another. Princeton scored a 16–12 victory over Dartmouth, but the turnout was a modest 7,000.

Designed as a horseshoe—in the Greek tradition—with a capacity of 42,000, the stadium was built at a cost of $300,000, a gift of Edgar P. Palmer, Class of 1903, in memory of his father, Stephen.

At the opening ceremonies, Princeton's Dean Howard McClenahan, likening the stadium to a "beautifully cut jewel," was carried away by the moment. He called the new home "Pedlar Palmer's polyhedric, polychromatic and princely present to Princeton."

Palmer Stadium may have been "princely," but Yale Bowl would be built on a far grander scale. Forsaking the classical-style horseshoe architecture favored by Harvard and Princeton, Yale designed its showcase as an ellipse. Constructed at a cost of $750,000 through a fund-raising drive, the bowl boasted 60,617 seats—the largest arena in America. It covered twelve and a half acres and required the removal of 320,000 cubic feet of earth.

Yale Bowl opened on the sunshiny afternoon of November 21, 1914, for the Harvard game before a crowd, including standees, estimated as high as 75,000. The Crimson romped to a 36–0 victory, their third straight triumph over the Elis, inspiring one newspaper account to note how "Yale had the Bowl but Harvard had the punch."

The previous autumn, Yale's last full season at 33,000-seat Yale Field, its home since 1884, the team had a letterman who would be far more prominent in the world of letters beyond the football field— Archibald MacLeish, a future Pulitzer Prize–winning poet, librarian of Congress, and assistant secretary of state.

In December 1969, MacLeish received the Distinguished American Award of the National Football Foundation and Hall of Fame, sharing the honor with that other renowned football expert Richard M. Nixon.

In his remarks, MacLeish reflected on his football years at Yale.

"I won my Y as an all-purpose, all-position substitute on a series of Yale teams which never beat Harvard.

"I have only one glorious memory of those four years, and its setting is not Soldiers Field in Cambridge but the bar of the long-vanished Tremont Hotel in Boston. We—we being the Yale freshman team of the fall of 1911—had just held the best Harvard freshman team in a generation to a 0–0 tie in a downpour of helpful rain, and we were relaxing, not without noise, when the coach of that famous Harvard freshman team approached us, looked us over, focused (he had had a drink or two himself) on me and announced in the voice of an indignant beagle sighting a fox that I was, without question, the dirtiest little sonofabitch of a center ever to visit Cambridge, Massachusetts.

"It was heady praise. But unhappily I didn't deserve that honor. I was little but not THAT little."

Autumn 1915 brought another new stadium—Cornell's Schoellkopf Field, built with contributions from the Schoellkopf family. Henry (Heinie) Schoellkopf, who played for Cornell and then coached the team in 1907 and 1908, would become the stuff of legend. He was said to have once dived 70 feet into a gorge pool at Ithaca to save a drowning dog, and one account had him losing his life in the rescue. There may be some elements of truth to the story, but Schoellkopf died not in Ithaca but Milwaukee, where he committed suicide by turning a gun on himself in 1912.

Cornell blessed the new stadium with its first undefeated football team, a squad cheered on by Touchdown I, a bear hailing from the Maine woods. He was a cuddly

Schoellkopf Field's distinctive crescent stands, added in 1924, nine years after the Cornell stadium opened. (CORNELL UNIVERSITY)

cub when he arrived at Ithaca, his specialty climbing the goalposts.

But Touchdown I's mascot career was to be brief.

"It was not cute and cuddly as it matured," Everett Hunkin, the student manager of the 1915 football team, would ruefully note. "It became perpetually mean, ill-bred and dangerous when allowed to climb the goalposts. It was hell trying to get him down and a menace to try and re-cage him."

While accompanying the Cornell team to a game at Michigan, Touchdown tore himself loose from a metal chain and ran amok in the lobby of Detroit's Tuller Hotel. En route to the Penn game, he rampaged through a saltwater taffy shop in Atlantic City, tipping over tables and chairs and terrifying customers.

Soon he would do his rooting from a zoo run by a Cornell alumnus in Rome, New York.

The human star for Cornell was quarterback Charley Barrett, an excellent runner, passer, and kicker.

Barrett was tested against Harvard's Eddie Mahan in midseason, both teams coming into the game undefeated. Early in the first quarter, Mahan fumbled and Cornell recovered on the Harvard 25. Six plays later, Barrett ran for a score, and then he kicked the extra point. He was later knocked unconscious in a collision with Mahan, but Cornell held on for a 10–0 victory.

In its final game, Cornell brought an 8-0 record up against Penn in Philadelphia. Penn led by 9–7 going into the fourth quarter, but then Barrett, who had scored Cor-

Charley Barrett, whose quarterback play led Cornell to an undefeated 1915 season. (CORNELL UNIVERSITY)

nell's first touchdown, put the game away. He went 40 yards around end for one touchdown, 25 yards for another, and kicked a field goal. Cornell emerged with a 24–9 victory and a perfect record.

Barrett died in 1924, his life cut short by tuberculosis contracted in an explosion aboard a navy ship during World War I. Soon afterward, Penn players erected a tablet in his memory at Franklin Field.

A decade after dropping the sport as too violent, Columbia began playing football again in 1915. But the administration was not ready to go big-time. It put the program on a five-year trial basis, during which the prominent Eastern teams—Harvard, Yale, Princeton, Penn, and Cornell—would not be on the schedule.

In an editorial, the *New York Times* congratulated Columbia for bringing back the game, observing that "a college or a university without a football eleven is like a church without a steeple, a steeple without a bell, a bell or a woman without a tongue."

Columbia enjoyed the only unbeaten season in its history in 1915, playing a none too formidable schedule. The victims were St. Lawrence, Stevens, Connecticut, New York University, and Wesleyan.

In the years before World War I, Dartmouth had some fine teams under Coach Frank Cavanaugh, a strapping man at 6 feet 1,230 pounds with a demeanor to match.

Coaching at Dartmouth between 1911 and 1916, Cavanaugh compiled a record of 42-9-3. His 1913, 1914, and 1915 teams lost only one game each.

Harvard beat Dartmouth in 1911 and 1912, by scores of 5–3 and 3–0, but then dropped Dartmouth from its schedule, evidently deciding that the bruises inflicted by Cavanaugh's men weren't worth the trouble.

"Harvard gave him a reputation as a dirty coach," the sportswriter Hugh Fullerton wrote years later.

Hubie McDonough, the Dartmouth quarterback in 1915 and 1916, would say of Cavanaugh: "If he produced rough

Dartmouth Coach Frank Cavanaugh, a rough customer whose combat exploits in World War I would bring him the sobriquet "The Iron Major." (DARTMOUTH COLLEGE)

teams, it was incidental to his attitude toward life and football, which he regarded as a man's game to be played by men. I don't remember when playing teams such as Penn State, West Virginia, Syracuse and Princeton that I ever met many Lord Chesterfields."

But Cavanaugh didn't abuse his players verbally—at least to excess—as McDonough recalled it.

"As for profanity, Cav had no need of it.

He had a marvelous vocabulary and a gift for sarcasm that could knock one down. Profanity would have been superfluous."

Cavanaugh was commissioned in the army at age 41 in May 1917—though he had six children—and was grievously wounded near Verdun less than three weeks before the armistice. He emerged from World War I highly decorated and known as "the Iron Major." After the war he returned to football but left the Ivy scene, coaching at Boston College.

Cavanaugh's successor at Hanover was Clarence Spears, better known as "Fat" or "Doc," an all-America guard at Dartmouth in 1914 and 1915.

A transfer from Knox College in Illinois, the 5-foot-7-inch, 235-pound Spears brought a rough edge from the Midwest in his undergrad years.

Raymond (Slats) Baxter, who played end for Dartmouth as a teammate of Spears, remembered how both were poor boys with one pair of pants apiece. So they found a roommate named Archie Gile who had some money. Archie was able to handsomely furnish a room they shared on the top floor of Sanborn Hall.

"It was palatial, but the beauty did not last long," Baxter would recall. "Spears had a curious habit of throwing all the furniture out the window to hear the crash four floors below. We wound up sitting on wooden boxes for two years."

In his four years coaching at Dartmouth, Spears compiled a record of 21-9-1. Meanwhile, he completed work on a medical degree and spent many hours treating

Clarence Spears—better known as "Fat" or "Doc"—an all-America guard and later the coach at Dartmouth. (DARTMOUTH COLLEGE)

influenza patients in the Hanover hospital during the great 1918 epidemic.

Spears was as tough on alumni as he had been on furniture, telling the old grads to keep their advice to themselves since they were ignorant about football. That attitude led to his turning up as the coach at West Virginia in 1921.

On New Year's Day 1916, a California spectacle began its modern run—with an Ivy League team in the spotlight.

Back in 1902, Michigan had faced Stanford at Pasadena in a game growing out of the Tournament of Roses festival. The crowd of 8,000 at Tournament Park had a most unpleasant afternoon. It was a hot, dusty day and the fans had to wait for hours in long lines for the one tiny entrance to open. When it did, there was a stampede, and the first 2,000 fans swooped down on the reserved seats whether they had tickets for them or not.

After that, Pasadena officials stuck to chariot races, pole-climbing contests, and greased-pig hunts to complement their rose parade. It wasn't until 1916 that football was again on the scene—the first modern Rose Bowl game. (The event was still called the Tournament of Roses back then, and Tournament Park remained the site. The Rose Bowl stadium wasn't built until 1923.)

The 1916 "home team" at Pasadena was Washington State, the best in the West, sporting a 6-0 record and having outscored opponents by 190–10.

The visitor was a team that had been far from the best in the East. Though Cornell went 9-0, it was not invited. Harvard and Dartmouth, each with one defeat, and Princeton, with two losses, were snubbed as well. The hosts wanted Syracuse, but having played several games in the Far West during the season, it declined. So the invitation finally went to Brown, which had a modest record of 5-3-1, though running up a 166–32 point differential.

The Bears were led by Frederick Dou-glass Pollard—better known as Fritz—a 5-foot-8-inch, 160-pound left halfback out of Chicago with tremendous speed (he was intercollegiate hurdles champion in 1916 and 1917) and an elusive close-to-the-ground running style.

Fritz Pollard stood out, however, for more than his ability to evade tacklers—he was the first black man to be a college football star.

His brother, Leslie, a football player at Dartmouth from 1907 to 1909, had encountered resistance that might have given a lesser man than Fritz pause.

"When Leslie played at Dartmouth, he was the only black on the team," Fritz would remember. "One year, Princeton protested because it didn't want to play against a black man, so I knew what I was getting into when I decided to go to college."

It didn't take long for Pollard to see the kind of welcome he would get at Providence.

"When I went out for football at Brown in the autumn of 1915, I was told the last practice suit had been given out," he would recall.

The athletic director, Frederick Marvel, saw to it that Pollard received equipment, but he got the oldest uniform in the gym and a pair of shoes at least two sizes too big.

Pollard remembered how "that first day they gave me a ball and told me to go over to one side of the field and practice punting. At dusk we quit and I trailed the rest of the players into Marston Field House. But when I walked into the shower room, my teammates moved out. I showered alone.

"On opening day I slipped into the field

A star running back for Brown, Fritz Pollard was the first black first-team all-American. (BROWN UNIVERSITY)

elusiveness to break away.

Pollard's running helped Brown score a 3–0 victory over Yale at New Haven, a triumph that propelled it to the Rose Bowl.

Years later, William Ashby, a black man who had been a Yale student back then, would recall how Yale's left tackle, an Atlanta native named Sheldon, had chased after Pollard on one play as the Yale fans yelled "Catch that nigger, kill that nigger." Sheldon collided with a teammate as they tried without success for a pincer tackle, and both were carried off on a stretcher.

Ashby later witnessed a little drama in the locker room.

"I was in the gym after the game hoping to shake Pollard's hand when Sheldon burst in. 'Where is he? Where is he?' he was calling. Pollard, having taken a shower, stepped out of a cage where he was dressing. 'You're a nigger but you're the best goddamn football player I ever saw,' blurted Sheldon, thrusting his hand out to Pollard."

house early to pick up my game uniform. But I found they hadn't assigned me one. I went over behind some game lockers, sat down by myself and cried."

But Pollard's talent won him acceptance, and he emerged as a star by midseason, developing a style on punt returns similar to Hobey Baker's: he took a running start, grabbed the ball at full speed, and used his

When Brown arrived at Pasadena for its Rose Bowl workouts, there was trouble for Pollard. A clerk at the Hotel Raymond, where the team was scheduled to stay, did not want to give him a room. But the head coach, Edward North Robinson, made it clear that if Pollard wasn't staying at the hotel, neither was the rest of the team. He got his room.

Brown had hoped to have Pollard run wide, but that strategy was taken away by rainy weather that brought slippery footing. Pollard couldn't get traction (he gained only 47 yards on 13 carries), and both clubs concentrated on plunges into the line.

After a scoreless first half, Washington State's runners tore through the right side of the Brown line, dragging would-be tacklers through the mud, en route to a 14–0 victory.

In 1916, Pollard became the first black player to make a No. 1 all-America team—a unanimous selection. Walter Camp wrote in *Collier's* that Pollard was "the most elusive back of the year, or of any year. He is a good sprinter, and once loose is a veritable will-o'-the-wisp that no one can lay hands on."

That autumn Pollard played against Paul Robeson of Rutgers, who in 1918 would become the second black to make a first-team all-America squad. Robeson, who would gain renown as a singer, actor, and civil rights activist, was bested by Pollard, who romped for 44- and 48-yard touchdowns in a 21–3 victory.

He ran wild in successive triumphs over Yale and Harvard, and Brown won its first eight games—outscoring its opponents 254–9 and rolling up six shutouts—before ending its season with a 28–0 loss to Colgate.

After his sophomore year, Pollard left Brown for service in World War I. Upon returning, he became the first black coach in

Edward North Robinson, the longtime Brown football coach who took the team to the 1916 Rose Bowl. (BROWN UNIVERSITY)

professional football, with the Akron Indians and Hammond Pros. He was later a highly successful businessman, newspaper publisher, and booking agent for black talent.

Pollard's college coach, Edward North Robinson, was to Brown as Walter Camp was to Yale. Robinson played football, baseball, and ran track for Brown, graduating in 1896, and then, after coaching at Nebraska for two seasons, became the Brown coach. He stayed on for 24 years, compiling a record of 140-82-12. Yet, in an era of tough coaches, Robinson did not fit the profile.

He was soft-spoken, shunned pep talks, and was loath to hurt a player's feelings.

The 1916 season saw the former Yale quarterback Tad Jones return to his alma mater as coach, and he took the team into the Harvard game with only one defeat, a 21–6 loss to Brown. Harvard had lost just twice, to Tufts and Brown.

Jones was a traditionalist. He gave a larger advisory role to Walter Camp, whose influence had waned when the former all-American Frank Hinkey coached Yale in 1914 and 1915. And the week before the Harvard game, Jones even brought Pudge Heffelfinger, 48 years old, back to New Haven. Heffelfinger scrimmaged with the varsity, was flipped up and came down with his right elbow smashing into star tackle Mac Baldridge, breaking two of his ribs.

But Baldridge would play 60 minutes against Harvard. He could hardly have done otherwise following Tad Jones's locker room speech.

"Gentlemen, you are now going to play football against Harvard. Never again in your whole life will you do anything so important."

The Yale boys responded with a 6–3 triumph after six straight years without a victory against Percy Haughton's Harvard teams.

That would be Haughton's last Harvard squad. He left to head a syndicate that bought the Boston Braves baseball team, then went into the chemical warfare corps during World War I. Upon return-ing, he entered the bond-trading business.

On New Year's Day 1917, an Ivy school once again represented the East in the Rose Bowl. This time Penn faced Oregon, traveling to Pasadena on a special train provided by a vice president of the Reading Railroad.

Penn had two players who would make a mark on football long after their college years.

The quarterback was Bert Bell, a future commissioner of the National Football League who would guide the pro game to prominence in the 1950s. When Bell was an all-around athlete at Haverford School in the Philadelphia area, his father, John Cromwell Bell, the attorney general of Pennsylvania and a trustee at Penn, had been asked where his son would go to college. "Bert will go to Penn, or he'll go to hell," he responded.

Penn's right tackle was Lou Little, who would become a coaching institution at Columbia.

But the stars were fullback Howard Berry and end Heinie Miller.

Penn was considered a better team than the

Tad (also known as T.A.D. for Thomas Albert Dwight) Jones, the Yale coach whose locker-room oration before a Harvard game rivals "Win One for the Gipper" in the annals of college football oratory.
(YALE UNIVERSITY)

Brown squad that played in the previous Rose Bowl, taking in a record of 7-2-1 but holding victories over strong Michigan and Cornell teams. The Quakers were a heavy favorite over an Oregon squad that had gone 6-0-1 against weaker opponents.

Playing before a crowd of more than 26,000 on a beautiful afternoon, Penn lived up to its notices in the early going, taking the football deep into Oregon territory three times. But it couldn't score.

The turning point came in the second period after Berry was hurt catching a pass on the Oregon 22-yard line. Penn got to the 3, but then a switch in strategy backfired. Although Penn had done well on line smashes, Berry's replacement, Bill Quigley, tried a run around right end. He was thrown for a 10-yard loss. Quigley then tried a field goal, but it was botched in the face of onrushing linemen. Suddenly, Penn did not seem invincible.

Oregon rallied for touchdowns late in the third quarter and again in the fourth quarter, the star of the game not Berry (he gained just 16 yards on nine carries) but Oregon's Shy Huntington, who threw a 19-yard touchdown pass for the first score, then intercepted a pass in the fourth quarter. After that grab, a

spectacular 42-yard run by Johnny Parsons put the ball on the 1, and Huntington carried it in.

Oregon's 14–0 victory was the first significant triumph by a Pacific Coast team over a squad representing Eastern football at its best.

The following autumn, college football felt the impact of America's entry into World War I. Penn played a full schedule, but Yale, Harvard, and Princeton fielded only informal teams. In 1918, the game was even more sharply curtailed.

When the doughboys came back from France, college football returned as well. The 1919 season would see a resurgence for Harvard as Ivy eyes looked westward again at year's end.

Best remembered as the National Football League commissioner who brought the pro game to prominence, Bert Bell was the quarterback for Penn's 1917 Rose Bowl team. (UNIVERSITY OF PENNSYLVANIA)

"TEAM OF DESTINY"

THE 1920S WOULD be known as the Golden Age of sports—Babe Ruth, Red Grange, Bobby Jones, and Bill Tilden were cast in heroic molds.

At the Ivy schools, the nation's frenzy for athletic spectacle spawned huge crowds at the new stadiums for old rivalries. Autumn afternoons were grand times for alumni and for the young men with their girls sporting the fashion of the day—raccoon coats and hip flasks.

At Harvard, Percy Haughton was gone, now busy selling bonds. Bob Fisher, a former Harvard lineman and captain of the 1911 team, was named coach when full-scale football returned after World War I.

Haughton was hardly missed. Harvard finished the 1919 season at 8-0-1—a perfect record spoiled by a 10–10 tie with Princeton—and was invited to play Oregon in the Rose Bowl, the third straight time an Ivy team was picked to represent the East.

(Military squads played in the 1918 and 1919 Pasadena games.)

Neither Brown nor Penn, the first two Ivy teams in the Rose Bowl, had been powerhouses, but this Harvard squad was indeed impressive, having shut out seven opponents. The Crimson boasted three current or future all-Americans—right halfback Eddie Casey, center Charles (Bubbles) Havemeyer, and left halfback Arnold Horween, whose brother Ralph played at fullback.

Harvard went to Pasadena as a slight favorite over a 5–1 Oregon team coached by Charles (Shy) Huntington, who had starred in the school's 1917 Rose Bowl victory over Penn. But the Crimson were burdened by considerable pressure. The Eastern football establishment, grouchy over the bowl losses by Brown and Penn, counted on Harvard to prove that the old football stock still had steel in it.

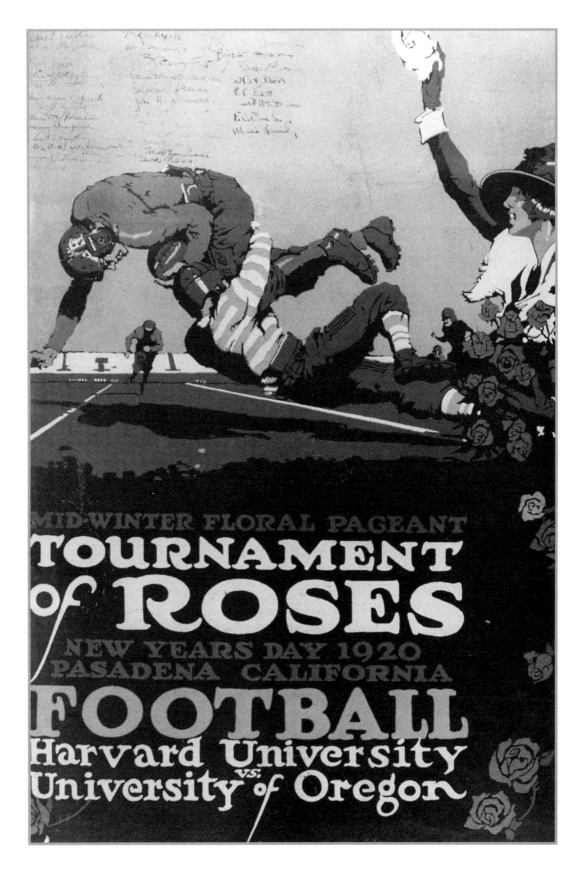

The first order of business on the rail trip to California was a bit of socializing. The team stopped off in Chicago for supper and a swim at the Harvard Club.

A brief layover at the Omaha train station brought a workout, Coach Fisher organizing a 15-minute signal drill and some sprints on an icy platform.

Before the train pulled out, Harvard received a pep talk from—of all people—a Yale man. Mac Baldridge, a tackle on the 1915 and 1916 Yale teams and now an Omaha resident, had some interesting news. He reported that another Yale player had been offered $150 and expenses by someone from the University of Oregon to go out there and give a blackboard talk on Harvard's style of play. The espionage mission was rejected because, said Baldridge, "Yale men want Harvard to win out on the Coast almost as much as if Yale's own team was playing."

"Remember that you are representing all the East," he pointed out.

Upon arriving in Pasadena, Harvard went Hollywood, visiting the Brunton movie studio to meet heavyweight champion Jack Dempsey, who was portraying an athlete working his way through college. Two players, Swede Nelson and Joe Ryan, had their pictures taken with Douglas Fairbanks Sr., who invited the team to return a few days later to see a preview of his movie *When the Clouds Roll By* and to witness a Wild West show. In gratitude, Harvard gave

Fairbanks and his guest, Charlie Chaplin, game seats on its bench.

There was one slight misadventure: a chauffeur-driven car carrying the captain, quarterback Billy Murray, and the star runner Eddie Casey on a visit to Hollywood was stopped for exceeding the 20-mile-an-hour speed limit. But Murray gave the cop two tickets to the game and that apparently fixed things.

By now, Casey may have been wondering if the fates were against him. Harvard was going to wear numerals for the first time, and he had been assigned No. 13. He refused the honor, and it developed that all-America rank had its privileges. Casey swapped for another number assigned to Babe Felton, a substitute quarterback.

The morning of the game, the Harvard players spent two hours on the lawn of the Elks Club watching the flower-bedecked floats of the Tournament of Roses parade go by.

Then it was off to the 32,000-seat Tournament Field, which was sold out. Thousands of fans gathered outside hoping for a stray ticket from scalpers seeking $25 for $5 box seats.

Armed with a good-luck telegram from the Massachusetts governor, Calvin Coolidge, Harvard took on an Oregon team led by running back Hollis Huntington, the coach's brother, and "Bad Bill" Steers, a second-team all-America quarterback.

Harvard had a chance to get the lead in

The 1920 Harvard-Oregon Rose Bowl game—called the Tournament of Roses back then—came up crimson. (HARVARD UNIVERSITY)

the first quarter. On third down, fullback Ralph Horween stood on the Oregon 45-yard line to attempt a dropkick field goal.

Seventy-five years later, Horween, at age 99, could vividly recall the moment:

"The pass from center was perfect and, as usual, I took my half-step forward when the ball was in the air. So the speed with which I got rid of the ball was within the limits as it was in the past.

"But I'm sure that Billy Murray, the quarterback, misread the signal. There's a photograph of that play showing him facing me with his hands in the air. It could be that the incoming linemen got through so quickly that they pushed Billy right into the ball. I did not see what happened because my eyes were glued to my feet, which were lined up with the center of the goalposts, which was the way I always worked."

The kick was blocked by an Oregon guard and rolled free.

"It was the first and only time I had a blocked kick," Horween remembered. "That goes for about 45 or 50 punts and about 10 or 15 dropkicks.

"Well, before I knew it, the ball kept rolling toward the sidelines. There was a scramble near the grandstand, where Jack Dempsey was sitting, and I hurt my shoulder and passed out."

Oregon recovered the ball. Having suffered a chipped collarbone and dislocated shoulder, Horween was replaced by the speedy Freddie Church.

Oregon's Steers opened the scoring in the second quarter with a dropkick field goal from 25 yards out.

But Harvard soon came back, Murray combining with Casey on pass plays of 25 and 15 yards in a drive to the Oregon 15. Then Church, playing only because Horween had been hurt, made the most of his opportunity. Taking the next snap deep behind the center, he raced around the left side and went into the end zone untouched. Halfback Arnold Horween, Ralph's younger brother, kicked the extra point. Now it was Harvard 7, Oregon 3.

Later in the second quarter, Steers ran for 18 yards, then was slammed by Arnold Horween and carried off the field.

At the Harvard Club on 44th Street in Manhattan, 500 alumni had gathered in the Georgian Room beside a small gridiron in a crimson frame flanked by blackboards with the players' names. A little football was moved along the gridiron to reflect each play as a telegraph operator received reports from Pasadena, then relayed the information to an announcer.

"Steers has been hurt," the announcer reported. "He wants to get back into the game, but is very wobbly."

Then, after a pause in the telegraph report, the announcer said that "the operator at the Boston Harvard Club has wired the operator at Pasadena asking whether the delay is due to the fact that they are burying Steers." Cheers erupted.

When the announcer reported that "a large section of the spectators are taking violent exception to Harvard's rough play," the old coach, Percy Haughton, rose from his seat, clapped, and smiled.

Steers did not return until the fourth quarter, and Harvard hung on for a 7–6 victory.

Centre College's Bo McMillin (*arrow*) breaking loose for the touchdown run that brought down mighty Harvard at Cambridge in 1921. (CENTRE COLLEGE)

Afterward, a Hollywood starlet named Viola Dana took all the credit, saying she had sent victorious thought waves to Harvard via mental telepathy.

In the autumn of 1920, mighty Harvard took on a tiny school that a few years earlier would never have dreamed of visiting Cambridge—Centre College of Danville, Kentucky.

Back in 1917, a Centre alumnus named Robert (Chief) Myers took over as coach after having coached football at North Side High School in Fort Worth, Texas. A few weeks later, evidently deciding the job was too complicated—even at a school with fewer than 300 students—Myers turned over the coaching to Charley Moran, a National League umpire and former college and pro football player whose son, Tom, was playing for Centre.

"Uncle Charley" would mastermind the strategy while Myers recruited talented youngsters who had played for him in high school.

After having lost to Kentucky by 68–0 in 1916, Centre won, 3–0, the following season under Myers and Moran. Before that second Kentucky game, the normally gruff Moran asked his boys to pray—and a public relations phenomenon was born. The team continued to win, continued to seek divine intervention, and came to be known as the "Prayin' Colonels."

Centre went unbeaten in 1919, defeating a West Virginia team that had shut out Princeton, a game that gave the school national recognition as quarterback Bo McMillin, one of those recruits from the Fort Worth high school, reeled off a series of running passes.

Eddie Mahan, Harvard's onetime star runner, scouted the Prayin' Colonels and helped arrange a matchup.

Centre drew a curious crowd of more than 40,000 for the 1920 game at Harvard, but was out of its league. The Crimson won by 31–14.

The following season, Centre returned to face a Harvard team with a 25-game unbeaten streak. As a crowd of 43,000 waited for the inevitable rout, Uncle Charley Moran delivered a fighting speech in the locker room. Following that up, A. B. (Happy) Chandler, the future baseball commissioner and Kentucky senator and governor—at the time a Harvard law student—sang "Dear Old Southland." Then everyone knelt for prayers.

Centre held its own in the first half, encouraged by Massachusetts Institute of Technology students who had appointed themselves a cheering section for the country boys. Harvard saw one field goal attempt blocked and another miss in a scoreless half.

Early in the third quarter, Centre got to the Harvard 32-yard line. McMillin then ran to his right and cut inside the Harvard left end. He got four big blocks, now veered to the left, received yet another block from lineman Red Roberts, who smashed the safety, and scored standing up.

That would be the only touchdown of the day. Centre emerged with an astounding 6–0 upset.

The MIT gang lifted McMillin on its shoulders, tore down the goalposts, and

Coach Gil Dobie, the eternal pessimist whose gloom was occasionally lifted by Cornell teams that went undefeated from 1922 to 1924. (CORNELL UNIVERSITY)

Seventy-five years after the upset of Harvard, the legend "C 6, H 0," written all over town during victory celebrations, can still be seen on Centre's campus post office building. (CENTRE COLLEGE)

snake-danced in ecstasy. Back in Danville, Centre students lit bonfires, then corralled a dozen milk cows, painted "C 6, H 0" on their hides, and herded them down the town's main street.

Twenty-nine years later, an Associated Press poll cited Centre's victory as the biggest upset in half a century.

Harvard lost to Princeton the week after the Centre game, finishing the season at 7-2-1, and would have only moderate success for the rest of the decade.

The king of the Ivies in the early 1920s was Cornell, its players driven relentlessly by Coach Gil Dobie, the epitome of the dour Scotsman.

Dobie arrived at Ithaca in 1920 after having compiled a record of 58-0-3 in nine seasons at the University of Washington before spending three years at Navy.

He produced a winning team in his first year at Cornell, then ripped off three straight 8-0 seasons as Cornell outscored the opposition by 392–21, 339–27, and 320–33.

The tall, lean Dobie was known as "Gloomy Gil" for his dire predictions and dissatisfaction with his players, no matter how well they performed. The sportswriters coined a word for gloominess— "Gildobian."

Walt Rollo, a Cornell guard in the 1920s, would remember how Dobie "was never known to congratulate a player in public, and seldom in private."

Apparently concerned that his men would become overconfident if lauded, Dobie had a habit of forgetting their names. There was one exception. "Gil always knew my name," recalled Andy Pierce, who played for Dobie in the 1930s. "He unerringly referred to me as Fat Ass Pierce."

A devotee of the ground game, and a perfectionist at drilling his teams until their timing was perfect, Dobie specialized in the off-tackle play. He had a pair of superb runners for his single-wing attack of the early 1920s in George Pfann, a powerful back, and Eddie Kaw, a shifty man in the open field who scored five touchdowns in the rain against Penn in 1921.

Pfann, who became a Rhodes Scholar, a prominent lawyer, and an aide to General George S. Patton in World War II, would recall how Kaw "was an exceptionally cocky

George Pfann, a star running back for Cornell and later a Rhodes scholar. (CORNELL UNIVERSITY)

individual" and "inclined to loaf." But, said Pfann, "I don't think he ever choked up when the pressure was on."

Despite all those unbeaten seasons, something was amiss at Cornell.

The *Cornell Daily Sun* ran an editorial in October 1924 titled "Soprano Cheering" in which it demanded that coeds be barred from the organized yelling at Schoellkopf Field.

"Our cheering has been deplorable," the editors complained. "If we are finally to boast of our cheering prowess, women must be prohibited from participation. Mixed duets of 'Cornell, yell, yell, yell, Cornell' do not particularly enhance the effect

Cornell's Eddie Kaw, who presumably elicited a rare smile from Coach Gil Dobie when he ran for five touchdowns against Penn in 1921.

of cheering. Feminine squeals of glee and screams of fear are charming in their place, but that place is not the cheering section of the Cornell crescent."

The state of cheering must have slid ever further downhill as the 1924 season moved along since Cornell went only 4-4, a 26-game winning streak ending with a 14–7 loss to Williams in the third game.

Sizing up his players before the 1925 season, Dobie made it clear there was something very wrong with their priorities. "They're just a lot of scholars dressed up as athletes with their minds on Phi Beta Kappa keys instead of interference," he complained.

That team would, however, go 6-2, and Dobie would be putting up with Phi Beta Kappa types for quite a while longer. He remained at Cornell through 1935.

Dobie's unbeaten team of 1922 wasn't the only impressive Ivy school that year.

Nobody expected Princeton to be particularly strong—tackle Herb Treat would be the team's only all-American—but the Tigers were an early surprise, winning their first four games by shutouts. Then they made the

school's first trip to the Midwest to face Amos Alonzo Stagg's powerhouse University of Chicago, which came in at 3-0.

Playing before a crowd of 40,000 at Stagg Field and one of the first radio audiences for college football (WOR's Gus Falzer at the mike), Chicago took an 18–7 lead into the fourth quarter on running back John Thomas's three touchdowns. (All three extra-point attempts were missed.)

But with six minutes to play, a botched snap on a Chicago punt play sent the football careening into the arms of Howard Gray, a Princeton end, who ran it back 40 yards for a touchdown. Now it was 18–14.

Princeton soon got the ball back, and Burly Crumm ran for a 1-yard score on fourth down. With the left-footed Ken Smith kicking his third extra point, the Tigers took a 21–18 edge.

Then Chicago moved down the field with a flurry of passes, finally getting to the Princeton 6 with two minutes remaining. Now Thomas assaulted the Princeton line. He carried for 3 yards, then picked up 1 yard, then 1 yard again. It was fourth down, only seconds remaining. Thomas plunged into the middle of the Princeton line once more, but Harland (Pink) Baker knifed in to tackle him. Princeton took the ball, punted out of danger and jubilantly watched the clock run out.

It was ostensibly a goal line stand for the ages. But as Don Griffin, a Princeton lineman, would remember things, the

Tigers had help—from the Chicago fans, whose exhortations kept Stagg's linemen from hearing their own signals. "We took credit for stopping them, but the truth is that their plays were messed up," Griffin recalled. "There was so much yelling and screaming going on, and Chicago's linemen didn't shift properly."

Nonetheless, the Princeton players were in a frenzy when it was all over.

"It was so emotional at the end that we thought we had won the Harvard and Yale games in the same afternoon," said Griffin.

Following that game, Grantland Rice bestowed a sobriquet on the Tigers befitting an age of ballyhoo—"Team of Destiny." It was a team that would go undefeated, finishing the season at 8-0.

The Princeton coach, Bill Roper, must have savored the nickname, for he specialized in whipping up his troops with emotional appeals.

Roper was no stranger to last-minute heroics. Playing end for Princeton, he had recovered a fumble late in the 1899 Yale game to set up the Arthur Poe field goal that brought a thrilling 11–10 victory.

"This game is ninety percent fight," Roper once said. "There is a great deal of bunk to all of this talk of system and involved plays. If a team hasn't the fight, the spirit and the courage to give just a little bit more when there doesn't seem to be anything left, it is not going to win very many important games."

To rally his boys, he would put out placards at team meals quoting the phrase coined by John Prentiss Poe Jr.—"A Team That Won't Be Beat Can't Be Beat."

Charlie Caldwell, a back on The Team of Destiny and later a renowned Princeton coach in his own right, would remember how Roper loved to say "if you had a Princeton jersey on and the other man didn't, you had him licked."

But Roper was no rah-rah simpleton. He was a lawyer, owned an insurance business in Philadelphia, and served three terms on its City Council while coaching at Princeton.

In the autumns of 1923 and 1924, Roper was pitted against another master psychologist when Knute Rockne brought Notre Dame into Palmer Stadium.

These were more than football games—they were encounters with a social context. Notre Dame, still yearning for institutional recognition in an era of widespread anti-Catholicism, was testing itself against the sons of the wealthy, powerful Anglo-Saxon establishment.

Notre Dame whipped Princeton, 25–2, in October 1923, ending a 10-game Tiger winning streak. The following October, a sports legend was manufactured after Notre Dame beat Army, 13–7, at the Polo Grounds. Grantland Rice, turning out the hyperbole once more, wrote his "Four Horsemen" lead. The Notre Dame publicist, George Strickler, then posed the backfield—Elmer Layden, Don Miller, Harry Stuhldreher, and Jimmy Crowley—on horseback, a classic public relations stunt. The Saturday after that, the Notre Dame backs arrived at Palmer Stadium as newly minted celebrities. Rockne used his second team for the first quarter and then, with Princeton worn down a bit, brought the

In the autumn before he joined the Yankees, Lou Gehrig was hitting the line for Columbia. (COLUMBIA UNIVERSITY)

prompting the well-known sportswriter Paul Gallico to write in the *Columbia Alumni News* how "Gehrig is the beef expert who has mastered the science of going where he is sent, for at least five yards. His plunges seem to carry force."

Gehrig wasn't the only baseball Hall of Famer who played football for Columbia. Fifteen years earlier, Eddie Collins—the future star second baseman for the Athletics and White Sox—also played both baseball and football for the Lions.

Gehrig's football season at Columbia was the team's final one at South Field.

As college football burgeoned into mass entertainment, more stadiums were being built or expanded around the nation. Pennsylvania demolished the wooden stands at Franklin Field in 1922 and replaced them with steel and concrete tiers, nearly doubling the capacity to 54,500. By the mid-1920s, a second deck had been completed, expanding the seating to 78,205.

Columbia's football team moved uptown from the dirt-top South Field at Morningside Heights to the Dyckman tract, a 26-acre complex on Upper Broadway overlooking Spuyten Duyvil, where the Hudson and Harlem rivers met. George F. Baker, chairman of the First National Bank

Four Horsemen in. Playing before a crowd of 45,000, Notre Dame won again, 12–0, as Crowley scored a pair of touchdowns.

Two years before the Four Horsemen rode into the public relations hall of fame, Columbia's football team had the Iron Horse. Nobody would be calling him that for some time, but Lou Gehrig—fresh out of Manhattan's Commerce High School—was already a name to know.

He would be best remembered at Columbia for clouting prodigious drives out of South Field toward the statue of Alma Mater on the Low Library steps. But Gehrig also played football for the Lions, a running back and lineman on the 1922 team. He scored two touchdowns in his first game, against Ursinus College, of New York, donated $700,000 for the property.

The Lions' new home—called, strangely enough, Baker Field—opened on September 19, 1923, with Columbia defeating Ursinus, 13–0, before a crowd of 15,000. (The fans watched from temporary stands since Columbia had not yet raised funds for a full-fledged stadium. Permanent seating wasn't in place until 1928.)

The Columbia administration figured a high-powered coach was needed in order to fill those Baker Field seats, temporary or not. So in a stunning move, Percy Haughton was enticed to forsake his business interests and his old school ties.

Haughton was hardly a traitor to Harvard, having been out of football since 1916, but for some purists the ideals of amateur athletics had been struck a blow. The *New Haven Journal-Courier*, putting aside its devotion to Yale, said of Haughton: "We hope to learn how he could be induced to desert his own college and transfer his genius to a field of instruction hostile to the pride of Harvard. The capture of Haughton by Columbia does raise interesting speculations upon the subject of modern collegiate sports."

Haughton, who reportedly was paid more than $15,000 to take the Columbia coaching job—a handsome sum back then—defended the switch to another Ivy school. He maintained that because Columbia had dropped football for a decade in the not-so-distant past, it lacked

John Heisman plots summertime strategy during training camp at Penn, where he coached from 1920 to 1922. (UNIVERSITY OF PENNSYLVANIA)

an alumni talent pool from which to pick a coach. He hoped to establish a system "that can be perpetuated by Columbia graduates."

Haughton's 1923 squad went 4-4-1, and things looked promising the following season when Columbia won its first three games. Then, a shock for the football world—Haughton died of a heart attack before the game with Penn. He was 48 years old.

Paul Withington, an assistant coach, finished out the season and then Charles Crowley, another aide, was hired as coach for 1925.

Columbia was 6-3-1 in 1925 and scored an upset victory over Army, but after the season it went hunting for another big-name coach. Early in December, Columbia looked to the top of the marquee, offering Notre Dame's Knute Rockne a three-year contract at $25,000 annually to make him the highest-paid coach in the country.

Rockne signed the deal, but the coup was supposed to remain a secret until he concluded his affairs at Notre Dame, then returned to New York for a formal announcement at the end of the month.

James Knapp, a Columbia alumnus who had been a key negotiator, couldn't keep a secret that long, so he leaked word of the signing. Grantland Rice promptly did handstands on his typewriter, predicting that Rockne "will have the Lion of the Hudson roaring before next fall is over."

Now everything unraveled as Notre Dame backers brought heavy pressure on Rockne. Embarrassed by premature word of his defection, he decided to stay at South Bend. Columbia would settle for rehiring Crowley, who had been a teammate of Rockne at Notre Dame in 1911.

While Haughton was building a program at Columbia back in 1923, Tad Jones was fielding one of the best teams in Yale's history.

Bill Mallory, the captain and fullback, a Tennessean known as "Memphis Bill," got a large share of the headlines for his powerful line plunges and blocking. But he had an impressive supporting cast, including four athletes who transferred from territory far beyond the Eastern prep establishment.

A 6-foot-4-inch, 220-pounder named Century Milstead (he'd been born on January 1, 1900) arrived from Wabash College in Indiana and teamed with Ted Blair, a Phi Beta Kappa man from Texas, to give Yale formidable tackles.

Mal Stevens, who had transferred from Washburn College in Kansas to study medicine, was a superb halfback. (He would later coach at Yale and then become a prominent gynecologist and obstetrician.)

Lyle Richeson, previously at Tulane, starred at quarterback. The fourth transfer was halfback Widdy Neale, who had played at West Virginia and Marietta of Ohio.

Yale was unbeaten going into the season-ender against Harvard, which was just 3-3-1, but stormy weather produced a mudbath that equalized things. The crowd of 55,000 at Cambridge was treated to 25 fumbles and 54 punts for its trouble. A couple of Yale players were, however, able to surmount the slop. Raymond Pond ran 67 yards for a touchdown after picking up a fumble (thereby gaining the nickname

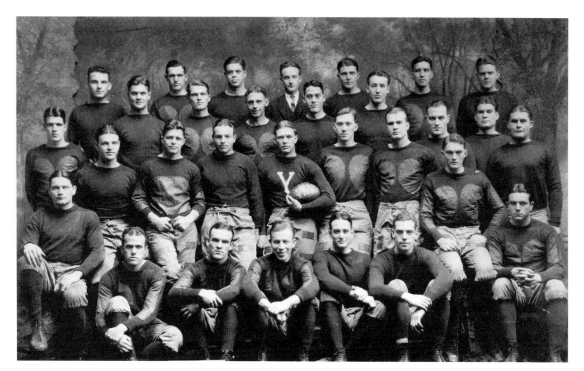

The undefeated Yale team of 1923, Captain Ted Mallory holding the football.
(YALE UNIVERSITY)

"Ducky") and Bill Mallory kicked 24- and 28-yard field goals. The Elis came away with a 13–0 victory, beating the Crimson for the first time since 1916 while scoring their first touchdown at Harvard in 16 years.

Yale students tore the goalposts down to celebrate an 8-0 season, then snatched the crimson flag from the Harvard Union building, an exuberant touch that embarrassed even the *Yale Daily News*, which apologized to Harvard for Yale's "rudeness and wretched sportsmanship."

The mid-1920s featured powerful teams at Dartmouth coached by Jess Hawley, Class of 1909, who was a man ahead of his times—he invited a psychology professor to address his players. It didn't hurt.

The 1923 team went 8-1, the 1924 squad finished at 7-0-1, and the 1925 team was 8-0.

Considered the Eastern champions, Dartmouth's 1924 team boasted an outstanding passer in Eddie Dooley. But the following season a bigger star emerged at quarterback when Andrew (Swede) Oberlander was switched from tackle.

Oberlander supposedly had a gimmick to guarantee passing accuracy:

"My secret of timing was to whisper to myself, 'Ten thousand Swedes jumped out of the weeds at the Battle of Copenhagen.' After reciting that jingle to myself, I'd let the ball go, confident my ends would be downfield by then."

**Quarterback Swede Oberlander led
Dartmouth to an unbeaten season in 1925.**
(DARTMOUTH COLLEGE)

ing off five touchdowns and 33 points
against Temple.

The 1925 Dartmouth team outscored
its opponents by 340–29, its biggest victory
a 62–13 thumping of Cornell at Hanover
on November 7 in a battle of unbeatens.
Oberlander threw six touchdown passes
and ran 50 yards around end for another
score.

(Cornell's Gil Dobie, a stickler for the
running game, supposedly said afterward:
"We won, 13–0. Passing isn't football.")

It was a sweet turnaround for Dartmouth, which had been beaten by Cornell,
59–7, in 1921 and had lost to the Big Red in
the game dedicating Dartmouth's Memorial
Stadium in 1923.

The 1925 season saw the Eastern
debut of a larger-than-life figure—Red
Grange of Illinois, the "Galloping Ghost."

It's doubtful that Oberlander really
recited poetry while dodging defensive linemen, but he connected often on long passes to George Tully and Heinie Sage. When
that didn't happen, halfback Myles Lane
picked up impressive yardage on the
ground. Lane, also a star hockey player,
rolled up 102 points in 1925, second best
in the nation. He would be the scoring
leader two years later with 125 points, reel-

**Myles Lane, a star running back for
Dartmouth, later a federal prosecutor in
the Rosenberg espionage trial and the
United States attorney in Manhattan.**
(DARTMOUTH COLLEGE)

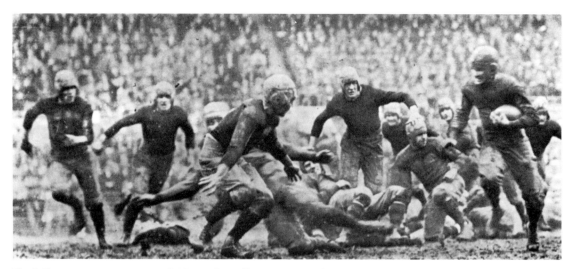

Red Grange en route to a 363-yard performance against Penn, proving to Eastern sportswriters that "the Galloping Ghost" was no phantom. (UNIVERSITY OF PENNSYLVANIA)

Grange had ridden a wave of press clippings with his five-touchdown extravaganza in October 1924 when Illinois opened its new stadium against Michigan. But the big-name Eastern sportswriters had yet to see Grange play. He still had something to prove to these provincials in order to be fully certified as a national sports deity.

Grange would recall how his coach, Bob Zuppke, "sent many personal letters to all of us on the squad telling how the eastern teams looked down their noses at midwestern football and that it was our duty to demonstrate to the football world that we were every bit as good or better than they."

He got his chance when Illinois met Penn on October 31, 1925, before 65,000 at a muddy Franklin Field. Penn was a national power. Its 1924 team had gone 9-1-1 and the 1925 squad was 5-0. This would truly be a test for Grange.

But he was hardly lacking support

against the hostile East. Thousands of Illinois fans made the trip to Philadelphia, and the 150-strong Illinois band—probably the biggest ever seen on the Eastern seaboard—tagged along, complete with a huge bass drum.

Playing the next-to-last game of his college career, Grange wasted no time in convincing the uninitiated. The first time he carried the ball he ran 55 yards untouched around left end for a score. He later ran for 12- and 20-yard touchdowns and gained 363 of Illinois's 450 yards in its 24–2 victory.

"This man Red Grange of Illinois is three or four men and a horse rolled into one for football purposes," wrote Damon Runyon. "He is Jack Dempsey, Babe Ruth, Al Jolson, Paavo Nurmi and Man o' War. Put them all together, they spell Grange."

Grange would tell how "a popular saying of the time was 'Penn rules the East,' but after our second touchdown in the first quarter our linemen became so cocky they stood up before almost every play and shouted, 'Illinois rules the East.'"

On a more modest scale, there were some lively moments at Brown in the mid-1920s.

Brown Stadium—replacing Andrews Field, the team's home since 1899—was dedicated on October 24, 1925, before a crowd of 27,000 that saw Brown fall to Yale, 20–7.

The 1926 season put Brown in an unaccustomed spotlight—it was the year of the unbeaten "Iron Men."

This was not a team with a bevy of stars. It had a fine passer and dropkicker in Dave Mishel and an outstanding end in its captain, Hal Broda. But only one player, 225-pound guard Orland Smith, would be named to the *Collier's* all-America team. (Smith, who would become a surgeon, evidently was a man of great endurance, since he worked his way through school by being on call every night as an ambulance driver at City Hospital.)

In the first of his 15 seasons at Brown, Coach Tuss McLaughry substituted freely in the opening four games, all victories. Then Brown went into Yale Bowl. Its vastness could intimidate most any team, but McLaughry—as Paul Hodge, a tackle on that team, would recall—told his players it was "just another hunk of concrete." Brown scored in the first period on a 2-yard run by fullback Al Cornsweet and held on for a 7–0 victory.

"It wasn't until the third quarter that I realized no substitutions had been made," McLaughry would remember. He thought:

"No one has been injured, the team is hot, winning and apparently fresh. Why break up a winning combination?"

So all the starters played 60 minutes, causing a sensation.

A large press contingent was on hand the following weekend when Brown played at Dartmouth before a sellout crowd of 13,000. The Bears rewarded the newspapermen by again going without a substitution in a 10–0 victory. When the team returned to Providence, it was greeted with a torchlight parade and a ceremony in which Brown's president conferred simulated honorary degrees on the players.

McLaughry started second-stringers the following weekend in a 27–0 romp against a weak Norwich team. Brown was now 7-0, having been scored on only in a 27–14 victory over Bates.

The next Saturday, a capacity crowd of 53,896 turned out for the Bears' game at Harvard—the largest crowd ever to watch a Brown team play. To placate Brown fans who couldn't get tickets, movies were shot of the game and shipped back to four Providence theaters. But not everyone was thrilled with the Iron Men—the Brown subs were getting restless, having become known as the "Wooden Men." So, with Brown holding a 14–0 lead, McLaughry put the bench warmers in for the final two minutes. They tacked on another touchdown for a 21–0 victory.

By now, the world of commerce was cashing in on all the publicity. Since McLaughry liked to give his players a pint of milk after practices, a farm publication called *The Rural New Yorker* pointed out how "in the great football game of life, you can have no finer friend than a cow."

But the hype had reached its zenith at the close of the Harvard game. Afterward, McLaughry sought to put things in perspective, telling a reporter: "They're not Iron Men. They are just 11 college boys having a good time playing football."

Brown beat New Hampshire next, but saw a perfect record spoiled in a 10–10 tie with Colgate on Thanksgiving Day that closed out its season at 9-0-1.

While Brown's Iron Men, Princeton's Team of Destiny and other products of the age of hyperbole like the Galloping Ghost and the Four Horsemen were taking breathers at halftime, big bands entertained the huge crowds filling the stadiums.

In the fall of 1919, Frederic Reynolds, a Harvard senior who had played in World War I regimental bands, recruited 40 fellow students for a marching band. By season's end it had doubled in size. Forty additional volunteers brimming with enthusiasm but

The Harvard drum, purchased for $1,500 in 1928 and thumped for 27 years until replaced by a similar giant. (HARVARD UNIVERSITY)

"My Time Is Your Time" crooner Rudy Vallee (*right*) spends time with fellow Yalies.
(YALE UNIVERSITY)

unable to play a note were enlisted for the sake of numbers. They held instruments aloft, marching alongside the real musicians when the band paraded from the campus to Harvard Stadium for the Yale game.

Sporting white flannel trousers, crimson sweaters, bow ties, and white sailor hats in its early years, the Harvard band would feature the baritone saxophone playing of Johnny Green, composer of "Body and Soul." In 1928, the band acquired the trademark Harvard drum from the firm of Ludwig & Ludwig. Costing $1,500 and mounted on a platform over four bicycle wheels, it was entirely handmade with each drumhead representing the seasoned skin of one whole cow. The drum would remain in use until 1955, when it lost its strength

and was replaced by a similar behemoth.

In 1929, a trombone-playing senior named Leroy Anderson—"Blue Tango" and "Sleigh Ride" in his future—became the Harvard band director. Serving as the band's first post-graduate leader in the early 1930s, Anderson brought a Broadway flourish to Cambridge, arranging tunes from Harvard fight songs around the melody "Wintergreen for President" from the Pulitzer Prize–winning musical *Of Thee I Sing*.

Yale's musical fortunes got a lift when a saxophone-playing transfer from the University of Maine named Rudy Vallee arrived on campus. The band's most inspired moment may have come in October 1929 when it played "Marching Through Georgia" to highlight Yale's game on the University of Georgia campus. Unamused by the Shermanesque touch, the southerners had the final say this time with a 15–0 victory.

What passed for campus humor played a role, meanwhile, in the great Ivy rift of the 1920s—a breakup of the Harvard-Princeton rivalry.

Relations first became strained when the Harvard Athletic Association—supposedly under pressure from alumni in the Midwest—suggested dropping Princeton from the 1927 schedule in favor of Michigan. But with Yale acting as a mediator, Harvard backed off.

The enmity resurfaced when the *Harvard Lampoon* put out a new issue hours before the 1926 Princeton game at Palmer Stadium.

The first page bore a picture of two pigs rooting in a trough with the caption: "Come, brother, let us root for dear old Princeton."

Elsewhere in the *Lampoon,* Princeton was described as a place "where the beer flows round the campus like a most exclusive moat."

An illustration showed a New England Puritan reproving his young son for bringing indoors a tiger cat that soiled the floor with his paws.

Joe Prendergast, a Princeton running back, would recall how the Princeton band leader handed Coach Bill Roper the *Lampoon* issue "as he was giving his usual pregame fight talk." Roper read it to the team and then said, "Now go out there and give them your answer."

Princeton went on to a 12–0 victory, but school officials proved to be sore winners upon further contemplating the *Lampoon*'s sophomoric wit.

Apologies were demanded—and received. President A. Lawrence Lowell of Harvard termed the humor magazine's anti-Princeton campaign "wholly repugnant to the sentiments of Harvard men." Even the *Lampoon* editors apologized for an "offensive" tone while expressing surprise that the issue had become a cause of contention.

But retaliation was swift. An elm tree in front of the *Lampoon*'s offices—a gift of Josiah Wheelwright, a founder of the publication—was sawed down.

That was minor compared with what happened the Wednesday after the game. Citing "an atmosphere of suspicion and ill will," Princeton broke athletic relations with Harvard.

It was the fourth rupture in the football rivalry, the previous one having lasted between 1897 and 1910 after Harvard accused Princeton of undue roughness.

The furor intensified the following January when Wynant Hubbard, who had played guard for Harvard in 1919 and 1920, wrote an article in *Liberty* magazine titled "Dirty Football" in which he asserted that Princeton had played brutally against Harvard during the 1920s, inflicting gouged eyes and broken limbs. His most sensational charge was that Al Miller, a Harvard fullback, came out of a Princeton game with the imprint of a signet ring on his nose. (Hubbard's credibility was, however, called into question. After graduating in 1921, he had spent five years overseas so was anything but a firsthand observer.)

Princeton responded by soliciting statements from game officials clearing the Tigers of foul play. W. R. Okeson, an official in the matchups between 1923 and 1926, stated that "the Princeton-Harvard games of the past four years have little to offer to the scandalmonger and male gossiper. They were just good, clean contests between a lot of fine, decent boys coached by gentlemen sportsmen."

But Harvard and Princeton would not meet again in football until 1934.

The big Ivy matchup of 1927 featured Princeton, at 6-0, finishing its season against a Yale team that had been beaten only by Georgia.

Yale suffered a setback before the game when Bruce Caldwell, its star running back, was declared ineligible under a rule curbing transfers. The *Providence Bulletin* reported that he had played two games for the Brown freshman team in 1923.

To lift his men's spirits, Coach Tad Jones called upon a friend who happened to be playing at the Shubert Theater in New Haven that weekend. Yale wasn't looking for a bowl-game bid, but Al Jolson turned up in the dressing room to serenade the team with "California Here I Come."

It proved inspiring enough. Yale trailed by 6–0 with 10 minutes to play, but halfback Johnny Hoben connected with Dwight Fishwick on a 40-yard touchdown pass, and Yale scored again after recovering a fumble. The final: Yale 14, Princeton 6.

The following Saturday, Yale finished at 7-1 with a 14–0 victory at Harvard on a frigid afternoon. It was the finale for Tad Jones, who had announced back in September that he would retire after eight seasons as coach. Mal Stevens, a star runner on the 1923 team, would take over.

Although hardly in the class of Yale or Princeton, Columbia had a winning team in 1927. The *Spectator* student newspaper found reason to grouse nonetheless, denouncing the student body as apathetic because it had quit holding pep rallies before home games.

The Thursday night before the season-ending game with Syracuse at the Polo Grounds, the apathy was shed with an exclamation point. Some 1,000 Columbia students snake-danced to South Field, the football team's former home, and lit a gigantic bonfire in the grandstand while members of the Alpha Delta Phi fraternity fired a cannon from their doorway on West 114th Street.

When firemen broke down a fence surrounding the field, the students pelted them with eggs and mud balls. The firefighters then turned hoses on their assailants, the police brandished billy clubs, 16 students were arrested, and scores more went home with bruised heads.

The next day, the revelers answered disorderly conduct charges in West Side Court, where Patrolman William Gaynor complained that they had derided him and his fellow officers as "Irish loafers."

Magistrate Dreyer, dismissing the whole thing as "youthful exuberance," imposed suspended sentences.

The following November, mayhem ranged well beyond Morningside Heights. After a pep rally for the Cornell game, Columbia students went on a rampage aboard a subway train they boarded at the campus, removing light bulbs, tearing advertisements from the walls, and throwing seats through car windows. They got off at Times Square, marched along 43rd Street to the Columbia Club near Fifth Avenue, serenaded a joint Columbia-Cornell football smoker, and were last spotted heading down Fifth.

The 1929 season saw the arrival of two great names whose fortunes would be linked—Barry Wood of Harvard and Albie Booth of Yale.

Wood, a dark-haired 6-footer, was the all-America boy—a superstar in athletics and academic life. He was a brilliant quarterback, a baseball and hockey player, and No. 1 man on the Harvard-Yale tennis team that faced an Oxford-Cambridge squad in 1929. He made Phi Beta Kappa, received the Francis H. Burr scholarship for academic merit, athletic ability, and leadership, and hoped to be a doctor.

In an era of hero worshiping, the sportswriters gushed.

Damon Runyon, in a sketch in the *New York American*, described Wood as "young, handsome, wealthy and brilliant. Also, I might add, modest, which is an attribute necessary to the complete rounding out of a real storybook hero."

Westbrook Pegler, writing for the Chicago Tribune Press Service, saw Wood as "close to the ideal conception of the American student, athlete, leader and sportsman."

And Paul Gallico of the *New York Daily News* called him "a really heroic figure."

At Yale, all eyes were on Albie Booth, a young man from New Haven known as "Little Boy Blue."

Only 5 feet 7 inches and 144 pounds, Booth was not extraordinarily fast, but he was a shifty runner and a terrific dropkicker and punter.

He became an instant star on the afternoon of October 26, 1929, when a crowd of 80,000 turned out at Yale Bowl for the Army game.

Booth came in during the second quarter with unbeaten Army ahead by 13–0, its first touchdown scored on a 57-yard run with an intercepted pass by the star halfback Chris Cagle. Now Booth would outshine Cagle, running for 223 yards and three touchdowns in a 21–13 victory, the last score coming on a 70-yard punt return on which every Cadet seemingly had a chance to nail him. And his dropkicks provided the extra points.

Barry Wood, Harvard's star quarterback from 1929 to 1931.
(HARVARD UNIVERSITY)

The following week, Yale played Dartmouth in a duel between Booth and the star running back Al Marsters.

Marsters got off to a disastrous start as Yale took a 10–0 lead, its touchdown coming when Alpheus Beane ran 22 yards after recovering a Marsters fumble. But in the third period, Marsters threw three passes for almost all the Dartmouth yardage on an 83-yard scoring drive, then ran 33 yards on three carries for another score after Yale had fumbled the kickoff. He would, however, suffer a vertebrae injury in a collision with a Yale player that ended his career.

Booth was also brilliant, running for 268 yards and unleashing a series of booming punts. He would have had much more yardage, but as Dick Williams, writing in the *New York World*, reported, "He was deprived of 43 yards when an official detected a Yale man in the act of sinking his teeth in the calf of a Dartmouth leg while both lay on the ground 30 yards behind the point to which the play had progressed."

Despite that little setback, Yale wound up with a 16–12 victory.

As Booth emerged on the football stage against Army before that roaring crowd of 80,000 at Yale Bowl, an era was ending for America. The stock market crashed a few days later. The raccoon coats favored by the Ivy sporting set would go out of fashion. For many Americans, even a cloth coat would be a treasure.

Barry Wood and Albie Booth would continue their rivalry, but the golden days of college football had run their course.

Albie Booth, the elusive Yale running back known as "Little Boy Blue."
(YALE UNIVERSITY)

"POMONA HIGH IN LIGHT BLUE JERSEYS"

IT WAS A frosty Saturday at Yale Bowl on a weekend when nobody would have expected to see an Ivy team take the field. But 23,000 fans had shown up to watch not one, but three football games.

The afternoon of December 5, 1931, had been set aside for a series of college football exhibition games around the nation raising funds for the unemployed. At New Haven, a charity affair comprising three 24-minute games brought in $46,000 as Yale defeated Holy Cross, 6–0, followed by 0–0 ties between Brown and Dartmouth and then Yale and Brown. (A three-judge panel awarded "victories" to Brown and Yale in the two scoreless games based on their domination of play.)

By the autumn of 1931 the Great Depression had gripped the country. In these grim times, there was little room in the popular imagination for casting college football players as heroic figures.

So it seemed fitting that as the 1930s began, the career of one of football's great romantics was ending. Bill Roper, coach of Princeton's 1922 Team of Destiny, master of the pep talk, announced in January 1930 that he would step down at year's end.

In the Tigers' final game of the season, against Yale at Palmer Stadium, the stage was set for heroics in the grand Roper tradition. Princeton trailed by 10–7 but seemed about to score with only seconds remaining.

It would not happen. The Tigers' Trix Bennett was stopped inches short of the goal line.

That was too much to bear for one sportswriter who was quite the old romantic himself—George Trevor of the *New York Sun*, still writing his game stories in longhand.

In those days, black-caped freshmen would ring the victory bell in the Nassau

Hall tower after a triumph over Yale. As Trevor walked through the campus in the gathering darkness after the game, he was struck by the silence. Though an old Yale man himself, he felt for Bill Roper.

"The mud-stained pigskin is four inches short of the yard pole, chain stretched taut," Trevor would write of that final failed touchdown drive by Roper's last team. "That's why the big bronze bells in Nassau Hall are silent as the dazed crowd slowly trickles out of Palmer Stadium, but Yale can hear the ghostly echoes of those muted chimes, and so can William Warren Roper. They never rang so loudly as the night they never rang at all."

The 1930 season brought Penn a bitter taste of what another famed coach could muster. Notre Dame—twice conqueror of Princeton in the early 1920s—once again met an Ivy team in a highly publicized intersectional game. This time Knute Rockne brought one of his strongest squads into Franklin Field.

Much of the buildup focused on the Notre Dame right halfback, Marty Brill, who had transferred from Penn, claiming he hadn't been given a chance in his two seasons there. Brill, now a senior, had been mostly a blocker for the Irish, but this time Rockne let him have the football. He scored touchdowns on runs of 66, 36, and 25 yards, picking up almost 200 yards overall, as Notre Dame drubbed Penn, 60–20.

Afterward, there were reports—promptly denied—that Brill's father, a well-to-do industrialist, had offered him $1,000 for every touchdown he scored against Penn.

Penn would now be closing out an era in which it had pressed hard for national recognition. During the 1920s, a booster named Otto Schwegler, Class of 1914, better known as "Uncle Otto," had funneled tuition fees, jobs, and gifts to players lured from the coal towns of western Pennsylvania, many with questionable qualifications as college students. In the autumn of 1930, Penn was one of only four universities to harvest more than $1 million in football revenue.

But that year, a Wall Street financier named Thomas Gates was named president of Penn and quickly decided "there was something radically wrong with the way we went after athletics." The Gates Plan would soon de-emphasize intercollegiate sports in favor of intramurals.

Up at Yale, however, some stirring afternoons loomed.

The 1931 season would bring an encounter that matched the excitement of the 1930 game against Princeton. This time the opponent was a Dartmouth team that came into Yale Bowl a decided underdog.

Albie Booth had his greatest performance since the 1929 Army game, scoring on a 94-yard kickoff return, a broken-field run of 54 yards, and a 22-yard pass from Kay Todd. But Dartmouth halfback Bill McCall also had a fantastic day, going for touchdowns on a 92-yard kickoff return, a 72-yard pass from Bill Morton, and a 60-yard run.

After trailing at halftime by 14 points, Dartmouth gained a 33–33 tie on a 23-yard field goal by Morton with three minutes left.

Two weeks later, Booth went up against Harvard's Barry Wood for the third time, and now each was a team captain.

The Crimson quarterback was still in superb form. Early in the season, he had enjoyed one of his greatest games in a 14–13 comeback victory over Army. The Cadets scored twice in the first quarter, but then Wood threw touchdown passes to Jack Crickard and Bernie White, kicked both extra points, and caught Army's Paul Johnson from behind in the fourth quarter as he raced toward the Harvard goal line. In a final flourish, he intercepted a pass on the Harvard 14. And he played all 60 minutes.

Three weeks later, Harvard was lucky to escape against Dartmouth, hanging on for a 7–6 victory. On that afternoon, Wood was not so spectacular, at least in the eyes of one well-known radio broadcaster.

A few days after the game, Harvard told the Columbia Broadcasting System's Ted Husing that he was unwelcome at any more home games because of his criticism of the team, particularly one word he used in describing Wood's performance.

"I don't think anyone speaking over the air has the right to refer to any boy of any team on the field as 'putrid,'" said Bill Bingham, the Harvard athletic director, who sent a letter of protest to the CBS chairman, William Paley.

Harvard and Wood bounced back from Husing's insult to post a 7–0 victory over Holy Cross.

The Crimson, 7-0 for the season, came into the Yale game unbeaten for the first time since 1913 and had shut out Yale the previous two years, Wood having thrown for a pair of touchdowns in his second encounter against Booth.

Playing before 60,000 at Cambridge, the teams were scoreless late in the fourth quarter. Then Yale's left end, Tom Hawley, blocked a punt attempt by Wood. Johnny Wilbur, the left tackle, recovered on the Harvard 45. Booth ran for 5 yards, then threw a pass to Herster Barres, his right end, down to the Harvard 12. The Elis got as far as the 4 on three running plays, and now Booth, who hadn't accomplished anything extraordinary in his two previous Harvard games, set up for a dropkick. His 14-yarder was good, and Yale held on for a 3–0 victory.

George Trevor, having bid an emotional adieu to Bill Roper, was overcome once more:

"The hero, thwarted and frustrated for three years by the machinations of the 'Red Villains,' finally casts off the winding sheets of an inferiority complex and, with three minutes to go in the big game, boots the goal that wins for Yale. Now we ask you— could Frank Merriwell himself have turned the trick more deftly?

"Albie is only a vest-pocket edition of 'infallible Frank,' but what are fifty pounds and five inches, more or less, when Booth comes through in the pinch with a typical Merriwell finish?"

The Yale men would have little sympathy afterward for Barry Wood, who, in a final indignity, had been smothered just outside his end zone on the game's final play.

"Wood was throwing passes from the one-yard line," Herster Barres would remember. "He was a sitting duck to be caught. I tackled him, and the game ended. Going home to New Haven, you could hear the whole train shouting:

*'Wood on his ass on the one-yard line.
Wood on his ass on the one-yard line.'"*

Booth and Wood traveled vastly different paths in the years to come. Booth married his high school girlfriend and stayed in New Haven, serving as an executive with a dairy company, a football referee and a counselor to boys' clubs. Wood became a professor at the Johns Hopkins School of Medicine.

Albie Booth died of a heart attack at age 51 in 1959. One of the mourners at the funeral service was Barry Wood.

After losing only one game apiece in 1931, Yale and Harvard were nothing special the following autumn. The king of the Ivies in '32 was Brown, which won its first seven games—each against an undefeated opponent.

In the Bears' traditional Thanksgiving morning finale against Colgate, the stiffest test of all was looming. Coach Andy Kerr's Red Raider team was not only unbeaten but had not been scored upon.

A record home crowd of 33,000 turned out at Providence for a game matching two teams with Rose Bowl ambitions. Colgate was hardly intimidated, scoring a second-quarter touchdown, but then Brown had the ball on the Colgate 1-yard line for the final play of the first half. Bob Chase plunged off right tackle, disappearing beneath a mob of Colgate players. The ref-

eree dived into the tangle as the crowd grew silent. Then two Colgate players jumped up, took off their headgear, and pranced toward the sidelines. Colgate had held inches from its goal. In the second half, Colgate pulled away for a 21–0 victory.

But there would be no Rose Bowl trip for the Red Raiders. Though Colgate outscored its opponents by 264–0, the invitation went to the University of Pittsburgh, which was also unbeaten. The honor was a dubious one as Pitt was trounced by Southern California, 35–0.

Up until the Colgate game, Brown's toughest time had come against Columbia, a 7–6 victory on the next-to-last Saturday. It would be the Lions' only loss of the season.

Football was flourishing at Morningside Heights under Lou Little, a man who seemed likely to end the revolving door for coaches.

Soon after his arrival at Columbia in 1930, Little was guest of honor at an alumni dinner. After a short speech in which he uttered the familiar platitudes praising a great educational institution, Little banged his right fist on the dinner table and roared, "I did not come to Columbia to fail."

That must have startled the old grads, who had seen Columbia go through six coaches in the 15 years since it restored football.

As Quentin Reynolds would put it in a *Collier's* magazine profile of Little: "Columbia University was known at that time as the coaches' graveyard. It was the first aggressive note ever heard from anyone associated with Columbia football."

Born in Boston as the son of a contractor who changed the family name from Piccolo, Little had been an outstanding tackle on the Penn team that went to the 1917 Rose Bowl. After seeing combat in World War I, he knocked around as a lineman and coach with several pro football teams. In 1924, he was named head coach at Georgetown, and he would post a record of 39-12-2 over six years.

Columbia was respectable in Little's first season, with a 5-4 record, but that only made him more determined. After a 52–0 thrashing by Dartmouth in 1930, he vowed to engineer a turnaround. The next season, preparing for the Dartmouth game, Little put himself into a scrimmage and emerged with a broken vertebra that kept him in a brace for four months. "I did what I told my kids never to do," he explained. "I charged and dropped my head." For the Dartmouth rematch, he sat in a specially constructed swivel chair, a leather brace holding his neck rigid. It must have been an inspiration, as Columbia won, 19–6.

The Lions went 7-1-1 in 1931, which presumably made most students happy. But not the editor of the student newspaper, Reed Harris, who wrote an editorial in the *Spectator* charging that college football was "a semi-professional racket."

As for the Columbia program, "It would be interesting to know where members of the coaching staff obtain sums they give to members of the football team," wrote Harris.

The day after the editorial appeared, two Columbia football players, Ralph Hewitt, the captain, and William McDuffee, confronted Harris in his office and threatened to beat him up if another editorial of that type appeared.

Little denied that any payments had been made, but that wasn't the end of Harris's crusading. He published an editorial attacking high-priced but poor-quality food in the student cafeteria and was eventually expelled from Columbia for what the administration called "innuendoes and misrepresentations."

Harris later wrote a book titled *King Football* in which he continued his attack on the college game.

In 1953, his editorials at Columbia became an issue for Senator Joseph McCarthy, who called Harris before his committee when he was deputy director of the International Information Administration. Harris later resigned from the government because of McCarthy's badgering—part of his wide-ranging attacks on State Department officials. But his career was resurrected eight years later when Edward R. Murrow, head of the United States Information Agency in the Kennedy administration, named him deputy director.

After weathering Harris's attacks, the Columbia football team rolled to a 7-1-1 record for a second straight season.

The 1933 team went 7-1, its only loss coming against undefeated Princeton. But the Lions weren't considered particularly fearsome. They had managed only a 15–6 victory over a Virginia team that was crushed, 75–0, by Ohio State. So what happened in December startled the college football world and certainly amazed everyone on the Columbia campus—the team was invited to the Rose Bowl.

The opponent was a Stanford team that had gone 8-1-1, significantly outweighed Columbia man for man, and had three players—fullback Bobby Grayson, tackle Bob (Horse) Reynolds, and guard Bill Corbus—who would be named to the College Football Hall of Fame.

Cliff Montgomery, the Columbia quarterback, would recall how the Lions almost turned down the bid.

"In those days the West Coast team was the home team and they could invite anybody they wanted to play. Al Masters, who was director of athletics at Stanford, called Lou Little to invite him. Lou hung up. He thought someone was kidding him. Masters called back, and Lou was finally convinced that the invitation was legitimate.

"But then the dean and the Columbia president, Nicholas Murray Butler, didn't go for it at all. They were worried about the team being disgraced."

Wild Bill Donovan, a former Columbia quarterback, then a member of the school's board of trustees and later head of the OSS—the World War II intelligence agency—saved the day for the players.

"He really convinced the board to accept the invitation," remembered Montgomery. "He was a very convincing guy."

Hardly anybody gave Columbia a chance.

One Los Angeles sportswriter called the Lions "Pomona High in light blue jerseys."

"The Marx Brothers should be the officials to really make it funny," said Dick Cullum of the *Minneapolis Star Journal*.

But this was not the mismatch it seemed to be. Columbia had beaten Penn State, Cornell, Navy, and Syracuse—hardly cream puffs—and Stanford had been defeated by a Washington team that lost four games.

Eighteen inches of rain fell in Los Angeles at year's end, the night before the game having brought Southern California's worst flooding of the century. "When we arrived in Pasadena from Tucson the day before the game, the Rose Bowl looked like a lake," Montgomery recalled. "The players' benches were floating up and down the sideline like small boats." The Pasadena Fire Department worked through New Year's morning to pump the field clear of water, but the turf remained muddy.

A crowd of 35,000 braved mud-soaked and virtually impassable roads. Among the spectators was former President Herbert Hoover, who had been a student football manager at Stanford but had also received an honorary degree from Columbia. It was questionable whether he could bring either team luck in these days of the "Hoover Depression" but, welcome or not, he would root for both teams, spending one half on the Columbia side and the other half overlooking the Stanford bench.

Lou Little had an answer for all those doubters: a trick play lurking in his single-wing offense. Its name was KF-79 (the letters and numbers stood for certain players and the holes they would hit) and it was part of a series—a pass, a reverse, and a spinner—all designed to look the same to the defense. Little had his men practice it until, standing in the defensive backfield, he couldn't tell who had the ball.

Later, the coach would recall how he

The starters for the 1933 Columbia team that would stun Stanford in the Rose Bowl: Top row (*left to right*), the backfield of Eddie Brominski, Cliff Montgomery, Al Barabas, and Bill Nevel. Bottom row (*left to right*), Red Matal, Joe Ferrara (replaced in the Rose Bowl lineup by Joe Richavich), Steve Dzamba, Newel Wilder, Lawrence Pinckney, Paul Jackel, and Owen McDowell. (COLUMBIA UNIVERSITY)

had Montgomery, Eddie Brominski, and Al Barabas go through the play for two hours at an armory. "I thought they'd punch me in the nose and quit the team," he said.

Columbia tried it in the first quarter, but the Stanford safety, Bobby Grayson, was left unblocked because the Lions thought he would be fooled and out of position. He tackled Barabas, the left halfback, on the Stanford 12. (Barabas fumbled on the next play, and Stanford recovered on its 18.)

In the second quarter, with the game scoreless, Columbia advanced to Stanford's 17-yard line following a 24-yard pass from Montgomery to his right end, Tony (Red) Matal.

It was time to try KF-79 again as Columbia lined up in a single wing strong to the right. Montgomery received the ball from the center and, midway in his spin, gave it to Barabas, who had been lined up to his right. Then Montgomery finished spinning and pretended to hand the football to Eddie Brominski, the right halfback, who charged over Stanford's right-tackle spot. Montgomery next headed for the hole between Stanford's left tackle and left end, seemingly tucking the football deep under his chest.

"Almost the entire Stanford team, ignoring Barabas, clawed at Brominski and me," Montgomery would remember.

This time, the Stanford safety was blocked out by Owen McDowell, Columbia's left end.

Barabas, meanwhile, was moving cautiously to his left, cradling the football with his hands at his sides. Then he took off around Stanford's right flank and raced into the end zone.

Newel Wilder's extra point made it 7–0.

After being outplayed in the first half, Stanford drove deep into Columbia territory four times, and Grayson ripped off four runs of more than 20 yards en route to a 152-yard game. But he fumbled the slippery ball five times, once at the Columbia 1, where Barabas recovered.

Columbia emerged with a shocking 7–0 victory.

Suddenly, the Lions were stars. The next day, Warner Brothers played host to the players, who met Joe E. Brown, Ginger Rogers, Edward G. Robinson (a Columbia graduate), and Dick Powell.

The team had a leisurely train ride home, stopping for an organ recital at the Mormon Tabernacle in Salt Lake City, an auto ride up Denver's Lookout Mountain to Buffalo Bill's grave, and a celebration at Columbia's University Club in Chicago.

On Sunday night, January 7, the players returned to New York and were given a motorcycle escort from Penn Station to a rally at the Columbia gym where a band played "Roar, Lion, Roar" but could hardly be heard over the din.

When the team had left New York for the West Coast on its own seven-car train, it was given a sendoff by John P. O'Brien, the Tammany Hall mayor of New York. Now there was a new mayor, that champion of the underdog Fiorello La Guardia, elected on a fusion reform ticket.

La Guardia had pledged to hold pomp at a minimum in his administration, but quickly broke that vow by welcoming the team back.

"I resolved that there would be no official greetings, and here in my first week I find myself greeting the Columbia football team," he said. "We have a great deal in common. Everybody thought that we didn't have a chance."

Following the celebration at the gym, 1,000 Columbia students did a victory war dance in the rain at South Field. But there was one untoward note. After the ceremonies, 500 students invaded the Nimo Theater at 110th Street and Broadway, where a packed crowd of 2,500 was watching a newsreel of the Rose Bowl game. Some of the revelers damaged balcony fixtures and others ran down the orchestra aisle shouting "Fire." That set off a panic, and several women fainted. When it was all over, 10 students had been arrested for disorderly conduct.

The Princeton team that handed Columbia its only loss, a 20–0 trouncing, would have been a candidate for the Rose Bowl had not the Big Three schools banned postseason play. The 1933 Tigers went 9-0, racking up shutouts in their first seven games before beating Rutgers, 26–6, and rolling over Yale, 27–2. They outscored their opponents by 217–8, the only touchdown against them—on a 60-yard Rutgers pass play—yielded by second-stringers.

After Bill Roper retired, his line coach, Al Wittmer, had taken over and proceeded to field a dreadful team. Wittmer's 1931 squad won its opener, against little Amherst, then dropped seven straight.

That debacle persuaded Princeton to break tradition. For the first time, a Big Three school went outside its alumni ranks for a coach when the Tigers hired Fritz Crisler, once a star end and assistant coach at the University of Chicago under Amos Alonzo Stagg and then head coach for two years at Minnesota. (Crisler, whose real first name was Herbert, supposedly got his nickname while playing for Stagg. The story goes that the coach was upset with his performance and began to call him Fritz in a derisive jest because his last name resembled that of the famous violinist Fritz Kreisler, whose agile hands provided a sharp contrast to Crisler's clumsiness.)

If Crisler believed in omens, he might have turned right around and headed back to the Midwest. He was hired by Princeton on March 1, 1932, the day the Lindbergh baby was kidnaped in nearby Hopewell. The next morning Crisler was caught up in a police manhunt, taken into custody because he was driving an auto that didn't belong to him. He was released after a Princeton alumnus who had loaned the car to him showed up at police headquarters to explain everything.

In his first season, Crisler's team went 2-2-3, but then came three extraordinary years—that unbeaten squad in 1933, a single loss (to Yale) in 1934, and then another undefeated season in 1935.

Looking back decades later, Gil Lea, an end on Crisler's three superb teams, would hail the coach for his meticulous preparation.

"At practices he had a seat overlooking the goalposts, and we'd run the same play 25 times against the scrubs. He knew every single move every one of us would make. If it wasn't right, we'd do it over and over."

Gil Lea happened to be the son of Princeton's first paid coach, Langdon (Biffy) Lea, a three-time all-America tackle for the Tigers who, in 1901, began the tradition of alumni coaches that Crisler had broken. But Biffy Lea's regime didn't last very long. As Gil Lea told the story: "Father loved football, but my grandfather, the president of a Philadelphia bank, didn't. After father was the coach in 1901 and got paid, he went to New York and took a whole floor at the Plaza Hotel and gave a party for a week for his friends and spent the money that he had been paid by Princeton. Grandfather Lea said, 'That's the end—no more football.'"

Fritz Crisler's 1933 squad had an all-sophomore backfield led by the 5-foot-9-inch Garry LeVan, who was also a sprinter on the track team, and a pair of outstanding tackles in Charlie Ceppi and Art Lane.

Ken Fairman, a receiver on that squad and a future athletic director at Princeton, would recall how Crisler had installed an effective single-wing formation.

"He put in reverse cross-body blocking,

trap blocking, and he had the ends slip the tackle to give another blocker," Fairman remembered. "Before that, the alumni coaches used to borrow plays from the opponents. It was an intellectual experience for the Princeton players."

But Crisler was challenged to show even more creativity by a Princeton man of the previous generation—F. Scott Fitzgerald.

Back in 1913, Fitzgerald had gone out for Princeton's freshman football team but quit after three days with an ankle injury, according to an account given to his biographer, Andrew Turnbull.

Late one night during Crisler's Princeton years, Fitzgerald, unable to sleep, phoned the graduate manager of athletics, Asa Bushnell, with "some suggestions for Crisler" on how to beat Yale.

"Princeton must have two teams," instructed Fitzgerald. "One will be big—all men over two hundred. This team will be used to batter them down and wear them out. Then the little team, the pony team, will go in and make the touchdowns."

Crisler wrote to Fitzgerald that his idea had merit but would be adopted only if it could be called "the Fitzgerald system" with the writer taking full credit for its success or failure. Fitzgerald replied that, under those circumstances, his system should be held "in reserve."

The 1934 season brought the end of the great Princeton-Harvard feud that had interrupted their rivalry for the previous seven years. The schools decided to forget about the *Lampoon*'s ridiculing of Princeton back in 1926 and Harvard's charges

that the Tigers had shown too many claws on the football field. Playing before 45,000 at Cambridge, Princeton beat Harvard, 19–0, amid a spirit of camaraderie. The *Lampoon* and the *Princeton Tiger* published a joint issue to mark the event, the seals of both schools on the editorial page. Before the kickoff, the Harvard band paraded across the field playing "Auld Lang Syne," and the Harvard and Princeton cheerleaders gave out with yells for the opposition. Afterward, Crisler led his players to Harvard's Lowell House for a joint dinner.

Harvard's timing in ending the split wasn't so great. For Princeton had another terrific team in 1934, following up its undefeated season by winning its first six games.

Then, on the next-to-last weekend, the Tigers went into Palmer Stadium against a Yale team that was only 3-3 under its first-year coach, "Ducky" Pond.

Princeton was indeed intimidating in the eyes of a sophomore end for Yale named Larry Kelley, about whom much would soon be heard.

Kelley would recall how huge the Princeton players looked before the kickoff, their shoulder pads supposedly the thickest used by any team and the orange stripes on their sleeves somehow making the jerseys seem larger. As if that weren't enough, as the Yale players went through their drills, the Princeton men formed a solid mass on the sidelines, staring them down.

But it was Princeton who faltered in the early going, fumbling the ball away several times. Yale then got an edge on a trick play. Kelley went down the middle and, as Stan Fuller pretended to punt, quarterback Jerry Roscoe hit Kelley with a 20-yard pass. Kelley had been a hurdler in prep school and his 6-foot-2-inch frame stretched high. He stopped the ball with his left hand and pulled it down with his right hand with his back to the goal line. Then he headed toward the sideline, cut back and scored, the play covering 43 yards. "I was as much surprised by the touchdown as anyone else," he would remember. "I was so nervous that I dropped the ball as I handed it to the referee."

The fake had not been called by the Yale coach. It was Roscoe's idea.

"In those days when you got on the field, there was absolutely zero communication between the coaching staff and the players," Roscoe remembered. "The coach never called anything when the game was in progress. You could send in a player, but he had to report personally to the referee and if he was caught making a gesture or talking until after one play was run, there was a penalty. It was a players' game. It was up to you to do what you'd learned."

As the game moved along, Fuller got off a series of superb punts, kicking the ball out of bounds to keep the star open-field runner Garry LeVan from breaking loose. Yale emerged with a huge 7–0 upset victory.

In the Yale locker room, Roscoe recalled, "There was pure elation but absolute exhaustion. It was about 70 degrees that day. I went in at 160 pounds. I had lost 11 pounds when I weighed in after the game."

For the Princeton players, the upset on their home field meant pure misery.

"After the game the people in the stands were so mad that they even spit on us as we were going out of the stadium," the Tigers' Gil Lea remembered. "The feeling was so intense against us that on Saturday night, Crisler had the team go down to the Lawrenceville School, where we had spent Friday night getting ready, and we sat up until about two o'clock in the morning talking about what we would do to Yale and Kelley in 1935—we were gonna knock the hell out of him."

Princeton finished its 1934 season by trouncing Dartmouth, and then, with all those sophomores from the unbeaten 1933 team now seniors, went on to a 9-0 record in 1935. (The Tigers did knock the hell out of Yale, a 38–7 drubbing in New Haven.)

The big matchup of the 1935 season came on November 23 when Princeton faced Dartmouth, both undefeated, in a snowstorm before a Palmer Stadium crowd of 56,000.

Dartmouth scored an early touchdown but then Princeton came back with four scoring drives—43, 48, 40, and 50 yards. Throwing only one pass all afternoon, the Tigers emerged with a 26–6 victory, outgaining their opponents by 200 yards to 3.

The game would be remembered long afterward—not for the Princeton comeback but for a bizarre moment in the fourth quarter. Princeton, leading by three touchdowns, was at the Dartmouth 3. Just as the ball was snapped, a spectator who had sneaked onto the field lined up with the defense. Princeton went ahead with the play and gained 2 yards despite the extra defender. Seconds later—with the 12th man having been escorted away—the Tigers' Jack White ran in for the score.

A few days later, a cook and counterman at a Rahway, New Jersey, diner named Mike Mesko garnered headlines by claiming to be the interloper, saying he had bet $2 on Dartmouth. "I saw they were taking a pretty rough shellacking and I wanted to help them," he told reporters while slapping together a ham sandwich.

But Mesko later admitted that his story wasn't true, and newspaper accounts suggested that the invader was a Princeton man liberally fortified with alcohol.

Many years afterward, an article in the *Princeton Athletic News* identified the culprit as Georg Larsen, an architect from Cranford, New Jersey, who evidently had partaken in a bit of partying. Larsen claimed neither Princeton nor Dartmouth allegiance—he had gone to the University of Cincinnati.

Dave Camerer, a Dartmouth tackle that

Princeton's undefeated 1935 team, whose seniors played in only one losing game over three seasons. At rear (*left to right*), the backfield of Ken Sandbach, Paul Pauk, Captain Pepper Constable, and Garry LeVan. On the line (*left to right*), Gil Lea, Fred Ritter, Bill Montgomery, Steve Cullinan, John Weller, George Stoess, and Hugh MacMillan. (PRINCETON UNIVERSITY)

day, later speculated that his helper had never experienced higher education of any sort.

"I don't think he was a college man," said Camerer. "At least what he yelled was, 'Kill THEM Princeton bastards.'"

Princeton's president, Harold W. Dodds, was unamused by what came to be called "The 12th Man Game." The following October, he imposed a ban on liquor at Palmer Stadium.

The Tigers' unbeaten 1935 team had no superstars—guard John Weller was the only all-American—but its fullback and captain, Pepper Constable, finished fourth in balloting for a new award going to the nation's top college football player, the Downtown Athletic Club trophy.

The University of Chicago running back Jay Berwanger captured the inaugural award. Then, the following October, John Heisman, the club's athletic director, died. The award was quickly renamed the Heisman Memorial Trophy.

Since Heisman's roots were in the Ivies—he had attended Brown and Pennsylvania and later coached at Penn—it was only fitting that Ivy Leaguers grab the Heisman.

The bronze statue went to Yale men in 1936 and 1937—end Larry Kelley and then running back Clint Frank.

Kelley was never an outstanding defensive player or blocker, but came up with many a timely catch and scoring play. His touchdown reception broke a 15-game Princeton winning streak in 1934, and by the time his career ended he had become the only player for Yale, Harvard, or Princeton to score a touchdown in each of his six Big Three games.

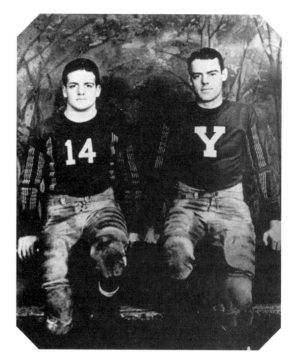

Larry Kelley, *right*, and Clint Frank of Yale, the Heisman Trophy winners of 1936 and 1937. (YALE UNIVERSITY)

The captain in his Heisman season, Kelley caught 17 passes for 372 yards in leading Yale to a 7-1 mark spoiled only by an 11–7 loss to Dartmouth.

Kelley was dubbed "Laughing Larry," but claimed that his quipster's reputation had been manufactured by sportswriters. The persona was born in that 1934 upset of Princeton. The way Kelley told it, a substitute halfback for the Tigers had been wandering around, looking haplessly for the man he was supposed to replace, when Merri Scott, Yale's left tackle, tapped the referee on the shoulder and said: "Maybe that sub is in for me, sir. I've been playing in Princeton's backfield all afternoon." The writers attributed the remark to Kelley, and he became an instant wit.

One day in the autumn of 1936, Kelley met a real comedian. Jimmy Durante and Bob Hope, appearing in New Haven with Betty Grable in the Cole Porter musical *Red, Hot and Blue,* joined the football team at its training table. Kelley asked Hope what kind of football player Durante might have been.

"With that Durante nose, he'd be offside on every play," Hope replied.

Kelley's touchdown against Princeton in 1934 was his biggest moment, but he would also be remembered for an incident in the 1936 Navy game in Baltimore. With Yale trailing by 1 point in the third quarter, Navy's Sneed Schmidt fumbled a punt, and as Kelley ran downfield he kicked the loose ball at the 25. It bounded to the Navy 3, where he recovered it. Clint Frank scored two plays later, and Yale went on to win, 12–7.

After the game, Kelley was accused of kicking the ball deliberately, which would have brought a penalty and nullified the recovery. He denied it, saying "I'm not that smart."

The following season, a rule change prohibited a player from recovering any loose ball he kicked without regard to whether it was done deliberately or not.

Kelley turned down a chance to play pro football and also rejected a Hollywood offer to play himself in a movie to be titled *Kelley of Yale.* He later coached and taught

Gerald Ford (*second from left*) with his fellow coaches at Yale. (YALE UNIVERSITY)

IVY LEAGUE AUTUMNS

at Peddie, the New Jersey prep school he attended.

Playing behind Kelley, and winning letters in 1934 and 1935, was John Hersey, who would receive considerably more notice as a writer. "My one decent ability was kicking," Hersey would recall, "but I only punted if I happened to be in the game, which wasn't often."

The Yale staff included a former University of Michigan center named Gerald Ford, who served as an assistant varsity line coach under Ducky Pond from 1935 to 1940, having been recommended by Michigan's head coach, Harry Kipke. Hired at $2,400 a year (his athletic duties also included coaching the freshman boxing team though he had never boxed), Ford took the job to pay his way through Yale Law School. The 1937 football team had an end named William Proxmire, who would be serving as a senator from Wisconsin when Ford became president.

Kelley's Heisman Trophy successor, Clint Frank, was a tough and speedy runner, a good passer, and a fine defensive back. The Yale captain in 1937, he ran for 630 yards and 11 touchdowns that season—four of them against Princeton—despite numerous injuries. When Yale went into the Harvard game at 6-0-1, Frank was suffering from a severe knee injury. But he played nonetheless. "He stuck it out when two iron men would have called it a day," remarked Tom Thorpe, the umpire. It was, however, in a losing cause, Harvard's 13–6 victory spoiling an undefeated season.

The Heisman Trophy was hardly big news in the 1930s.

Kelley would remember how "I got the telegram telling me that I had won it, and I didn't even know there was such a thing."

Long after being voted the Heisman winner, Frank would note how "the Heisman Trophy was only two years old when I received it, and there was little of the contemporary fanfare surrounding the award. Financially, it meant nothing."

Frank, like Kelley, passed up pro football. He returned to his native Chicago area after college and became an advertising executive.

The Heisman winners didn't think the honor was an especially big deal, but to hear William Proxmire tell it, the Yale campus was consumed with football and social life while the rest of the nation worried about the Depression.

Looking back many years later on his times as a football scrub in the mid-1930s, Proxmire would write how "most of my classmates were wholly preoccupied with sports and girls and grades, and bull sessions about sports and girls and grades—in that order. New Haven in the thirties was a temple to sports. The focus of university attention was not on the best drama school in the country or its relatively small but tremendously impressive law school. To many—probably most—Yale meant Kelley and Frank and football."

The pair may have gathered high honors for Yale, but Harvard came out ahead in off-the-field shenanigans. The Yale bulldog Handsome Dan II, purchased with pennies collected by the freshman class, disappeared when the Harvard swimming team left New Haven after a meet in the fall of

1934. It was a dognapping coup. Handsome Dan was eventually returned, but not before he appeared in a photo licking John Harvard's boots, ground beef having been thoughtfully applied to the statue in Harvard Square.

The bulldog incident aside, there wasn't much fun for Harvard football fans as the 1930s moved along. Although Coach Eddie Casey—the old Harvard backfield star—produced a 7-1 team in 1931, some unremarkable seasons followed. Harvard went 3-5 in 1934, finishing with a 14–0 loss to Yale, the third time in four years that the Crimson had been shut out by the Elis.

And Harvard's football profits had turned tepid, going from an all-time net gain of $706,000 in 1929 to a more modest $266,000 in 1934.

The school was getting desperate for a football turnaround. As Bill Bingham, the athletic director, put it: "When it got to the point where we started counting the house the minute we got into the stadium and began looking up almanacs a year in advance to see if there was a possibility of rain on the day of the Holy Cross game, we decided the time had come to do something about football."

Harvard looked for a coach outside its alumni ranks for the first time and came up with Dick Harlow, a former Penn State tackle coaching at Western Maryland who was said to have turned down 17 offers from first-rate schools. Harlow had racked up a 61-13-7 record since taking over at

the Westminster, Maryland, school in 1926. But rural Maryland was a universe or two distant from Cambridge.

"Where is Western Maryland?" asked the *Lampoon* in an issue greeting Harlow.

The new coach made good newspaper copy when it was learned he was an expert on the study of birds' eggs, having reportedly navigated every river in the eastern United States via canoe during his summers.

But at his introductory news conference in the spring of 1935, Harlow told of a summertime mishap that could hardly have inspired confidence. He was in Pennsylvania seeking out ravens' eggs when "all 250 pounds of me slid down a rope over a cliff and crumpled into unconsciousness at the bottom."

As for the football field, Harlow looked to deception on offense, his specialty the spinner play. He would remain at Harvard for 11 years, counting time out for World War II service.

There was also a new man at Dartmouth in the mid-1930s. Earl (Red) Blaik, an assistant at Army, was hired in 1934 to replace Jackson Cannell, whose teams finished at .500 the previous two seasons.

While they sought housing, Blaik and his assistants lived in the guest quarters above the bedroom occupied by Dartmouth's president, Ernest Hopkins, and his wife. The first night, the new regime banged around the furniture trying out the single-wing plays Blaik envisioned. That brought an inquiry from Mrs. Hopkins

Before his championship years at Army, Earl (Red) Blaik coached Dartmouth teams that lost only three games between 1936 and 1938. (DARTMOUTH COLLEGE)

around 3:00 A.M. "Do you plan to have all the season's major games played upstairs?" she wondered.

Blaik, a West Point graduate, was dismayed by "the spirit of good fellowship" on Dartmouth's football team. He imposed what he called a "Spartan approach" emphasizing physical conditioning and discipline.

Dartmouth won its first five games under Blaik by shutouts before tailing off to finish at 6-3. And his teams kept improving, going 29-5-3 from 1935 to 1938. At one stretch, Blaik's men went 22 games without a loss, posting 19 victories and 3 ties.

Blaik's best player was Bob MacLeod, an all-American who specialized in running deep reverses behind a wall of single-wing blockers. One particular weekend in the fall of 1937 saw MacLeod and a dozen teammates carrying on in the rugged vein demanded by Blaik. Although felled by dysentery from rancid spinach only two days before the Yale game at New Haven, the players suited up. And they held Yale to a 9–9 tie as MacLeod—having lost 18 pounds over a couple of days—ran 85 yards with an intercepted pass for a touchdown. It was the game of the season: Dartmouth would finish unbeaten while Yale would lose only to Harvard.

While Dick Harlow and Red Blaik were emerging on the Ivy scene in the mid-1930s, Cornell's Gil Dobie was on the way out.

Dobie had his first losing season in 1934, when Cornell went 2-5. The next year brought a debacle. After dropping its first three games (two to such nonentities

Bob MacLeod, an all-America halfback for Dartmouth in 1938. (DARTMOUTH COLLEGE)

as St. Lawrence and Western Reserve), Cornell was drubbed by Princeton, 54–0.

Going into the Dartmouth game with an 0-4-1 record (Cornell had managed a tie with Columbia), the normally gloomy Dobie was in an exceedingly dark mood.

He took his team on a tour of the field before the kickoff. Pointing to the 40-yard line, he said, "You kick off here." Then he walked to the bench and said, "This is where you sit when you're not playing." Finally, he went to the 10-yard line and observed, "Here is where you'll be all afternoon with your backs to the wall."

Duly inspired, Cornell was clobbered, 41–6, and finished at 0-6-1. The administration then bought out the last two years of Dobie's contract, but he departed with a record of 82-36-7.

The late 1930s saw the emergence of a homegrown star at Columbia—Sid Luckman, a passing, running, and kicking threat at tailback.

A native of Brooklyn—he starred at Erasmus Hall High School in Flatbush—Luckman received 40 offers from colleges all over the country and had been planning to go to Navy.

When Navy played Columbia at Baker Field, he was taken into both teams' locker rooms by Rip Miller, the Navy athletic director.

"As soon as I met Lou Little I was impressed—the way he dressed, the way he spoke," Luckman would recall. (Little was known as the game's best-dressed coach. By the mid-1940s, he admitted to owning 40 suits and 10 hats and coats, 30 pairs of shoes and 500 ties.)

"I knew I wanted to play for him. And then Columbia contacted me. Columbia had no athletic scholarships then so I had to work my way through—painting walls, washing dishes in the fraternity house for my room and meals."

Luckman's greatest game came on October 8, 1938, at West Point. The Cadets led at halftime, 18–6, but Luckman threw for a touchdown in the third quarter and his passing engineered another drive in the final minutes to give the Lions a 20–18 victory.

Luckman was nonetheless modest, to hear the press tell it. A profile in the *New York Herald Tribune* described him as extremely popular on campus, "a handsome Jewish boy with a shy and charming manner, and there never was a more-effacing hero."

He wasn't looking to play pro football, but George Halas, the owner and coach of the Chicago Bears, scouted him and was told by Little that Luckman had an excellent football mind. Halas would relate how "when I saw him with the Lions I knew I had found the quarterback I was looking for to make the T formation go."

Though having played in the single

Sid Luckman, a Brooklyn boy who made good uptown. (COLUMBIA UNIVERSITY)

wing at Columbia, Luckman starred with the Bears through the 1940s as the first pro quarterback to master the techniques of the modern T.

Columbia was developing a string of outstanding passers. Before Luckman, there was Cliff Montgomery, whose teams compiled a 22-3-2 record and staged the Rose Bowl upset of Stanford. After Luckman came Paul Governali, a star in the early war years.

Down at Penn, there was a coaching change in 1938. Harvey Harman departed after seven seasons, his final one a dreary 2-5-1, including a 0–0 tie with Georgetown in which a field goal by Penn's Ned Fielden was nullified because 12 men were on the field.

The administration reached for a local favorite, George Munger, a sports star at Philadelphia's Episcopal Academy and then a Penn running back from 1930 to 1932 and winner of the 1932 decathlon at the Penn Relays. Only 28 years old when he took the coaching job, Munger would remain for 16 seasons, building a succession of strong teams through the 1940s.

At Cornell, Carl Snavely, hired in 1936 as Gil Dobie's successor, had a losing team in his first year but followed that up with a pair of winning squads and then, in 1939, perfection—an 8-0 record.

Propelling Cornell were Jerome (Brud) Holland, an all-America end in 1937 and 1938, and Nick Drahos, a tackle named an all-American the following two seasons. Holland, a husky 215-pounder and one of

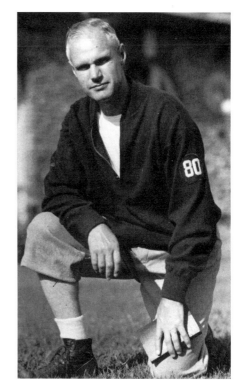

Coach Carl Snavely, who restored Cornell to national football prominence in the late 1930s. (CORNELL UNIVERSITY)

the few black players starring in the pre-World War II years, later served as president of Hampton Institute in Virginia and ambassador to Sweden. (The nickname of "Brud," short for brother, was supposedly given him by 12 brothers and sisters when he was growing up in Auburn, New York.)

Snavely, hired away from the University of North Carolina, was noted for his meticulous preparation and his studying of football films in an era when movie projectors were usually confined to the Bijou.

Coach George Munger, about to embark on his first season at Penn, shares burdens with his captain, Harlan Gustafson. (UNIVERSITY OF PENNSYLVANIA)

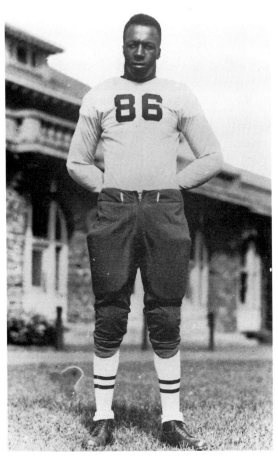

Jerome (Brud) Holland, an all-America end for Cornell who would serve as ambassador to Sweden during the Nixon administration. (CORNELL UNIVERSITY)

He would spend the first three days of each week going over slow-motion pictures of the previous week's game, then send his players notes analyzing their performance.

But he stopped short of using movies to scout the opposition—it was considered less than sporting, a sort of high-tech espionage.

"If movie scouting was accepted practice, in no time we'd all be scrambling for films of every game our opponents played," Snavely remarked in 1940, an astute prediction. "Inevitably, some smart guy would set up a movie service and we'd all be forced to subscribe."

Sometimes the technology wasn't so impressive. Lou Little persuaded the Columbia athletic department to invest in a new camera in 1938 and it functioned perfectly during practice before the game at Yale Bowl. But when the game shots were developed, the film was a blank. The fade-out shutter had inadvertently been closed. (Columbia won, 27–14, but Yale wasn't a sore loser. The Elis gave Little a copy of their own film.)

Cornell's 1939 team proved it could play with the big guys when it traveled to Columbus to face Ohio State. The Buckeyes took a 14–0 lead, but then Cornell's Walter Scholl ran 80 yards off tackle for a score and connected on a 62-yard scoring pass to Jack Bohrman, a substitute wingback. Mort Landsberg, a 160-pounder, picked up good yardage on deceptive spinner plays, and Snavely's boys emerged with a 23–14 victory over a team that would win the Big Ten title.

The Rose Bowl committee was interested in matching Cornell up against Southern California, but Cornell's president, Edmund Ezra Day, vetoed a trip to Pasadena. Studies came first.

The victory over Ohio State was a great highlight in Cornell football history but a sad finale for the tradition of a live bear

Jim Schmuck, Cornell's left end, picking up yardage during a 23–14 victory over Ohio State at Columbus in the Big Red's undefeated 1939 season. (CORNELL UNIVERSITY)

mascot. Touchdown IV, stopping off in Cleveland to be feted by Cornell alumni on his way back from Columbus, became rowdy in a nightclub, wound up in police custody, and found himself a ward of the local Animal Protective League, which deposited him in Cleveland's Brookside Park Zoo.

All future Cornell bears would be furry-costumed undergraduates.

Cornell won its first six games in 1940, yielding only two touchdowns, and once again beat Ohio State, this time by 21–7, before a record crowd of 34,500 at Schoell-kopf Field.

But the victory was tarnished a bit when the Ohio State athletic director, L. W. St. John, accused Snavely of "bad ethics" for illegally signaling offensive plays from the sideline by wigwagging a light-colored cylinder in various positions.

"We got so proficient at lifting their signals, we were able to call every play they

ran toward the end of the game," said E. P. Maxwell, an Ohio State alumnus with a quarter-century experience as an official, who was sitting next to St. John on the Buckeye bench.

Cornell denied having cheated. But remembering that game decades later, Walt Matuszak, Cornell's 1940 captain and blocking back in the single wing, would recall with much laughter how "there was no question about it. We had a few things Snavely called. I went over the signals with him, and Hal McCullough, the halfback, was the other man that knew the signals. Snavely called special plays off and on. What coach didn't?"

Soon that controversy was overshadowed by another one that would be remembered long beyond the Ohio State tiff.

Cornell went up to Dartmouth on November 14 with a 6-0 record, an 18-game unbeaten streak, and the No. 2 national ranking, figuring it would have an easy time with a Dartmouth team that was only 3-4.

But Coach Red Blaik's defensive schemes stopped Cornell's tricky ball handling, and Dartmouth held a 3–0 lead as the clock wound down. Cornell mounted a final drive and faced fourth down on the Dartmouth 6-yard line with seconds to play. Cornell's Walter Scholl then fired a pass into the end zone intended for Bill Murphy. It was batted down by Dartmouth's Ray Hall.

The referee, W. H. (Red) Friesell, began to take the ball to the 20-yard line, where Dartmouth would presumably get it on a touchback. But then Friesell turned around and marched back to the 6, insisting over the protests of the Dartmouth captain, Lou Young, that Cornell still had one down left. There were 3 seconds remaining. This time Scholl raced to his right and hit Murphy with a scoring pass. The extra point was good and the game ended as Cornell 7, Dartmouth 3.

At first, it seemed there might have been a double offside called on that first Cornell pass, negating the play. But that was not the case—the referee had simply blundered.

More than 1,500 Dartmouth students held a "victory" rally anyway, convinced that their team had really triumphed, whatever the official score.

The following Monday, Cornell's players received some bad news.

Captain Matuszak would long remember the moment.

"On Sunday, in the late afternoon, they were going over the films. The pictures did not show that both teams were offside. The big question was: what are you going to do about it?

"We were called together on Monday afternoon, and President Day, who incidentally was a Dartmouth graduate, came in and said: 'I'll tell you what we should do. We'll be good sports and give it to them.' Dartmouth will be better sports. They won't accept it.'"

But, Matuszak would observe, "It didn't happen that way."

Upon receiving a telegram from Day conveying "hearty congratulations" on winning the game, even though the scoreboard said otherwise, Dartmouth accepted the victory and saluted Cornell as an "honorable and honored opponent."

The fiasco became known as "The Fifth Down Game."

Blaik's big victory came at the end of his Dartmouth career. In December, he returned to West Point, where he would coach two national championship teams in the era of Glenn Davis and Doc Blanchard.

Cornell suffered another blow the following Saturday against Penn, which had held the Big Red to a scoreless tie in the 1938 season-ender.

Penn was no patsy, having routed Army and Yale, and it boasted an all-America tailback in Frank Reagan. Cornell took a 13–0 lead, playing before more than 79,000 at Franklin Field, but then Reagan scored a pair of touchdowns and kicked a field goal to put the Quakers ahead by 16–13 at halftime. Cornell gained a 20–16 edge, but

Penn's all-America back Frank Reagan returns an interception during a 23–0 victory over Yale in October 1938. (UNIVERSITY OF PENNSYLVANIA)

Reagan wasn't through. He ran 16 yards on an off-tackle play for the winning score in a 22–20 triumph.

That wasn't Reagan's only spectacular performance of the season. He ran for five touchdowns, rushed for 200 yards, and scored 31 points against Princeton.

Penn finished at 6-1-1 in 1940, just the beginning of its decade of dominance among the Ivies. The following season, Penn rolled to a 7-1 record, losing only to Navy.

After a succession of so-so teams, Harvard came on strong in 1941. The Crimson lost only their opening two games—to Penn

and Cornell—and boasted an all-America guard in Endicott (Chub) Peabody, a future governor of Massachusetts and grandson of the Reverend Endicott Peabody, founder of the Groton prep school.

Peabody caught the attention of the press after Harvard managed a 6–6 tie with a Navy team ranked No. 1 in the country. Navy Coach Swede Larson told reporters that Peabody had been "the fifth man in our backfield."

Two weeks later, when the Crimson prepared to play a strong Army team, Harvard Coach Dick Harlow was asked by reporters whether Peabody could also block.

Peabody would remember how the question was answered in the Army game (a 20–6 Harvard victory) with help from a fellow lineman.

"There was one play through the line where Dick Pfister trapped a tackle, making a huge hole through which I would go, leading the runner to take out the backer-up. This time the backer-up was conveniently one step too slow, and as I picked up steam I hit him in the chest with my head, knocking him ass over teakettle. I can still see Coach Harlow playing and replaying that film for the press. 'Are you asking me, can he block?' he roared. The real credit belonged to Dick Pfister, who opened up the hole."

Two hours after graduating from Harvard the following spring, Peabody was commissioned in the navy. By then, many of the men who had been wearing Ivy football jerseys were in uniforms of another kind.

One day in the autumn of 1941, the Columbia football team had paused during a workout and put aside its single wing. The players posed for a team photograph in an alignment reminiscent of the nineteenth century wedge. This one, however, was borrowed from Winston Churchill—the "V for Victory" formation.

Two months before Pearl Harbor Sunday, Columbia's football team is already proclaiming "V for Victory." (COLUMBIA UNIVERSITY)

"VICTORY WITH HONOR"

HARVARD-YALE? HOW about Harvard versus the Camp Edwards, Massachusetts, army base instead.

College football was sharply curtailed during World War II, 190 schools dropping the sport by 1943. With most of the athletes off to war, the continuation of a football program depended on muscular freshmen, 4-Fs sufficiently able-bodied for football combat, and members of a school's navy V-12 officer training program, which allowed its participants to engage in intercollegiate sports. (The army confined its officer trainees at colleges to intramurals.)

Harvard fielded an "informal" team in 1943 and 1944—among its opponents Camp Edwards and the Melville, Rhode Island, PT boat squad, composed of navy men in the motor torpedo boat squadrons. Casual games between Harvard and Boston College in both seasons—their first

matchups since 1919—were nonetheless a major attraction. The second game, a 13–0 Crimson victory at Harvard Stadium, drew a crowd of 44,000 with seats going for 50 cents apiece.

Substitution rules had been liberalized in 1941, ending the era of one-platoon football. But by 1943, Princeton was so strapped for manpower that Coach Harry Mahnken remarked, "I'll put 11 men on the field, but if anything happens to them I won't be able to do anything except start praying." Princeton was limited to an informal team in 1944, playing such football luminaries as Muhlenberg, Swarthmore, and the Atlantic City Naval Air Station.

Yale, however, played full wartime schedules under Coach Howie Odell, a former assistant at Harvard and Penn, and went unbeaten in 1944, yielding just four touchdowns. The Elis won their first seven games, then saw a perfect season spoiled by a 6–6 tie with Virginia.

Yale's 1945 team produced the 500th victory in school history when it romped over the Coast Guard Academy by 41–6 on November 17.

But overshadowing the success was a reminder of the motto "For God, for Country and for Yale." Three former Yale players died in military service. Hovey Seymour and Frank Gallagher were killed in action in 1944. Bill Mallory, captain of the unbeaten 1923 team, an Army Air Forces major who won the Legion of Merit for a tactical plan cutting German supply lines in Italy, died in the crash of a plane taking him home for discharge in 1945.

Columbia boasted a war-era star in quarterback Paul Governali, who won the Maxwell Trophy—given by the Touchdown Club of Philadelphia to the player it deemed best in the nation—and finished second in the Heisman balloting in 1942.

An obscure member of the 1942 Columbia team would make a name for himself far removed from the football field.

In the fall of 1940, Jack Kerouac arrived at Columbia and joined the freshman team as a wingback. But he broke his leg in the third game and thereby discovered the literary life.

"I was out all the rest of the season on crutches, sitting in front of the fire in the Lion's Den, eating big steaks and hot fudge sundaes," Kerouac would recall. "It was great. And that's when I started reading Thomas Wolfe."

After service in the navy and merchant marine, Kerouac returned to Columbia in October 1942 and was invited by Lou Little to play for the varsity. But before the season was over, he quit again.

Kerouac would tell how "I was just sitting in my room and it was snowing, and it was time to go to scrimmage, time to go out in the snow and the mud and bang yourself around. And then, suddenly, on the radio it started—Beethoven! I said, 'I'm going to be an artist. I'm not going to be a football player.' That's the night I didn't go to scrimmage. And I never went back to football."

When he wasn't pursuing the likes of a Jack Kerouac—obviously desperate for manpower—Lou Little kept busy with correspondence. He sent out 15-page, single-spaced mimeographed letters three times a year to 600 former Columbia players in the armed forces, supplying them with the latest football news, campus gossip, and military addresses of other Columbia athletes. The coach accumulated a file of 2,500 letters in response.

Dartmouth benefited greatly from navy V-12 manpower, posting a 6-1 record in 1943, its only loss a 7–6 defeat by Penn. Navy trainees who had transferred from 16 different colleges were on the Dartmouth roster, among them Don Kasprzak, who played behind Paul Governali at Columbia in 1942. Kasprzak, emerging as one of the East's best passers in 1943, would return to Columbia in 1946 and be named captain.

The fortunes of wartime might see a halfback scoring a touchdown against the very team he had played for the previous autumn. It happened to Anthony (Skip)

Minisi, a freshman starter for Penn's 1944 team but a Navy player the next season.

Minisi had signed up for the Naval Academy upon graduating from high school in June 1944, but because he was only 17 he had to wait a year before going to Annapolis. So he enrolled in Penn's Wharton School of Commerce and soon saw plenty of action at halfback.

In June 1945, Minisi transferred to Navy, and on October 27 he was playing for the Naval Academy against Penn before 73,000 at Franklin Field.

"It was sort of strange," he would remember. "I had mixed emotions because there were still a lot of people I knew at Penn. I knew all the coaches. But when you play football, you put all those thoughts aside and your goal is to win."

The score was tied, 7–7, late in the fourth quarter though Navy had lost the ball on fumbles seven times.

"We were very heavily favored but Penn came out well prepared and we were over-confident," Minisi recalled. "We were stymied through practically the whole game. We were in a state of utter confusion.

"But we got the ball down to the Penn side of the field and we made up a play. Hunchy Hoernschemeyer, the quarterback, would pretend to run. I would go down and out. I caught the pass for the touchdown that won the game."

The 22-yard toss to Minisi, with 25 seconds remaining, gave Navy a 14–7 victory.

After 14 months at the Naval Academy, Minisi resigned—"it was not my life"—returned to Penn, joined the reserve offi-cers' training program, and went back to the football team, starring during the 1946 and 1947 seasons.

The fall of 1945 saw a wounded war veteran named Meryll Frost serve as an inspiration merely by his presence on the field. Frost had been terribly burned when his bomber was shot down over Italy, and he was hospitalized for 18 months. A new face, including new ears, was grafted onto him. Nevertheless, he made the Dartmouth back-field, was named co-captain, and scored two touchdowns that season. When he was removed from the game with Penn at Franklin Field, he drew a standing ovation.

Cornell boasted the nation's top passer for 1945 in Al Dekdebrun, though his statistics were modest—94 completions in 190 attempts for 1,227 yards. Dekdebrun was voted the most valuable player in the East-West Shrine game at San Francisco on New Year's Day 1946, scoring on a 42-yard run in a 7–7 tie. Big things were expected of him for the following season, but his career ended with that all-star game. He was declared ineligible because he had technically played four seasons, having enrolled as a freshman at Columbia in 1942 and seen a total of 4 minutes 5 seconds action against Fort Monmouth in the season's opener. Dekdebrun never attended classes at Columbia, returning to his Buffalo home and a war plant job, but that brief appearance would count as a season's play.

By the autumn of 1946, the Ivy football teams were fully stocked with veterans, and fine crowds were turning out again.

Princeton's Val Wagner getting behind Penn captain Art Littleton at Franklin Field during the Tigers' 17–14 upset in 1946. (PRINCETON UNIVERSITY)

The season's most memorable game was played on November 2 when Princeton, only 2-2, came into Franklin Field to face a Penn team that was 4-0 and ranked No. 3 in the nation.

"Penn was favored by at least four touchdowns—we were not expected to win by any stretch of the imagination," Princeton wingback Ernie Ransome would recall. "People from Penn told me afterward that some players said to their coach, George Munger, 'Do you really think we should put our pads on today?' That's how confident they were."

Playing before a crowd of 72,000, Penn twice took a one-touchdown lead, but each time Princeton came back with a score, and it was 14–14 at halftime. "All of a sudden, by the half, we thought Penn was no longer invincible," Ken Keuffel, who had replaced Ransome, would recall. "Everybody was noisy and excited. We were saying, 'Hey, we can beat these guys.'"

With one minute to play, Princeton was deep in Penn territory, the game still tied. But Ransome, the Tigers' regular placekicker, was in a hospital. Soon after scoring Princeton's first touchdown on an outstanding reception, he had suffered a dislocated hip.

Now Keuffel, who had previously done some kicking, took charge. With Princeton on the Penn 19, "I told Charlie Caldwell, 'I can kick one from here.' He was so carried away by that time that he never even said, 'Go in the game.' I just went in. We ran the ball in front of the posts and kicked it."

Keuffel, who had seen an earlier extra-point attempt blocked—the quarterback threw to an end for the 1 point—booted the ball through the uprights and Princeton emerged with a huge 17–14 upset victory.

When Princeton had returned to a full schedule in 1945, it looked back to the glory days of the 1920s in selecting a new coach. Charlie Caldwell, a sophomore back on the 1922 Team of Destiny and a basketball player and star pitcher for Princeton (he had a brief stint with the 1925 Yankees), took over after 15 seasons as head coach at Williams.

Caldwell proved a master of the single wing, befuddling opponents with spinner plays, lateral passes, flankers, and backs in motion.

George Munger, later recalling the 1946 loss to Princeton, noted how "I didn't recognize his damn offense. Everything was different. He had two flankers out. He had men in motion. He moved an end and played five men on one side of the center."

But the Princeton-Penn game would be remembered more for what happened after the final gun.

"As we ran off to the dressing room, the mounted police came riding up," Keuffel would remember. The Philadelphia police had told Penn authorities they expected "serious trouble" and were permitted to place 100 officers on foot inside Franklin Field. The school denied a request that 30 mounted policemen be stationed on the sidelines. When the game ended, hundreds of Princeton fans swarmed onto the field and tore down the goalposts. The mounted police now moved inside and charged, roughing up many Princeton students and arresting a goodly number for inciting to riot.

Afterward, the Penn president, George W. McClellan, told Princeton he had never given permission for the cavalry to arrive and said he was "deeply sorry" about the police intervention.

With the travails of wartime behind them, a little thing like a stampede by mounted police couldn't dim collegians' spirits.

Later in November, a fiery *P* was branded onto the turf of Yale Bowl in the days before the Princeton game. Retaliation was swift. A dozen Yale students seized Princeton's campus radio station, WPRU, overpowering the four-man staff shortly after 11:00 P.M. one weekday, then played Yale songs followed by uncomplimentary comments on the Tiger football team. Accomplices painted a blue *Y* 10 feet high on the side of the Foulke Hall dormitory, daubed the stone Princeton Tiger at Palmer Stadium so it resembled a blue-spotted leopard, and burned a *Y* into the lawn of the Nassau Tavern.

Penn's stunning 1946 loss to Princeton was only a blip on an outstanding string of seasons. After going 6-2 in both 1945 and 1946, the Quakers produced their first undefeated team since 1908.

Penn's Chuck Bednarik, an all-America center who would later star for the Philadelphia Eagles. (UNIVERSITY OF PENNSYLVANIA)

The 1947 squad went 7-0-1, a perfect season foiled by a tie with Army. It recorded four shutouts, including a 21–0 blanking of Navy, racking up a point margin of 219–35.

Penn students were understandably enthusiastic. Before the Princeton game at Palmer Stadium, they staged a pair of nighttime raids, armed with a plentiful sup-

ply of red and blue paint, leading to an automobile chase in which the Princeton Borough police nabbed four invaders. "I don't mind the painting of the tigers and the cannon, but this business of being waked up at 3:30 and 5:30 every morning is getting on my nerves," said Francis R. H. Godolphin, the Princeton dean.

Penn's 1947 team featured three all-Americans: center Chuck Bednarik, later a star linebacker with the Philadelphia Eagles; tackle George Savitsky, named to an all-America squad for a fourth straight season, and running back Skip Minisi—the former midshipman—all of whom would be inducted into the College Football Hall of Fame.

Bednarik, 6 feet 2 inches, 215 pounds of steel, had forged his toughness before arriving at Penn.

Raised in Bethlehem, Pennsylvania, the son of a Czech immigrant who worked in the steel mills, Bednarik would remember how "I spent a few summers in the mills myself. It's not a boys' camp."

The family lived in a small house, five children sharing the same room. "I got my first football when my father saved the tops of twenty-five coffee bags and sent away for a free premium," Bednarik would recall. "The ball was made of cheap imitation leather. I used tape to keep it in one piece."

After starring in football, baseball, and basketball at Bethlehem High School, Bednarik went into the Army Air Forces in 1943 and served as a waist-gunner on a B-24, flying 30 missions over Germany. One time his plane, damaged by flak, crash-landed on returning to base. He escaped by

George Savitsky, a four-time all-America tackle for Penn.
(UNIVERSITY OF PENNSYLVANIA)

kicking out a window and jumping 20 feet to the ground.

When Bednarik came home, John Butler, his high school coach, recommended him to George Munger, and he would play for Penn from 1945 to 1948, an all-American his final two seasons and winner of the Maxwell Trophy in 1948.

Bednarik's fellow all-America lineman, the 6-foot-3-inch, 250-pound tackle George Savitsky, was an instant star as a freshman back in 1944 after being discharged from the Marine Corps because of a head injury.

"Rather than take a desk job, I was sent home," he would recall. "I was home a very short while when all hell broke loose. Penn, Notre Dame, Villanova were all on the phone."

Savitsky broke into the Penn lineup wearing a helmet with special rubber padding to guard against another head injury.

"I didn't think I needed that special helmet, but they did," he noted. "Foam rubber wasn't going to help that much if you got a good shot to the head in the ol' leather helmet days."

The postwar years saw a succession of exciting Penn-Army games at Franklin Field, played before crowds of more than 70,000.

Penn came into the 1947 Army game with a 6-0 record but an unhappy recent history against the Cadets, having lost by 62–7, 61–0, and 34–7 the three previous seasons when squads led by Glenn Davis and Doc Blanchard were pummeling just about everybody. Davis and Blanchard were gone now, but Army was still strong.

With the score tied at 7–7 in the fourth quarter, it seemed that Penn would finally break through.

"It was raining and it was very late in the game," Skip Minisi would remember. "I took the ball and went through the center of the line and got clear. There was no one in front of me. An Army guy was on the ground, but he slammed my foot. With the mud and everything else, I just lost my balance and went down. Other than that, I would have scored."

Penn settled for a tie that deprived it of a perfect season and would be edged by Army the following two autumns. In 1948, the Cadets rallied for a 26–20 triumph on Arnie Galiffa's touchdown pass in the final seconds. In 1949, Army won by 14–13 as end Hal Loehlein blocked a field goal attempt to save the victory.

Columbia had floundered through the war years, winning only eight games between 1941 and 1944, but then came a revival. Led by running backs Gene Rossides and Lou Kusserow, the Lions turned in an 8-1 record in 1945 and a 6-3 mark in 1946.

They opened with victories over Rutgers and Navy in 1947, but some Columbia students figured the team needed a special boost. Presumably inspired by the naming of Dwight D. Eisenhower as school president the previous June, they hired a blimp and staged an air raid the Thursday before the Yale game at Baker Field, dropping 5,000 "propaganda" leaflets over New Haven. The leaflets offered "safe conduct" to any Yale men who would surrender at Columbia the following Saturday while reminding "the hungry and bewildered bulldog" of his leaders' "empty promises of victory."

But Yale was hardly in a capitulating mood, racking up a 17–7 victory. Columbia lost to Penn, 34–14, the following Saturday, and then more trouble loomed—a visit by an Army team with a 32-game unbeaten streak.

Army arrived at Baker Field with four straight shutouts—three victories and a scoreless tie with Illinois. Quarterback Arnie Galiffa and fullback Rip Rowan weren't exactly Glenn Davis and Doc Blanchard, but they seemed far too talented for Columbia.

The Cadets took a 20–7 lead into the fourth quarter with Columbia showing minus yardage on the ground. Then the Lions got back in the game when end Bill Swiacki made a spectacular diving catch for a touchdown on a 28-yard pass from Rossides. Army thought that Swiacki trapped the ball, but the official thought otherwise. The extra point by Ventan

Bill Swiacki, whose pass-catching acrobatics enabled Columbia to snap Army's 32-game unbeaten streak in 1947.
(COLUMBIA UNIVERSITY)

Princeton bonfire on cannon green celebrates a victory over Yale in November 1948 that brought supremacy among the Big Three, the Tigers having beaten Harvard earlier. (PRINCETON UNIVERSITY)

Yablonski, the Columbia fullback, made it 20–14.

"It was a down-and-out pass," remembered Rossides. "They had a player in front of Bill and one behind him. I was moving out of the pocket to get away from Army's Joe Steffy and I threw the ball over the safety's head toward Bill as I got hit by Steffy. I didn't see the rest of the play. All I heard was a roar."

Columbia then stopped an Army drive and took over on its 34 with eight and a half minutes left. Three plays later the Lions were at the Army 29, the big play a 22-yard run by Rossides.

Now Rossides found Swiacki again on a pass to the Army 3, another down-and-out play. "He broke clear," recalled Rossides. "The Army defender had fallen down."

In the next instant, though, it seemed that the play would be botched.

"I'm hit," Rossides remembered. "I'm going down, and all I see is Bill turning his head the wrong way. I nearly died. He turned his head to the inside. Then I saw his head starting to roll toward the outside as he was following the ball."

On the next play, Rossides ran for a yard on a quarterback sneak, and then he handed off to Kusserow, who went in to tie the game at 20–20. Yablonski made his third extra point, and the crowd of 35,000 went wild.

On Army's next possession Kusserow intercepted a pass by Galiffa as the Lions held on for a 21–20 victory, Columbia's finest moment since the Rose Bowl stunner over Stanford and one of the biggest upsets in college football history.

Columbia set a school record for pass completions with 20—18 by Rossides and 2 by Kusserow. Swiacki snared nine passes for 148 yards, several of them on brilliant grabs, and the senior from Southbridge, Massachusetts, was carried off on his teammates' shoulders.

W. C. Heinz of the *New York Sun* wrote that Swiacki "catches passes the way the rest of us catch the common cold. He knows where he gets some of them, and the rest he just picks up in a crowd."

Columbia fans had one more man to thank for the passing game that day—Sid Luckman.

Like Luckman—his boyhood hero—Rossides had starred at Erasmus Hall High School in Brooklyn.

"I had written Columbia off because one of my teammates couldn't get in," Rossides would remember. "At our Erasmus championship banquet in December 1944, I got a phone call. It was from Sid Luckman. He said, 'You go play for Lou Little at Columbia.' And that was it. I didn't get a full scholarship. I turned down two full scholarships elsewhere."

Luckman helped insure that Rossides would succeed. He tutored him, at Little's request, during 1947 spring practice, when Rossides was shifted from left halfback to quarterback, and donated his fee to a Columbia scholarship fund.

Following the shocker over Army, Columbia shut out Cornell, Dartmouth, and Holy Cross, then finished with a 28–8 victory over Syracuse for a wonderful 7-2 season.

In February 1948, Yale offered Little the posts of athletic director and football coach, Coach Howie Odell having moved to the University of Washington after four straight winning seasons. Little apparently

Levi Jackson, named Yale's first black captain in 1949. (YALE UNIVERSITY)

agreed to a deal but then was persuaded to stay by Eisenhower. He would remain at Columbia through 1956 but had only one more winning season, a 5-3 mark in 1951.

Following the 1948 season, the Yale squad elected halfback Levi Jackson as the first black football captain in school history, a milestone producing a page-one story in the *New York Times*.

Jackson would remember how the vote was announced just before the team was about to board its bus for a practice session one day.

"Bill Conway, who was the captain in 1948, raised a glass of champagne and said: 'Here's to the 1949 captain.' When he mentioned my name, I almost fell out of my seat."

What Jackson would look back on as "the most satisfying moment of my life" came after a string of outstanding seasons for him.

After playing football for Camp Lee, Virginia, he was an instant success as a freshman in 1946, awarded the George Lowe Trophy by the Gridiron Club of Boston as the best player in New England. And he led the 1948 team in every offensive category except passing.

But Jackson, once an all-round athlete at Hillhouse High School in New Haven, had arrived at Yale—most of his tuition financed under the GI Bill—amid much trepidation.

"I was a townie, which meant I grew up in the town, and now I was becoming a gownie, or a Yale student. My father was a chef at Yale's Trumbull College and my mother worked. I was the last of six kids—the only one who got a college education. I had the feeling that I did not belong in a rich man's institution. I'm a high school graduate and I'm going to school with a lot of prep school grads who went to Choate and Exeter."

But Jackson would thrive, and he would recall only one instance of anything approaching a racial taunt on the field. It came near the end of a 35–0 loss to Vanderbilt at Yale Bowl in 1948.

"One of their centers, a fellow named Hoover, got in the ball game. He said, 'You better watch yourself, brother' and started jawing, 'Nobody comes through here, particularly you.' He was pointing at me. One of our guards stood up and said, 'Hey, Hoover, if you were any good you would have been in the game a long time ago.' That shut him up."

Jackson, who would become an executive with the Ford Motor Company and a Detroit civic leader, was not the first black player to be an Ivy captain. Back in 1893, William Lewis, a center for Harvard, was named acting captain for the Penn game after the regular captain was injured. Lewis, then attending Harvard Law School, would become one of the first blacks admitted to the American Bar Association, a Massachusetts state legislator, and assistant attorney general of the United States under President William Howard Taft. He also found time to serve as a Harvard line coach.

The late 1940s brought outstanding teams at two schools who hadn't captured

Before the Nittany Lions there were the Bears: Joe Paterno, the 1949 Brown quarterback and co-captain.
(BROWN UNIVERSITY)

back, an Army Air Forces veteran who had won the Silver Star and had parachuted into enemy territory three times, escaping on each occasion with help from the underground.

With that résumé, a broken nose didn't mean much. Dorset was clobbered in the first half of the 1949 Penn game, and at halftime Cornell was trailing by 21–7. But the quarterback, who hadn't even taken time out when he was hurt, brought Cornell back in the second half before a crowd of 75,000 at Franklin Field. He connected twice with left end Walt Bruska on one touchdown drive, then put Cornell ahead with a 25-yard, fourth-down pass to Bruska. What his coach called "the greatest second half I have ever seen" produced a 29–21 victory.

Matching Cornell's record, Brown went 8-1 in 1949 under Coach Rip Engle, in his sixth and final season, losing only to Princeton. The Bears finished up on a spectacular note against Colgate on Thanksgiving Day when their quarterback and captain, a fellow named Joe Paterno, put on a passing and running show to overcome a 19-point third-quarter deficit.

much notice for some time—Cornell and Brown.

Under Lefty James, who would coach at Ithaca for 14 seasons, Cornell went 8-1 in 1948 and 1949, losing only to Army and Dartmouth.

The Big Red were led by Pete Dorset, their 5-foot-8-inch, 155-pound quarter-

Paterno ran 42 yards on a bootleg to the Colgate 3 in the fourth quarter, then threw a touchdown pass to Frank Mahoney. He later went 40 yards with an interception, setting up a 15-yard touchdown run by his brother George, the Brown fullback. Scoring four touchdowns in a span of six minutes, Brown came away with a 41–26 victory to conclude its best season since 1932.

The combination of Engle and Paterno would loom larger at Penn State, where Engle took over as coach in 1950, followed by Paterno in 1966.

Harvard posted winning seasons in 1945 and 1946 with Coach Dick Harlow returning from the navy.

The 1947 season began on a bright note with a 52–0 romp over Western Maryland, Harlow's old school, in a game marking the career highlight for a slender end named Bobby Kennedy.

Bobby was continuing a family sports tradition at Harvard.

His father, Joseph Kennedy Sr., had played first base for the Crimson in 1911. Bobby's eldest brother, Joe Jr., won minor letters for varsity football in 1935 and 1937 despite breaking an arm and suffering a knee injury that required surgery.

The next brother, John, was on Harvard's 1936 freshman football team but spent most of his time on the bench, prompting a story he would later tell.

After six weeks of doing little but working out, he walked up to the coach, Henry Lamar, in the late stages of the Yale game, tapped him on the shoulder and said, "Coach, how about putting me in?"

John would recall how "the coach turned to me and said, 'Who the hell are you?'"

A spark of recognition evidently did dawn on Lamar that afternoon since Harvard records show that JFK got into the Yale game as a substitute right end. He won a minor letter the following season as an end on the jayvee team.

Bobby Kennedy, only 5 feet 10 inches and 165 pounds, was never considered an outstanding offensive threat. He would be remembered by Lamar—still on the coaching staff after giving brother John the brushoff a decade earlier—for his "tenacity, drive, competitive push."

Teammate Ken O'Donnell would recall how "after the war, there were eight men on the team, all high school stars, all-scholastic or all-prep. Some had returned from the war bigger and stronger. They used to knock Bobby down. Then he'd be right back up and make a tackle."

Playing in his third season, and finally a starter, Bobby caught the first and only touchdown pass of his career in the Western Maryland game, a 6-yarder from O'Donnell. The following week, he suffered a major injury during practice, and though he showed considerable grit, it essentially ended his football career. He would return only for brief appearances against Brown and Yale.

"Bob tried to block an opposing back near the sidelines and missed," O'Donnell would recall. "He crashed heavily into a red equipment wagon. Bob returned to his position immediately, but three days later

Herman Hickman, storyteller, broadcast personality, devotee of the classics, and Yale coach. (YALE UNIVERSITY)

he collapsed and was carried from the field. An examination proved that he had been playing with a broken leg."

Later an aide in the Kennedy White House, O'Donnell was a fine football player at wingback and quarterback on offense and safety on defense. He intercepted eight passes in 1949, a school record.

O'Donnell had plenty of opportunity to see defensive action in 1949 since it was a dismal year for Harvard, which went 1-8, losing all of its six games to Ivy opponents. Soon after the season ended with a 29–6 loss to Yale, that old all-American Hamilton Fish sent a letter to the athletic director,

Bill Bingham, demanding the firing of Coach Art Valpey, who had succeeded Harlow the year before. Fish insisted that the whole Harvard coaching staff be fired "at all costs" for having produced "the most ineptly coached team—offensively, defensively and in forward passing—in the history of Harvard football."

Valpey was indeed out before long, succeeded by Lloyd Jordan, who would remain for seven seasons, only three of them yielding a winning record.

When Yale couldn't get Lou Little in 1948, it reached out for a colorful character in Herman Hickman, an all-America guard at Tennessee in the early 1930s, later a professional football player and wrestler and then line coach for Army's powerful teams.

Hickman found his Yale men quite a contrast to his Cadet squads.

As Levi Jackson remembered it: "In our first practice he looked and said, 'Okay, here's the backs. Now where's the linemen?' Meaning we were all relatively small. He was used to all those big guys.

"Herman used to say, 'Somewhere in the world God must have made a couple of tackles, 6 feet 4, 230 pounds, who had enough intelligence to attend Yale, and they were agile, mobile and hostile.'

"We all roared."

Hickman, who weighed in the neighborhood of 300 pounds, was famed for his prodigious appetite, hillbilly storytelling, and penchant for poetry and the classics. He became a broadcast personality while at Yale, playing host on a weekly radio show with a national hookup and appearing as a panel member on television's *Goodrich Celebrity Time Show*. And he was much in demand as a banquet speaker.

He failed—at least publicly—to take defeat with any degree of solemnity.

While Yale was in the last throes of that 35–0 shellacking by Vanderbilt in 1948, "he put his feet up on the table and lit a cigar as if he were winning," recalled Levi Jackson. "I think that disturbed some of the alumni pretty much."

One day in 1949, Hickman told an audience that his aim was "to keep the alumni sullen but not mutinous." He remarked that "there were a couple of times back there when I was real worried; I was afraid I would make too good a record for me in the first year. We went into the last periods leading both Harvard and Princeton, but I gathered the boys around me and said, 'Fellows, how about losing this one for old Herman.' Bless 'em, they obliged."

(Yale had, in fact, dropped both games, closing out its 1948 season by losing 20–14 to Princeton and 20–7 to Harvard.)

Hickman claimed to have remembered one game where Yale lost the ball on fumbles four times inside the opponent's 10-yard line while the opposition scored on its only opportunity.

"We were coming off the field at the halftime intermission just as the Yale band was marching on. The drum major was really strutting. He threw the baton 30 feet up in the air and, without missing his stride, dropped it. Unperturbed, he twirled it skyward again and missed again. Suddenly, a big voice, sounding as if it came from the loudspeaker, boomed out of the Bowl: 'Hey Hickman, are you coaching the band today, too?'"

In the summer of 1952—coming off a 2-5-2 season—Hickman received an offer from the General Cigar Company to do a weekly football commentary show at a higher salary than he was earning under a long-term contract at Yale.

By then there were rumblings of discontent over his outside pursuits. After the dismal 1951 season, Yale's trustees had decided to bar a coach from participating in sponsored broadcast programs except in rare cases.

Hickman went before Yale's football advisory committee and, as he recalled: "When I explained to them my dilemma, and the wonderful television offer I had, they seemed a little too optimistic and enthusiastic. I looked around to see if somebody was pushing me."

He got out of his contract and took a sports broadcasting job at NBC.

Jordan Olivar, a former head coach at Villanova and Loyola of Los Angeles and a newly named assistant line coach at Yale, replaced Hickman. He envisioned the post as an "interim" one, saying he intended to keep his job with a life insurance company in Los Angeles and have his family remain there. But he stayed at Yale for 11 seasons.

The class of the Ivies in the early 1950s would be Princeton.

The Tigers went unbeaten in 1950 and 1951—their first undefeated squads since 1935—and captured the Lambert Trophy as the top team in the East both years. The trophy, first awarded in 1936, had only

Dick Kazmaier, winner of the 1951 Heisman Trophy, led Princeton to two straight unbeaten seasons.
(PRINCETON UNIVERSITY)

An all-around high school sports star in Maumee, Ohio, Kazmaier had been coveted by two dozen schools. But his physique did not particularly impress Princeton. When he applied, he weighed only 155 pounds, prompting Princeton's director of admissions, C. William Edwards, to write: "Fine boy. Excellent record. Has played football and other sports in high school. But too small to play college football."

Coming from a small town in the Midwest did not, however, hurt Kazmaier—Princeton's effort to achieve geographic diversity helped him gain entrance.

Kazmaier didn't play full-time in 1949, his sophomore season—Coach Charlie Caldwell was apparently worried that he couldn't take a pounding—but he led the Ivy teams in total offense with 1,155 yards.

once before gone to an Ivy team, the undefeated Cornell squad of 1939.

Princeton's dominance was mostly the work of tailback Dick Kazmaier, a superb runner, passer, and kicker and Heisman Trophy winner in 1951, the first Ivy recipient since Larry Kelley and Clint Frank in the 1930s.

In his junior season—by now all of 171 pounds—Kazmaier put on a series of spectacular performances, confounding opponents on pass-run option plays. He accounted for four touchdowns, either running or passing, in three separate games—against Rutgers, Harvard, and Yale.

Kazmaier's most memorable game came on one of the worst days ever for football—November 13, 1950, the afternoon of Hurricane Flora. He ran through Dartmouth, and the torrential rain and 75-mile-an-hour winds, for a 37-yard touchdown and a 23-yard run setting up another score in a 13–7 victory at Palmer Stadium witnessed by all of 5,000 fans. (A total of 31,000 had bought tickets.) But Kazmaier wasn't perfect. One time when he tried to punt, the wind sent the ball flying back over his head.

Princeton's single-wing attack swept through nine opponents in 1950, rolling up a point margin of 349–94 and a No. 2 national ranking in total offense and rushing.

It seemed that the following year's team might have its troubles since 6 of 11 defensive starters and 10 of 11 offensive starters had departed. But the one offensive player still around was Kazmaier, and he was better than ever.

The Tigers romped over New York University, 54–20, to start the 1951 season, but Kazmaier encountered a problem the following Saturday that hampered his gripping the football. "At Navy, in the heat, Kaz ran out of saliva," recalled Homer Smith, Princeton's outstanding fullback. "I would spit on his hands so he could pass." With that assist Princeton topped Navy, 24–20.

Princeton's next big test came on the final Saturday of October when it played Cornell. Both teams came in undefeated, Princeton ranked No. 8 nationally with a 17-game winning streak and Cornell No. 12 behind quarterback Rocco Calvo, the country's most accurate passer.

Smith would remember how "Charlie Caldwell called us together after the Friday workout and said: 'There has been a lot of talk about the streak. To hell with the streak. The world won't come to an end if we lose. But we're not going to lose.'"

Princeton went on to a 53–15 rout as Kazmaier outgained the entire Cornell team on the ground and in the air, picking up 126 yards rushing to the Big Red's 98, and 236 yards passing (completing 15 of 17 passes) to Cornell's 112. He threw for three touchdowns, ran for two more, and added 2 points on a safety.

Two weeks later, Kazmaier passed for three touchdowns in a 54–13 romp over Harvard, the worst beating a Princeton team had ever given the Crimson.

Kazmaier finished his career on a woozy note when Princeton defeated Dartmouth, 13–0, at Palmer Stadium.

As he threw a second-quarter pass completion putting the ball on the Dartmouth 3, Kazmaier was hit by George Rambour, a 235-pound tackle, and suffered a broken nose and mild concussion. He sat things out until the last minute when he returned to share in the exuberance of another undefeated season, carried off the field by his teammates.

Kazmaier wasn't the only player hurting that afternoon. Dartmouth quarterback Jim Miller suffered a broken left leg and a total of 12 players had to be helped off the field. Following the third quarter, the referee, John Coles, went to both benches to tell them "there are 40,000 people who came out here to see a football game and not a free-for-all."

Afterward, Charlie Caldwell, angered over the injury to Kazmaier, called for automatic ejections for unnecessary roughness.

"Fifteen yards is a cheap assessment for slugging, kicking and other flagrant violations," complained the Princeton coach. "What do 15 yards mean to a team if it can get the star player of the other side out of the game?"

The *Daily Princetonian* charged that Dartmouth's main objective wasn't winning the game but "'getting' the Ivy League champions—with Dick Kazmaier as their primary target."

Rambour, who hit Kazmaier as he was running to his right on a pass-run option play, denied trying to hurt him, and Dartmouth Coach Tuss McLaughry called the allegation "outrageous." The referee did not call a penalty on the play. As for Kazmaier, he said: "I don't remember anything about it. I don't remember who hit me or how."

Kazmaier finished with career totals of 20 touchdowns rushing, 35 touchdowns passing, and 4,354 yards running and throwing. His 1950 and 1951 teams each finished No. 6 nationally in the Associated Press media poll.

Like the previous Ivy winners of the Heisman, Kazmaier did not pursue pro football. He went on to the Harvard Business School and a career in the business world.

But he had been pursued by the national media, making the cover of *Time*. The magazine's November 19, 1951, issue hailed Kazmaier as "a reminder, in a somewhat fetid atmosphere that has gathered around the pseudo-amateurs of U.S.

sports, that winning football is not the monopoly of huge hired hands taking snap courses in football factories."

The world of college sports had indeed been troubled, the Kazmaier injury controversy only one among a string of unsavory episodes. For 1951 had brought the basketball point-shaving arrests, a cheating scandal that rocked the West Point football team, and a general upsurge in college football violence. The most notorious incident was the broken jaw suffered by a black football player at Drake University named Johnny Bright, the nation's leading ground-gainer, in a Missouri Valley Conference game at Oklahoma A&M. Charging that Bright was slugged, Drake quit the conference.

Out of all this came a report by the American Council on Education—representing all the major colleges in the country—calling for a "back to purity" code. That formed the model for actions to be taken by the Ivy presidents—the first steps toward de-emphasis of football.

Back in November 1945, the eight Ivy schools—bound by common goals yet still unaligned in a formal league—had joined together in a code pledging commitment to high academic standards for athletes. They agreed to ban athletic scholarships and hold football players to the same expectations as other students.

Now, in February 1952, the Ivy presidents announced an eight-point program that ended spring practice and abolished postseason participation by players, coaches, and teams. The presidents agreed to "reaffirm the principle of the control of athletics by the academic authorities" and created a policy committee that would meet at least twice a year to keep an eye on things. They also decreed that beginning in the fall of 1953, every Ivy school would play every other college in the group at least once every five years, the first step toward formal, round-robin play.

Reaction was swift—and in some circles unfavorable.

Lloyd Jordan, the Harvard coach, maintained that a ban on spring practice would simply bring more intense recruiting of schoolboy stars to make up for lack of training time. Tuss McLaughry, the Dartmouth coach, saw the spring ban as putting Ivy schools at a "distinct disadvantage" with outside opponents, something that would certainly prove true.

There was even grousing that the Ivy postseason ban would hurt crippled children. Officials of the East-West game played each December in San Francisco to aid the Shriners' hospital complained about the prospect of losing an occasional Ivy presence. (Tuss McLaughry and Herman Hickman had been coaching in that game, and Dick Kazmaier had played for the East in 1951.) The ban would stand, however, and it would include the Shriners' game.

On the playing field, 1952 brought a flourish for Columbia, which hadn't had much to gloat about since its shocker over Army in 1947.

The Lions were host to Army again in late October before a crowd of 31,000 that included a certain presidential candidate. On leave from the Columbia presidency, Dwight D. Eisenhower had campaigned in Harlem that morning, then went up to Baker Field. He sat on the Columbia side for the first half, then crossed to the Army side where he was greeted with a rousing "Ike, Ike, Ike, Hooray" before resuming his joust with Adlai Stevenson. He missed a terrific finish.

Army held a 14–7 lead early in the fourth quarter and was driving for another touchdown, but was stopped on the Columbia 1-yard line. A little later the Cadets were threatening once more, only to be stymied when defensive tackle John Casella recovered a fumbled handoff on the Columbia 33. The Lions couldn't match the Cadets' running attack, but had yet another fine quarterback in Mitch Price, who set a school career record for passing yardage with his first completion of the day, breaking the mark set by Gene Rossides. Now Price threw a 19-yarder to end Al Ward. Then he tossed three more passes, but all were incomplete. Finally, Price faded back again, went to his right, then to his left, then found Ward alone in the end zone and hit him with 16 seconds remaining. Ward kicked the extra point and Columbia came away with a 14–14 tie.

It would be a satisfying autumn as well for Yale, which was enjoying a turnaround under Coach Jordan Olivar after winning only two games in Herman Hickman's final season.

Yale entered the Harvard game at 7-1, but Harvard was experiencing a revival as well, coming in at 5-3 after having won a total of five games over the previous three seasons.

The Elis romped by 41–14, but it wasn't just the final score that rankled the Crimson—it was the way Yale's final point was scored.

After taking a 40–7 lead in the third quarter, Yale seemed ready for a routine conversion as quarterback Ed Molloy got set to hold the ball for the kicker, Bob Parcells. But after getting the snap, Molloy ran to his right and threw into the end zone for his right end, No. 99.

There was, coincidentally, a drawing of a Yale player wearing No. 99 on the game's program cover. But Harvard could be forgiven for not noticing the real 99, who wasn't listed in the program's lineups and could easily have disappeared in a football crowd, being only 5 feet 5 inches and 140 pounds.

He was Charlie Yeager, Yale's student manager, who was supposed to hand out footballs at practice, not catch them in games.

Yeager had been running pass plays for fun during workouts, so with Yale leading by two touchdowns at halftime, Coach Jordan Olivar let him don a uniform. When the game turned into a rout, Yeager was sprung from the bench.

"Angelo Bertelli, the former Notre Dame quarterback, had been brought in by Olivar to help with the backfield, and I used to get a kick out of playing catch with Bertelli," Yeager would remember.

"Olivar and an assistant spotted me one day after practice and said: 'We've got an idea. We want to put you in for an extra point in the Harvard game if we get far enough ahead.' I said, 'Well, I'll start trying to kick and see if I can get the ball high enough up in the air,' but they said, 'No. We've been watching you play catch. We're gonna put you in at end to catch a pass.'"

"I had a little trepidation," Yeager recalled. "I was afraid of the consequences. They kind of laughed and said, 'Well, it's end or nothing.'"

The Friday before the game, Yale had practiced a fake extra-point attempt, with the ball being thrown to Yeager. When the Elis took a 33-point lead, Yeager lined up at right end on the conversion play.

Then, as Yeager would tell it, everything went wrong.

"When the ball was snapped I didn't get off on the count, and a Harvard defensive player who was coming in to block the extra point hit me pretty hard and knocked me into our right tackle, Pete Radulovic. He sort of picked me up and I staggered out in the end zone."

Now would come even more improvisation.

"By this time they were chasing Eddie Molloy, our quarterback. He could have run the ball into the end zone. One Harvard defender who was laying back went after Jim Ralston, one of our backs. I kind of sneaked out behind him. Molloy saw my jersey, threw an easy pass and I caught it.

"It was kind of a busted play."

Yeager remembered how "toward the end of the fourth quarter there was an announcement that the last point for Yale had been scored by the manager. They gave my name and there was a groan from the Harvard side and a cheer from the Yale side."

Why was Yeager wearing No. 99, the number on the Yale player drawn on the program cover?

"It was pure coincidence. That was the number on the smallest jersey they had."

While Yale and Harvard were starting out on the road to their bizarre finale, Princeton won its first two games in 1952—the start of the post-Kazmaier era.

Then the Tigers faced a Penn team that held Notre Dame to a 7–7 tie two weeks earlier and was the only Ivy squad still playing an ambitious national schedule.

Hardly intimidated by the crowd of 40,000 at Palmer Stadium, Penn took a 13–0 lead in the second quarter on a 2-yard run by fullback Joe Varaitis and a 46-yard pass from halfback Walter Hynoski to end Jack Moses. Then Princeton struck back on the left-handed tailback Bob Unger's 12-yard touchdown pass to the captain, Frank McPhee.

Princeton dominated the second half, driving deep into Penn territory four times, only to be halted by a pair of interceptions, a fumble, and a major penalty. Late in the fourth quarter the Tigers were threatening once more, but Unger was injured after completing a 20-yard pass. Bill Tryon, his replacement, came in with a minute remaining and the ball on the Penn 30. He fired a pass into the end zone, but it was intercepted by Penn's George Bosseler.

Penn had a 13–7 victory that snapped Princeton's winning streak at 24.

Princeton's Homer Smith would remember how "the last two to shower, Captain Frank McPhee and I, sat down on the floor of the shower, let the water rain over us and just let ourselves collapse. We thought we had let down all the guys who had built the streak."

But Princeton rebounded for another terrific season. Led by Smith, their fullback, and McPhee, a receiver later cited by Charlie Caldwell as the best all-around player he had ever coached, the Tigers went 8-1.

Penn won all four games it played against Ivy teams in 1952, also beating Dartmouth, Columbia, and Cornell, but finished only 4-3-2. The rest of its season was decidedly un-Ivy-like—losses to Penn State, Georgia, and Army and ties against Notre Dame and Navy.

By then, Penn's high-powered program had stirred a major controversy.

In August 1950, Penn's president, Harold Stassen—the political "Boy Wonder" elected governor of Minnesota at age 31 and a Republican presidential contender in 1948—announced a "Victory with Honor" program. While pledging to refrain from improper recruiting and stating that the prime objective for athletes was working toward a degree, Stassen said that Penn was "moving with ingenuity" within the National Collegiate Athletic Association code.

"We want to appeal to star high-school athletes," he told a gathering of sportswriters at Philadelphia's Warwick Hotel. "I foresee a remarkable future of strong teams."

Stassen brought in a new athletic director, Fran Murray, a former Penn football

Penn's George Munger, who would depart as coach after 16 seasons amid a battle against the administration's ambitious football program. (UNIVERSITY OF PENNSYLVANIA)

star and talented promoter, with orders to oversee an ambitious football program.

Penn's 1950 team had four Ivy opponents, one of whom—Dartmouth—probably wished that the Quakers could play Notre Dame every Saturday. The all-America halfback Francis (Reds) Bagnell gained 490 yards in total offense and connected on 14 straight passes during one stretch for Penn in a 42–26 victory over Dartmouth.

In January 1951, Joe Williams of the *New York World-Telegram and Sun* wrote

that the other Ivy schools, with the exception of Cornell, would boycott Penn as a protest over its moves toward a major-college schedule while the rest of the Ivies were beginning to de-emphasize football.

Stassen claimed that Penn was being ostracized because it had scheduled Notre Dame for a 1952 game and wouldn't back off. The Ivy athletic officials supposedly felt that Notre Dame's academic standards didn't match theirs, but they wouldn't say so for the record, stating only that there were problems fitting Penn into rotating schedules.

After going ahead with its imposing 1952 schedule—four Ivy opponents and five national powers—Penn arranged an even tougher agenda for 1953. The only Ivy opponent was Cornell, for the traditional Thanksgiving Day meeting. The first eight games were with Vanderbilt, Penn State, California, Ohio State, Navy, Michigan, Notre Dame, and Army.

Now a split erupted at Penn pitting Murray, the new athletic director, against George Munger, the longtime coach. Murray was pressing ahead with a big-college schedule in the hopes of getting games on television for nice paydays, but Munger wanted more games with the traditional Ivy opponents.

Before the powerhouse 1953 schedule could be played, the dispute became public. The Penn players wrote a letter in March to Murray, Munger, and Acting President William Du Barry (Stassen had resigned to become mutual security administrator in the Eisenhower administration) complaining that the schedule was too dif-

John Culver, a future congressman and United States senator from Iowa, runs for a 35-yard touchdown in Harvard's 1953 victory over Yale. (HARVARD UNIVERSITY)

ficult for a team now barred by Ivy regulations from holding spring practice.

A team "harmony" dinner a few days later was anything but. Murray used the forum to assail Munger for interfering with his responsibilities by pressing for an easier schedule. Du Barry, meanwhile, named former Supreme Court Justice Owen J. Roberts, a Penn alumnus and former law professor, to head a review of the university's athletic policies.

Two months later, Murray was fired,

and a few days after that Munger announced his resignation effective after the 1953 season, saying he would become the school's director of physical education.

Penn held its own in 1953, going 3-5-1. But it was Munger's only losing team. He departed with a record of 82-42-10 over 16 years.

The season proved a satisfying one for Harvard, which had not had a particularly good year since Dick Harlow's 1946 team went 7-2.

Now, in Coach Lloyd Jordan's fourth year, the Crimson were turning things around behind their captain and star runner, Dick Clasby, and an outstanding passer in Carroll Lowenstein. The Harvard-Yale game matched two good teams, the Crimson having lost only twice going in and the Elis having been beaten once with two ties. Harvard proved better this day, the game's biggest play a 35-yard touchdown run in the third quarter by fullback John Culver. The Crimson came away with a 13–0 victory, deprived of a perfect season only by 6–0 losses to Columbia and Princeton.

In January 1954, Penn named Steve Sebo, an assistant coach at Michigan State, to succeed Munger. Sebo would stay for six seasons, but he had to weather a disastrous start. The 1954 and 1955 schedules—still packed with strong teams, leaving Cornell and Princeton as the only Ivy opponents—brought a debacle. Penn finished 0-9 both years.

But relief was in sight. Early in 1954,

Cheerleaders are surrogate moms for the Brown bear at the 1953 game against Rhode Island.
(**BROWN UNIVERSITY**)

Brown's homecoming queen arriving in fine style in the autumn of 1955. (BROWN UNIVERSITY)

the Ivy presidents took a step beyond the tightened code they adopted in 1952 and went further on the road toward de-emphasis. They announced creation of a formal Ivy football league, starting in the 1956 season, with round-robin play. (Since the Ivies had already limited themselves to a nine-game schedule, that meant only two games against outsiders.) The schools would now vie for a championship trophy, presented by Penn's Class of 1925.

Yale looked to be the Ivies' dominant team in 1954, winning its first four games. But then came a tie with Colgate and, after a victory over Dartmouth, a 48–7 loss to Army at Yale Bowl before a sellout crowd of 73,000 in their first matchup since 1943.

For the second straight autumn, an otherwise fine season for Yale ended on a down note when Harvard overcame a 9–0 deficit in the fourth quarter for a 13–9 victory at Cambridge. A substitute halfback named Frank White, playing only because of an injury to a starter, threw for the winning score on a reverse, tossing the ball to left end Bob Cochrane, who did a juggling act, then held on for a 39-yard touchdown play.

Yale featured an outstanding backfield in 1955—two fine quarterbacks in Dean Loucks and Dick Winterbauer and strong runners in Dennis McGill and Al Ward. The Elis got another shot at Army, and by the end of the afternoon it was possible to forget about those two previous season-ending losses to Harvard. In a major upset, Yale stunned Army, 14–12, before 61,000 at Yale bowl. Army Coach Red Blaik, relying on quickness, was unhappy over muddy spots on turf left uncovered during a day and a half of rains that stopped just before the kickoff. Yale, which spotted Army a touchdown, then came back on Loucks's soaring pass to Paul Lopata and Al Ward's 4-yard touchdown run, was thrilled.

The following Saturday, Yale met Princeton at Palmer Stadium in the matchup of the year for the Ivies. Yale was 6-1, having lost only to Colgate. Princeton, led by Royce Flippin, considered the nation's top single-wing tailback, came in at 5-2. Flippin ran for one score and the Tigers got another touchdown on an interception for a 13–0 victory.

On the final weekend, Yale took a 14–0 lead over Harvard, but the Crimson rallied

West Point cadets march past the Walter Camp memorial arch before game at Yale Bowl. (YALE UNIVERSITY)

Ted Kennedy, the fourth Kennedy brother to play football at Harvard and the most talented of the bunch, caught two touchdown passes for the 1955 Crimson. (HARVARD UNIVERSITY)

in the third quarter on Walt Stahura's 7-yard touchdown pass. It was caught by a senior end named Ted Kennedy.

"Jack could always throw a football real well, and so it was natural for the rest of us—Joe, Bob, and I—to be his ends, shagging on the beach all summer," Ted would remember.

It was his second touchdown catch in two years of varsity play, the first one a 20-yarder against Columbia earlier in 1955. But it wasn't enough as Yale got the clinch-

er on McGill's 39-yard interception return and emerged with a 21–7 victory.

The 1955 season brought a coaching change at Dartmouth, which hadn't had a winning team since 1949. Tuss McLaughry stepped down after 12 years and was replaced by Bob Blackman, a hard driver who would gain a reputation for intensity, careful preparation, imaginative offenses, and methodical recruiting.

Blackman's football career was spawned at the University of Southern California, which gave him an athletic scholarship in 1937. But he never played for USC. In his freshman year, he was stricken by polio. He became a coaching assistant as an undergrad, later a highly successful coach in the navy, then a high school and junior-college coach before moving to the University of Denver in 1953. The school had gone 0-7 in 1952, but in his second season Blackman brought Denver its first Skyline Conference title in 27 years. Before signing on with Dartmouth, he was reportedly close to getting the Los Angeles Rams' coaching job.

Blackman was stunned by the environment at Hanover, underlined by a train trip early on. As soon as his players were settled in their seats, out came the books and newspapers.

"They were reading the *Wall Street Journal*," Blackman would remember. "I wouldn't even know how to read it myself. I was flabbergasted. When I was coaching at Denver University, the first time we went on the road the kids either pulled out decks of cards or stacks of comic books."

Bob Blackman, who brought Dartmouth seven Ivy League championships, leads his boys onto the field. (DARTMOUTH COLLEGE)

Blackman's first Dartmouth team went only 3-6. After that he would rip off 12 straight winning seasons, producing two teams with perfect records.

But a new era was unfolding beyond Dartmouth as well. The Ivy schools were approaching their first season of round-robin play. They would vie for a true league championship and a brand-new trophy for whoever dominated the nation's oldest football rivalries.

PART

TWO

"THIS BOURGEOIS GAME"

HE WOULD NEVER be confused with Walter Camp as a football pioneer, but Dick Bence of Brown produced a couple of firsts for the Ivy League.

On the afternoon of Saturday, September 29, 1956, the Bears' left end and captain scored the first touchdown of formal Ivy play. One week later, he blazed a trail again, mixing it up in the inaugural fistfight of the Ivies' new era.

Over four decades to come, Brown would often keep company with Columbia around the bottom of the Ivy League. But the Bears stood alone atop the Ivies as round-robin competition finally got under way 87 years after Princeton and Rutgers first kicked a round canvas ball in anger.

Playing before 12,000 at Baker Field, Brown defeated Columbia, 20–0, in the lone all-Ivy game played on opening day, getting the only score it needed when Bence caught a 29-yard pass in the sec-

ond quarter from quarterback Frank Finney.

The other teams faced nonconference opponents on that first Saturday, emerging with assorted indignities. Penn lost its 19th straight in a 34–0 trouncing by Penn State. Dartmouth tackle Bill Pettway incurred a personal travail, suffering burns of the arm when a blank charge from a fan's toy cannon went off near him in the game against New Hampshire.

The following Saturday, good fortune seemed to be with Brown again when the Bears played at Yale. A gaffe by an official gave the Elis only three downs on a first-quarter series. The first Ivy fight broke out in the third quarter when Bence traded punches with the Yale quarterback, Dean Loucks, emptying both benches and bringing an early departure for the two miscreants. Despite losing a down and a quarterback, Yale won its Ivy opener, 20–2.

streak had come against Navy on October 24, 1953. Navy was back with a vengeance this year, ripping Penn by 54–6 at Franklin Field as the Midshipmen in the stands shouted "We want more" during the final minutes while fifth-stringers were in the game.

The Quakers finished at 4-5 but experienced a sour finale, a 20–7 home loss on Thanksgiving Day to Cornell, which hadn't won a single game all season, its star runner, Bo Roberson, hampered by a knee injury. The Cornell players carried Coach Lefty James off on their shoulders. But Penn students were considerably less charitable toward their coach. A few days later, Steve Sebo was hanged in effigy.

A coach who had remained enormously popular even when losses were piling up closed out his career in the autumn of 1956. Lou Little would be retiring after 27 seasons at Columbia, and tributes were in the works.

The first ceremony unfolded on an afternoon to forget. At halftime of the Columbia-Army game at Baker Field, the West Point brigade commander presented Little with a plaque, and the corps of 2,400 cadets saluted him. But the Army players weren't so kind. They drubbed Columbia, 60–0.

Columbia coach Lou Little is honored by West Point in a 1956 retirement ceremony at Baker Field.
(COLUMBIA UNIVERSITY)

Penn ended its losing streak by topping Dartmouth, 14–7, at Franklin Field. With a half-minute remaining, Penn fans participated in a ritual that most were rusty at—tearing down the goalposts. It would get to be a habit. Two weeks later, Penn again won at home, this time by 14–7 over Brown, and once more the goalposts were trashed.

Penn's last victory before its losing

The following Saturday, Little was honored again at his final home game as a crowd of 12,000 stood at halftime and sang "Auld Lang Syne." It was a far happier occasion than the Army game. Claude Benham threw for three touchdowns and scored another himself, playing all 60 minutes, in a 25–19 victory over Cornell.

There was a final round of honors when Columbia ended the season with its first visit to Rutgers since 1902. Former Columbia stars—among them Al Barabas and Bill Swiacki, the respective heroes of the Rose Bowl victory and the 1947 upset of Army—turned out as Little ended his Columbia career with an 18–12 victory and an overall record of 110-116-10.

League honors went to the preseason favorite, Yale, which rolled to a 7-0 Ivy mark behind the outstanding all-senior backfield of Loucks, Dennis McGill, Steve Ackerman, and Al Ward, and a good backup quarterback in junior Dick Winterbauer. Yale finished at 8-1, a perfect season spoiled by a 14–6 loss to Colgate.

Aldo (Buff) Donelli succeeded Lou Little in 1957 and got off to a splendid start. The coach's son, Dick, replacing the departed Benham at quarterback, threw a pair of touchdown passes in a 23–20 upset of Brown. But that would be Columbia's only victory for the season.

A venerable coach was gone at Princeton as well. Charlie Caldwell, stricken by cancer, went on leave a few weeks before the 1957 season opened and would die in November. Dick Colman, an assistant coach, took over.

There was also a new coach at Harvard as John Yovicsin, recruited from Gettysburg College, succeeded Lloyd Jordan and scrapped his single wing in favor of the T formation.

Princeton, favored to take the Ivy title, won its first five league games, then played at home on the next-to-last Saturday against Yale, which was just 2-2-1 in conference play. On a tumultuous day that saw fights break out in the stands, the Elis'

The Ivy League championship trophy, donated by the University of Pennsylvania. The sculpture atop the trophy, "The Onslaught," depicts a Harvard-Penn game of the 1890s.
(HARVARD UNIVERSITY)

Handsome Dan IX almost met disaster when he fell into the Housatonic River accompanying the Yale crew, but he recovered to lead Yale to the first Ivy League football championship in 1956. (YALE UNIVERSITY)

Winterbauer threw two touchdown passes to Mike Cavallon, and fullback Gene Coker tossed another one on an option play as Yale sprang a 20–13 upset.

The following Saturday, Yale rolled to the biggest rout in the history of The Game, trouncing Harvard by 54–0. Winterbauer threw for three scores and set a Yale career record of 20 touchdown passes with the last one.

But the Ivy title was decided at Palmer Stadium, where a crowd of 46,000 turned out on a snowy afternoon to see Princeton (5-1) face Dartmouth (5-0-1).

In the opening minute of the fourth quarter, with the Tigers leading by 20–14, Dartmouth quarterback Bill Gundy, the Ivy League's best punter, was forced to kick. The ball, heavy from snow, stayed low, and freshman tailback Dan Sachs caught it on the run at his 40. Sprung by a block from fullback Hewes Agnew, he cut to the right and ran for a touchdown, breaking the game open. Sachs, from nearby Hopewell, New Jersey, ran for three scores and passed for another in a 34–14 victory that gave Princeton the championship.

If there were any doubts that the Ivies were de-emphasizing football, they were dispelled in the early weeks of the 1958 season.

The opening Saturday saw the end of a long series between an Ivy team and an outsider who had obviously become too strong when Penn was drubbed by Penn State, 43–0, at Franklin Field. The Nittany Lions romped to their seventh victory in the last eight games with Penn, which only a few years earlier had played an ambitious national schedule. It wasn't a good Saturday for Princeton, which lost to Rutgers for the first time since 1948 as tailback Billy Austin starred in a 28–0 triumph at Palmer Stadium. And two weekends later, Cornell closed out its series with Syracuse on a dismal note, a 55–0 romp by the Orangemen.

Dartmouth and Princeton emerged again as the class of the league. Dartmouth had the Ivies' top runner in Jake Crouthamel

Jake Crouthamel, an outstanding running back and later head coach and athletic director at Dartmouth. (DARTMOUTH COLLEGE)

while Princeton featured a surplus of good tailbacks, with Hugh Scott, a sophomore, stepping in when Dan Sachs and John Sullivan were hurt.

The conference championship would again be decided on the final Saturday when Princeton met Dartmouth at Palmer Stadium.

Crouthamel struck early in the first period with a 55-yard run to the Princeton 3 that set up the game's first touchdown. But in the second quarter, while playing defense, he was incensed by a controversial call. John Heyd, a Princeton receiver, turned the wrong way and fell against Crouthamel, but field judge Ray Barbuti threw a flag for defensive interference. Crouthamel tore off his helmet and advanced menacingly on the official while someone threw a smoke bomb onto the field from the Dartmouth side amid much jeering. Crouthamel was restrained by two teammates and was lucky not to be thrown out.

But Crouthamel and Dartmouth went home happy with a 21–12 victory for the Ivy title.

In March 1959, a football controversy erupted at Brown, not usually known for passionate debate over the sport's pros and cons.

Wade C. Thompson, a member of the English Department, placed a classified ad in the *Brown Daily Herald* stating "we really ought to get rid of this bourgeois game of football and get down to the real business of being a university."

Thompson, a graduate of the once-powerful University of Chicago, which abolished football in 1940, groused that the sport symbolized "the anti-intellectualism which a university should oppose."

The argument was thrashed out in a debate—Thompson on one side and the Brown athletic director, Paul Mackesey, and the new football coach, John McLaughry, son of the former Brown coach Tuss McLaughry, on the other—with students invited to attend.

Whatever debating points Thompson may have scored, Brown was still playing football the following September. But the Bears calmed any concerns about overemphasis by dropping their opener to visiting Columbia, 21–6. The Lions suffered a loss as well. When the 35 players returned to their locker room, they discovered that their wallets had been stolen.

Yale dominated early in 1959, shutting out Connecticut, Brown, Columbia, Cornell, and Colgate to become the first major team to post five shutouts at the outset of a season since Southern California in 1943. The streak ended on a rainy afternoon at Yale Bowl with a 12–9 loss to Dartmouth.

The season's big surprise was Penn, which had not managed a winning year since 1951 and had only 11 lettermen returning. Led by outstanding runners in Dave Coffin and Fred Doelling, the Quakers won their first four games and then played a 22–22 tie with Navy, the best showing by an Ivy team against a strong outside opponent since Yale beat Army in 1955. But then came a 12–0 loss to Harvard.

Going into the final week, Penn was in first place with a 5-1 record, followed by Dartmouth at 4-1-1 and Yale at 4-2. Penn, concluding on Thanksgiving Day against

Cornell, would not play its last game until its two pursuers had finished up the previous Saturday.

Harvard knocked Yale out of a chance to tie for the title with a 35–6 rout at Yale Bowl before 66,053, the biggest crowd there since the 1954 Army game, as quarterback Charlie Ravenel displayed clever ball handling and ran for two touchdowns.

Dartmouth stayed alive with a 12–7 victory over Princeton at Palmer Stadium as Bill Gundy threw an 11-yard touchdown pass in the final minute to halfback Alan Rozycki, who dragged a host of Princeton players the final 5 yards.

So Penn played Cornell at Franklin Field with the title on the line. The Big Red took a 13–0 lead in the third quarter, but the Quakers surged back on George Koval's three touchdown passes for a 28–13 victory.

Coach Steve Sebo had taken Penn (7-1-1) to its best record since 1947. But he would be strangely rewarded. School officials celebrated their Ivy championship by firing Sebo and hiring John Stiegman of Rutgers.

After concluding its 1959 season with a dismal effort against Harvard, Yale won its first seven games in 1960. But Princeton was also unbeaten in conference play, setting up the season's big matchup when they met at Yale Bowl before a crowd of more than 62,000.

Princeton had the edge when it came to colorful nicknames—its alternating tailbacks were Hugh (Great) Scott and John (Silky) Sullivan. They ran for 156 and 89 yards respectively, but it was hardly enough. Yale's Tom Singleton threw only

seven times but completed six passes, two of them for touchdowns to Ken Wolfe and another for a score to John Hutcherson. And he carried the ball seven times for 83 yards, including a 2-yard rollout for a touchdown, leading Yale to a 43–22 victory that clinched the Ivy title.

All that remained for Yale to celebrate its first unbeaten season since 1923 was a triumph over Harvard, which had drubbed the Elis—28–0 and 35–6—the previous two seasons. No problem this time. Wolfe ran 41 yards for a touchdown and Yale kept piling it on, recovering three fumbles and intercepting four passes in a 39–6 rout, its largest margin of victory in the history of The Game.

Yale did not normally have much in common with New Mexico State University, but now they shared an honor, finishing as the only major unbeaten teams, Yale 9-0 and New Mexico State 10-0. The Elis, with an all-America center in Mike Pyle, were rated No. 14 nationally in the Associated Press poll, the first time an Ivy team had been ranked since Princeton's 1952 squad.

Columbia had made modest progress in 1960, moving from last place the previous year to fifth. When the 1961 season got under way, uncommon optimism bloomed on Morningside Heights, centering on an outstanding backfield: quarterback Tom Vassell, halfbacks Tom Haggerty and Russ Warren, and fullback Tom O'Connor.

The Lions opened with a 50–0 walloping of Brown, then were beaten by Princeton. On the third Saturday, they bounced back at New Haven as Al Butts, a sophomore fullback, ran for a touchdown and

The Columbia Lions, co-champions of the Ivy League in 1961. (COLUMBIA UNIVERSITY)

O'Connor kicked a 23-yard field goal in an 11–0 victory snapping an 11-game Yale winning streak.

Columbia followed with a 26–14 triumph over Harvard, achieving a modest milestone—it had won on successive Saturdays for the first time since 1951.

As the season moved along, more good things were happening for the Lions. On November 4, Haggerty ran from scrimmage for two touchdowns and scored another on a punt return, his runs of 84, 64, and 47 yards bringing a 35–7 triumph over Cornell. The following Saturday, the largest Baker Field crowd since the 1952 Army game—25,106—saw the Lions top Dartmouth, 35–14.

Going into the next-to-last Saturday of league play, Columbia stood at 5-1 with Princeton and Harvard both 4-1.

The Lions—finishing their Ivy schedule early—assured themselves of a tie for the title with a 37–6 romp over Penn as Haggerty scored his 10th touchdown of the season and added a 2-point conversion for an Ivy-record 62 points.

Princeton beat Yale while Harvard was defeating Brown, each remaining a half-game behind the Lions. If both won on the following weekend, there would be a three-way tie for the championship.

The Harvard-Yale game at New Haven promised an added attraction—the *Yale Daily News* reported that President Kennedy had made a last-minute scheduling change and would attend the game. With the crowd in high anticipation, the public address announcer said: "Ladies and gentlemen, the president." A cheer went up. That just about drowned out the conclusion of the announcement..."of the *Harvard Crimson*." A convertible entered the field with an escort of Secret Service look-alikes, and the figure in the back seat waving to the crowd certainly seemed to be JFK. But it was Robert E. Smith, Harvard's Class of 1962, wearing a rubber Kennedy mask. The edition of the Yale student newspaper reporting Kennedy's visit was actually a counterfeit printed by the *Harvard Crimson*.

Harvard had the last laugh as well. Yale was out of the Ivy race and had nothing to lose except the football, which it did with abundance. The Elis gave up the ball on fumbles five times, and their first two turnovers brought Harvard touchdowns within 1 minute 20 seconds of the first period. The Crimson went on to a 27–0 victory to share the title with Columbia.

Princeton lost its hopes for a third piece of the championship when it was beaten by Dartmouth, 24–6. Bill King, a sophomore quarterback, ran for one score, passed for another, and spent his spare time starring at safety.

Columbia was drubbed by unbeaten Rutgers, 32–19, at New Brunswick in its finale—the Scarlet Knights scoring 25 points in the fourth quarter—but there was consolation aplenty on Morningside Heights since the Lions had already clinched a tie for their first Ivy title.

Over the next three decades, Columbia would never repeat, and for much of the time the Lions would be at the bottom of the league. One-platoon football, reinstituted in the early 1950s, was on its way out as the 1960s moved along. As substitution rules gradually became more liberalized, teams deep in talent could wear down opponents whose manpower pool was thin. Columbia, with a small student body by Ivy

standards and lacking the athletic facilities to attract a host of good players, couldn't come up with the depth to stay competitive.

The 1962 season featured three terrific quarterbacks.

Dartmouth boasted King, an outstanding passer and rollout runner adept at directing Coach Bob Blackman's multiple offense. Cornell had Gary Wood, a junior emerging as an exciting runner as well as a passing star. And at Columbia, a heralded sophomore would live up to his notices, breaking the league record for pass completions in a season.

Archie Roberts—actually Arthur James Roberts—had been an all-American at Holyoke (Massachusetts) High School, where he was coached by his father, Arthur Henry Roberts, also known as Archie, who had starred at quarterback for New York University in the late 1920s.

Columbia scored a coup in getting him, and soon the image of the all-America boy grew grander. According to one newspaper profile, Roberts addressed his elders as "sir" and had taken on a morning newspaper route to help meet expenses, pushing a handcart around campus at 7:00 A.M. each day.

He seemed so perfect that, as the *New York Times* put it, "There are those who believe that Archie Roberts does not exist, that he is merely a pasteboard figure from a Wheaties box."

But the quarterbacks weren't alone in stirring up excitement. Harvard's band decided to give Yale a wakeup call five weeks before The Game.

Archie Roberts, Columbia's star quarterback of the early 1960s, picking up yardage.
(COLUMBIA UNIVERSITY)

A group of Harvard bandsmen en route to Columbia on the third Saturday of October took a detour and found themselves, of all places, on the Yale campus. At 4:30 A.M., they blasted away with "Ten Thousand Men of Harvard."

The Yale police arrested seven bandsmen—still carrying their instruments—and charged them with disturbing the peace and parading without a license. They were quickly released after posting $50 bail apiece.

"We actually felt a little sorry for them

and wound up giving them coffee," said John Powell, Yale's director of security.

By the end of October, Dartmouth had breezed to five straight victories and a 3-0 Ivy mark behind King, halfback Tom Spangenberg, and center-linebacker Don McKinnon, only 215 pounds but the Ivies' top lineman.

But the last Saturday of the month belonged to Gary Wood, who engineered a 35–34 upset of Princeton at Ithaca, passing for 212 yards and running for another

125. Wood threw for three touchdowns and ran for two more, winning the game on a 6-yard scoring toss to Al Aragona with just under two minutes left.

The following Saturday brought rain and high winds when Wood dueled with Roberts at Baker Field. Trailing by 2 points, Columbia took over at its 16 with 2:06 remaining. Roberts completed five passes, misfired on another, then threw a 24-yard touchdown pass to halfback Al Butts for a 25–21 lead. Wood had one more chance, but Roberts, who also punted and played safety, batted down his final pass.

The next weekend, Roberts went up against Dartmouth's King at Hanover on another soggy afternoon. The night before the game, the Dartmouth quarterback lifted campus spirits at a traditional bonfire rally. "Columbia has a fine football team and Archie Roberts is a great passer," King conceded. "But come out tomorrow anyway and see who's better."

Roberts hit on 10 of 21 passes, giving him 71 completions for the season—an Ivy record with two games to go—but was dumped for losses seven times. On this day, Dartmouth and King were far better. King threw touchdown passes of 31, 51, 36, and 48 yards and ran 7 yards for another score in a 42–0 victory.

The circle of quarterback duels was completed when King vied with Wood at Ithaca in a light snow on the next-to-last Saturday. Dartmouth came in having allowed only a touchdown and a field goal all season, but Wood ran for 161 yards. King, however, closed out his career by scoring three touchdowns as Dartmouth

came away with a 28–21 victory and the Ivy crown.

Dartmouth closed out the season with a 38–27 triumph over Princeton and a 9-0 record, its first unbeaten and untied team since another terrific quarterback, Swede Oberlander, led the 1925 squad to an 8-0 mark.

Archie Roberts and Gary Wood were back in 1963, but with mediocre supporting casts. Princeton was hoping to contend for a title behind Cosmo Iacavazzi, a line-smashing fullback who had scored seven touchdowns the previous year.

Harvard, meanwhile, received a boost on October 19 when President Kennedy

Cornell quarterback Gary Wood, a fine passer and a scrambling runner who would later play for the Giants. (CORNELL UNIVERSITY)

visited Harvard Stadium for the Columbia game. Flanked by aides David Powers and Larry O'Brien, Kennedy sat on the Harvard side above the 50-yard line—in the midst of the crowd, in the open stands. He saw the Crimson settle for a 3–3 tie.

When Dartmouth visited Harvard on the final Saturday of October, a pair of unbeaten streaks were on the line—15 games for Dartmouth, 8 for Harvard. Playing in 83-degree weather before a sellout crowd of 38,000 (the stadium capacity had been reduced from the original scale), the Crimson won, 17–13, sparked by a 36-yard run by Scott Harshbarger, the first touchdown on the ground against Dartmouth all season.

At Palmer Stadium that afternoon, it was a duel of the Hungarian-born Gogolak brothers—Princeton's Charlie and Cornell's Pete, masters of the then novel soccer-style placekicking—as the Tigers went for their fifth straight victory of the season.

Anything that happened on a football field promised to be tame compared with the ordeal of their boyhoods.

Pete was 14 years old and Charlie almost 12 when their father, a doctor, and their mother, who was pregnant, plotted an escape to Austria after the Russians crushed the 1956 Hungarian uprising. The family left everything in Budapest, took a train to a town near the border, then paid a guide to find a spot for a crossing.

As Pete recalled: "We could see tanks on patrol and we knew there were border guards and electrified fences. The thing that scared us the most were the flares that went up every five minutes, lighting up muddy fields dotted with haystacks. Every time a flare went up, we grouped together tightly and froze in position so that we'd look like a stack of hay."

It took 12 hours of walking—the guide got lost and led the family across the same stretch of railroad tracks four times—and the father had to carry the mother for the last few hours until the Gogolaks escaped across the border.

The family eventually settled in Ogdensburg, New York, and Pete tried out for the high school football team. Kicking with his instep instead of the toe, he lined his first field goal attempt at practice under the crossbar. His teammates thought his style was hugely funny, but he persevered, making the adjustment from a soccer ball to a football.

Charlie had most of the work when Princeton faced Cornell, kicking a 15-yard field goal and converting six of seven extra-point attempts as the Tigers romped by 51–14.

At New Haven that day, the niftiest play was made by a fan who swiped the feathered headdress from a cheerleader for the Colgate Red Raiders, raced along the sidelines, and then tossed it to an accomplice. Under a new coach, John Pont, who had replaced Jordan Olivar, the Yale team did the rest, dispatching Colgate by 31–0.

The following Saturday, Pont was carried off the field on his players' shoulders

Cornell's Pete Gogolak connecting on a 33-yard field goal against Yale in 1963.
(CORNELL UNIVERSITY)

The Princeton Tiger makes sure Charlie Gogolak's toe won't be tarnished. (PRINCETON UNIVERSITY)

13th touchdown of the season, tying a school mark that had stood for more than half a century.

Going into what was supposed to be the final day of the season—November 23—Princeton stood atop the league at 5-1, followed by Harvard at 4-1-1 and Dartmouth at 4-2.

The sports sections in the Eastern newspapers of Friday morning, November 22, looked ahead to the Dartmouth-Princeton game at Palmer Stadium and Harvard-Yale at New Haven.

Princeton's Dick Colman was wary in the best tradition of college coaches. "Dartmouth always plays its best football against us," he was quoted as saying in one pregame story. Yale wasn't anything special this season, but Harvard Coach John Yovicsin told a reporter that the 80th edition of The Game "figures to be a real dogfight."

The travails of the coaches amounted to nonsense by the time the newspapers were brought home that evening—President Kennedy had been assassinated.

At four o'clock—two and a half hours after Kennedy was shot—the Harvard president, Nathan M. Pusey, and the Yale president, Kingman Brewster Jr., issued a joint announcement calling off Saturday's game.

The Harvard players had concluded their workout and were heading back to their headquarters, the Yale Motor Inn in

following Yale's surprising 10–6 victory over Dartmouth. For Harvard, there was disappointment, a 7–2 upset defeat at the hands of Penn. At Ithaca, Gary Wood and Archie Roberts played out Chapter II of their rivalry. Columbia had won in the final seconds the previous year, but now Wood scored from the 1-yard line with 14 seconds to go, then pitched out to Bob Baker, who ran around right end for a 2-point conversion and an 18–17 victory.

Princeton's Cosmo Iacavazzi went over three times from the 1-yard line that Saturday in a 34–13 victory over Brown, but the Tigers finally stumbled the following weekend, losing to Harvard by 21–7 at Cambridge on a rainy, windy afternoon. Princeton came back to beat Yale, 27–7, at Palmer Stadium as Iacavazzi scored his

Wallingford. "There was not a word said on the bus going back to the inn," Adolph Samborski, the Harvard athletic director, would recall.

Princeton-Dartmouth was also called off as were many other college games, though the National Football League went ahead with its Sunday games while dropping television coverage.

The two big Ivy games were rescheduled for Saturday, November 30.

Princeton took a two-touchdown lead over Dartmouth but saw its edge cut to 21–15 early in the fourth quarter. The Tigers later stopped Dartmouth on two running plays just short of their goal line, Cosmo Iacavazzi joining in the defensive charge. But moments after that, Iacavazzi—now back at fullback—was hit by linebacker Dave DeCalesta and fumbled. Dartmouth's defensive end and captain, Scott Creelman, fell on the ball at the 2. On the next play, John McClean ran around left end to tie the game with 5 minutes 24 seconds remaining. Gary Wilson kicked the extra point and Dartmouth held on for a 22–21 victory that pulled it even with Princeton atop the league at 5-2.

There was little sense of excitement in New Haven the day of the Harvard-Yale game, the president's death having muted any show of exuberance. Store windows were without the customary banners and bunting, and the Midtown Motor Inn, a favorite for visitors, had vacancies.

Harvard, having lost only one game in Ivy play, got off to a good start. Playing in wind gusts up to 30 miles an hour, the Crimson managed a 39-yard touchdown

pass from Mike Bassett to Scott Harshbarger in the first quarter. But it was all Yale after that. Fullback Charlie Mercein ground out yardage up the middle, and the Elis scored three times on short runs. The final: Yale 20, Harvard 6. The Crimson could have won the championship, but now were also-rans.

Elsewhere, the Ivies' season had ended on Thanksgiving Day with the traditional Cornell-Penn game and Columbia-Rutgers, which had been rescheduled from the previous Saturday. (The Brown-Colgate finale was canceled.)

Gary Wood, playing his final college game, picked up 192 yards running and passing in Cornell's 17–8 victory to wind up as the league's offensive leader, accounting for 1,151 yards, 42 more than Archie Roberts. Pete Gogolak, who had already established a college record for consecutive extra points, concluded his career with 44 in a row.

Roberts finished his junior season with a flourish as well, running and passing for 278 yards—his career high—and scoring the winning touchdown on a 38-yard run in the fourth quarter as Columbia beat Rutgers, 35-28, at New Brunswick after losing a four-touchdown lead.

But these final games seemed bizarrely irrelevant—with the death of President Kennedy, there was little for anyone to cheer about.

The following season brought a change in traditional scheduling. Since 1946, Princeton and Dartmouth had ended their seasons with a matchup at Palmer Stadium. But in 1964, the game was shifted to

Hanover and moved up to mid-October. The league title was on the line in the 1963 season-ender, but now the teams had gone in different directions. Princeton was clearly superior and enjoyed a 37–7 romp.

Going into the Yale game at New Haven in mid-November, Princeton had swept to seven straight victories, including shutouts in its previous four games. The Tigers were 5-0 in Ivy play, but Yale took a 4-0-1 mark into the game. The Elis' only stumble had been a 9–9 tie against Columbia when they drove 84 yards for a late touchdown only to have Chuck Mercein's extra-point attempt blocked by the Lion end Bob Donohue.

Playing before a crowd of 60,173, Yale took a 14–0 lead, the first time Princeton had trailed all season.But by halftime it was 14–14, and then Cosmo Iacavazzi took over. He rumbled 23 yards in the third quarter to set up the go-ahead score and

Princeton's star fullback Cosmo Iacavazzi (No. 32) with his 1962 and 1963 backfield teammates (*left to right*) Jim Rockenbach, Dick Springs, and Pete Porietis. (PRINCETON UNIVERSITY)

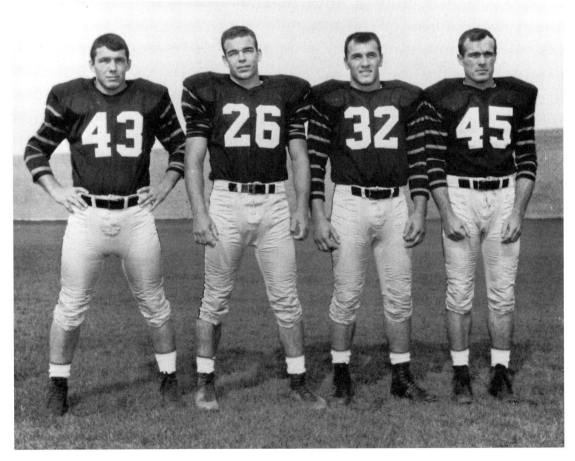

then, in the fourth period, scored on runs of 39 and 47 yards, shedding tacklers and concluding each jaunt by firing the football into the stands. He gained 185 yards on the day, a Princeton record, as the Tigers emerged with a 35–14 victory.

Princeton completed a 9-0 year—its first perfect season since Dick Kazmaier's 1951 team—with a 17–12 victory over Cornell at Palmer Stadium. Iacavazzi's 1-yard touchdown run gave him 186 points for his career, exceeding the school mark of 180 set by Hobey Baker in the pre–World War I years. And his total yardage for the season—909—surpassed Kazmaier's school-record 861 yards in 1951.

But Princeton was denied the Lambert Trophy as the East's top team. It went instead to Penn State, only 6-4 for the season but with a much tougher schedule.

What had been a bright year for Yale finished on a down note as Harvard slipped past the Elis for second place with an 18–14 victory at Cambridge.

Archie Roberts concluded his spectacular career with Columbia's game at Brown. When it was all over, Roberts didn't feel like celebrating, but the likes of Bob Seiple, Alan Miller, Neil Anderson, Ron Ferraris, and Ralph Duerre certainly did. They led a Brown defense that sacked Roberts 14 times for 89 yards in losses as the Bears emerged with a 7–0 victory.

Roberts finished with Columbia season records in passing yardage (1,444) and total yardage (1,618), exceeding marks set by Paul Governali in 1942, to go with a flock of Ivy League records. Like Barry Wood—the Harvard quarterback of six

decades earlier who could do no wrong—Roberts would go on to medical school.

The 1965 season brought a coaching change at Yale. After only two years at New Haven, John Pont abandoned the Ivy League for the Big Ten, taking over at Indiana.

His successor was Carmen Cozza, a former quarterback at Miami of Ohio who later coached there under Pont, then joined him at Yale as backfield coach in 1963. Ten years later, Cozza would become the winningest coach in Yale football history—his 69 victories two more than Walter Camp had achieved—and 20 years after that he would still be going strong.

But Cozza's debut was not a happy one as Yale lost to Connecticut, 13–6, the first defeat for the Elis against an in-state opponent in 87 games going back to 1875.

Three weeks later, there was another first for Yale. When the Elis went down to Baker Field, they took along eight cheerleaders from Connecticut College for Women in New London. George Brown, Yale's chief cheerleader, said the recruitment was part of a campaign to have Yale go coeducational.

But it seemed that nothing could inspire Yale that day. As a *New York Times* headline put it: "8 Girl Cheerleaders Shout in Vain for Elis to Hold 'Em." Final score: Columbia 21, Yale 7.

Four days later, DeLaney Kiphuth, Yale's athletic director, bid farewell to the young women. "It doesn't even have anything to do with sex," Kiphuth maintained. Cheerleading, like all other undergraduate activities, he explained, "is limited to undergraduates."

"I might like Leontyne Price's voice, but that doesn't mean she should sing in the Yale glee club," said Kiphuth.

Otherwise, all Ivy eyes focused on Dartmouth and Princeton.

Charlie Gogolak, now a senior, kicked an NCAA-record six field goals in Princeton's opener against Rutgers. Two weeks later, Gogolak was faced with an intriguing challenge when the Tigers visited Cornell. After a drive stalled at the Big Red 19, Gogolak came on to try a field goal. Cornell then went into a vertical shift, or a "twin towers" defense. Jim Docherty and Dale Witwer, a pair of defensive backs, climbed upon the shoulders of two 6-foot-5-inch tackles, Reeve Vanneman and Harry Garman, the Ithaca version of the Berlin Wall.

Gogolak aimed his kick slightly to the left, seeing an opening, but he missed. "It was like a bad dream," he said later. "I would have liked to hit one of those guys in the head."

Cornell was penalized, however, for being offside, giving Princeton a first down, and the Tigers went on to score a touchdown.

Cornell builds a wall to defend against field-goal attempt by Princeton's Charlie Gogolak. Dale Witwer (No. 49), a 6-foot defensive back, and Jim Docherty, a 5-foot-8-inch back, get a boost from a pair of 6-foot-5-inch tackles, Harry Garman (No. 74) and Reeve Vanneman. (CORNELL UNIVERSITY)

The Big Red tried the towers maneuver twice more, but Gogolak connected for field goals of 44 and 54 yards as Princeton went on to a 36–27 victory. (The scheme was banned by the NCAA rule-makers after the season.)

The following Saturday, Gogolak set an

NCAA career record for field goals, kicking his 21st and 22nd in a 27–0 victory over Colgate. The weekend after that, he had field goals of 43, 44, and 47 yards against Penn for a single-season NCAA record of 14. And he added six extra points—giving him 34 straight—in a 51–0 romp.

If it wasn't Gogolak, it was Ron Landeck. On the final Saturday of October, the tailback threw four touchdown passes and ran for another score in a 45–27 pasting of Brown. The Bears' quarterback, Bob Hall, wasn't bad either, throwing for three touchdowns and carrying the football over for another score. He would go on to set Ivy single-season records with 111 completions and 1,133 passing yards.

Princeton-Dartmouth had been returned to the final Saturday after the one-year experiment with an October date. The timing was superb. Each carried 8-0 records into the game at Palmer Stadium, and the Tigers had a 17-game winning streak on the line. A sellout crowd of 45,725 gathered for the most eagerly anticipated matchup since formal Ivy League play had begun.

Dartmouth tried a variation of Cornell's twin towers in the first quarter when Gogolak attempted a field goal. Coach Blackman had Sam Hawken, a reserve back wearing light, cross-country shoes, take a running start and then vault off the backs of linemen equipped with foam rubber padding. But before the snap Dartmouth was off-side, just as Cornell had been when it attempted an anti-Gogolak scheme. Perhaps unnerved, Gogolak then missed a shorter field goal attempt.

Princeton took a 7–0 lead, but quarterback Mickey Beard ran the deceptive Dartmouth offense superbly while scoring twice on 1-yard runs in the second quarter. He had his finest day of the season, throwing for 229 yards and completing the longest scoring play to date in Dartmouth history, a 79-yard pass to Bill Calhoun in the fourth quarter.

Landeck totaled 249 yards running and passing, giving him 1,949 for the season and exceeding the school mark set by Dick Kazmaier in 1951 by 122 yards. But Dartmouth prevailed, racking up a 28–14 victory and a perfect season, its second one of the 1960s and the third in school history.

Up at Hanover, 2,000 Dartmouth students and townspeople watched the victory over closed-circuit television at the Hopkins Center. Then the chapel bells began to ring and continued to sound until 5:00 P.M. the next day, when the team returned.

On Saturday night, Dartmouth students celebrated with a bonfire, feeding the flames with copies of *Time* and *Sports Illustrated*, which had predicted a Princeton victory. Soon Dartmouth would be named winner of the Lambert Trophy as the best team in the East, an honor the Ivy League would savor as it concluded its first decade of formal competition.

Brown's 1965 co-captains, Bob Hall, an outstanding passer, and end Dick O'Toole, plot strategy with the bronze Bruno outside Marvel Gymnasium. (BROWN UNIVERSITY)

"YOU CAN'T EVEN TRUST YOUR OWN EYES"

EXCITEMENT WAS BUBBLING at Yale as the autumn of 1966 approached. Two heralded young men were waiting to make their debuts and perhaps make Saturday afternoons reminiscent of the good old days when "Bulldog, Bulldog, Bow, Wow, Wow" echoed from packed stands at Yale Bowl.

One was a child of privilege, the other raised in an inner-city neighborhood. Neither had known the experience of losing.

Brian Dowling and Calvin Hill were presumably about to restore Yale to its once-familiar place atop the Ivies.

At 6 feet 2 inches and 195 pounds, Dowling had good size—certainly by Ivy standards—but he would become a larger-than-life figure.

As a quarterback in junior high and then at St. Ignatius High School in Cleveland, Dowling had never played in a losing football game. He had been a star as well in basketball, baseball, and tennis and had

received 100 scholarship offers. His father, an executive with a steel company, decided to pay for his son's education. So Brian chose Yale.

Dowling led the Yale freshmen to a 6-0 record in 1965—a triple threat as a passer, runner, and punter—and before he had proved himself with the varsity, he was being likened to that heroic fantasy Yalie Frank Merriwell.

"I expected to win," Dowling would later say. "After all, I'd won all the games I'd finished since seventh grade."

Dowling's co-star on the freshman team was a 218-pounder touted by Coach Carm Cozza as "the kind of runner who will bring fans to their feet."

Calvin Hill had grown up in Baltimore, but entered a new world in the ninth grade when he arrived at Riverdale Country Day School in New York on a scholarship earmarked for a black student from the South.

The son of an unemployed construction worker, he was a bright student and, like Dowling, would excel in several sports. Hill, too, was a high school quarterback who never appeared in a losing game.

He chose Yale in part because he hoped to make the team as a quarterback. But with Dowling in the same backfield, he would never get the chance.

Both Dowling and Hill seemed ready for big things when Yale faced Connecticut to start the 1966 season.

UConn's opening kickoff bounded near the sideline at the Yale 8. Hill picked it up and then, wriggling away from three would-be tacklers, brought the ball to the 38. Hill scored in the third quarter on a 12-yard pass from Dowling, who ran impressively, tossed for another score, and delivered a booming punt that was fumbled, leading to a Yale field goal, in a 16–0 victory.

Hill quickly established himself as an outstanding running back, but this opening Saturday proved the highlight of Dowling's first season. He suffered a leg injury in a loss to Rutgers the following week and was supplanted by Pete Doherty, who emerged as a fine passer. In mid-October, Doherty threw for five touchdowns against Columbia, which had an even better quarterback in sophomore Marty Domres, who tossed for three scores in Yale's 44–21 victory.

Harvard also had a passing threat that autumn in the left-handed Ric Zimmerman and outstanding runners in Bobby Leo, who had scored the winning touchdowns against Yale the previous two seasons; Vic

Gatto, a chunky 5-foot 6-inch, 180-pound sophomore; and Tom Choquette, a powerful fullback.

By early November the Crimson had rolled to a 6-0 record, and after a 27–7 victory over Penn, the Harvard bass drum proclaimed in six-foot-high letters, "We're No. 1." Harvard, in fact, led the nation in rushing at that point with an average of 325 yards a game.

But the Crimson's hopes for their first perfect season since 1913 came to an end the following Saturday with an 18–14 loss to Princeton at Palmer Stadium.

Going into the final weekend, Harvard, Dartmouth, and Princeton were in a three-way tie for the Ivy lead.

Harvard faced Yale at Cambridge on a cold, blustery day that limited both passing games—Zimmerman completed only three passes, Doherty just five, and neither had a single completion in the first half. But the weather was no problem for Bobby Leo, who tormented the Elis for the third straight season, scoring two touchdowns and running for 106 yards in the Crimson's 17–0 victory. Leo became the first Harvard player to score against Yale in each of his three varsity seasons as the Crimson built a three-game winning streak against the Elis for the first time since 1928–30.

Dartmouth rolled over Penn, 40–21, with a 413-yard rushing game while Princeton beat Cornell, 7–0, on Dick Bracken's 5-yard touchdown run in the fourth quarter.

So the final Saturday ended as it had

Yale's Brian Dowling gets in the face of a Harvard man. (YALE UNIVERSITY)

begun, with a three-way tie for the Ivy championship.

As the 1967 season neared, Brian Dowling ran into more bad luck, fracturing his right wrist early in September during a drill. He missed the opener—a 26–14 loss to Holy Cross—remained sidelined in a victory over Connecticut, and got in for only one play in a triumph over Brown. But then he took over as the starter for the first time since being injured in the second game of 1966.

Now Yale really began to roll.

Dowling was at his most scintillating in a matchup against Dartmouth on a rainy afternoon at Yale Bowl. The Elis jumped off to a 28–0 lead by the time two minutes had elapsed in the second quarter. Dowling ran for a score on a 30-yard bootleg play, hit Bruce Weinstein with a 69-yard scoring pass, and tossed a 4-yard touchdown pass to Jim Fisher. Calvin Hill threw a 53-yard pass to Lew Roney to set up another score. Yale came away with a 56–15 rout, its highest point total in 319 games dating back to 1930. (Could anyone forget that 66–0 drubbing of Alfred?)

Two weeks later Yale locked up the Ivy title, its first since that unbeaten 1960 sea-

Calvin Hill of Yale experiencing a weary moment.
(YALE UNIVERSITY)

son, with a 29–7 victory over Princeton.

The supporting casts had tried to psyche each other out before the game, which Yale entered with a 5-0 league mark to Princeton's 4-1. Yale cheerleaders ran along the field with a banner proclaiming "Blue Power" while the Princeton Tiger wore a button reading "I Hate Dogs."

Once the preliminaries were dispensed with, Dowling took over, scoring two touchdowns and passing for two more. On the first touchdown, Hill took a handoff from Dowling and ran to the right as Dowling slipped downfield, running to the left. Then Hill fired a 60-yard scoring pass to Dowling, whom nobody had bothered to cover.

Yale seemed ready to top Harvard as well after three straight losses to the Crimson, coming in at 7-1.

Playing before 68,135 at Yale Bowl, the largest crowd there since the 1954 Army game, Dowling threw a touchdown pass to Bruce Weinstein in the second quarter. Later in the period, eluding a host of Harvard tacklers and seemingly trapped 17 yards behind the line of scrimmage, he spotted Hill, who had broken free from a curl pattern and had raised his hand. They connected for a 53-yard touchdown play. "I knew he would see me," Hill said afterward.

Yale took a 17–0 lead, but Harvard rallied behind the passing of Ric Zimmerman and running of Vic Gatto and Ray Hornblower. With just over three minutes left in the game, the Crimson gained a 20–17 edge on a 31-yard pass from Zimmerman to Carter Lord.

Two plays after the kickoff, Yale had the ball on its 34. Dowling, who had been intercepted four times, sent split end Del Marting down the sideline. Dowling ran to his right, then looked left and heaved a pass. Marting caught it as Harvard's Mike Ananis slipped on a turf left wet by midweek rains, and he ran into the end zone. It was only the fifth completion by Dowling in 19 passes, but Yale took a 24–20 lead.

Harvard came back for one last threat as Zimmerman threw completions to Gatto, Lord, and Hornblower. He was now 14 for 29 for 289 yards, all school records. But then fullback Ken O'Connell, playing with a broken rib he had hidden from his coaches, fumbled at the 10 after picking up 10 yards. Yale's Pat Madden recovered, and the Elis had the victory.

Afterward, Rod Watson, the Yale captain, remarked: "It was a bad day for Brian Dowling. But Brian Dowling on a bad day comes up smelling like roses."

"We were never worried," said Watson. "We knew Brian would do something."

The Princeton band, meanwhile, got a few notices of its own in 1967 when the Tigers' game with Harvard was televised nationally by ABC. The band's irreverent reputation preceded it, so nervous ABC producers decided to televise the halftime show without sound—no double entendre narration, thank you. The band began its show with a formation spelling out "ABC." Its announcer told the crowd how "in a blatant attempt to get television exposure from ABC, the band forms a plug on the field." But then, with the cameras still focused, the "A" turned into an "N." Now plugging ABC's competitor, the band played "Who's Sorry Now?"

In the autumn of 1968, the Ivy quarterback with the gaudiest statistics was not Brian Dowling, but Columbia's Marty Domres. The Lions were consistent, posting their fourth consecutive 2-7 record, so the 6-foot-5-inch Domres was really a one-man team. When Columbia broke a nine-game losing streak on the first Saturday of November by beating Cornell, 34–25, Domres ran or passed on 66 of its 81 plays

Marty Domres, a superb entry in the gallery of outstanding Columbia quarterbacks. (COLUMBIA UNIVERSITY)

On September 30, a comic strip to be known as "Bull Tales" made its first appearance in the *Yale Daily News*, its creator a sophomore named Garry Trudeau. As the season moved along, the strip that would eventually become "Doonesbury" began to feature a helmeted football player wearing No. 10 and known as B.D.

As Frank Deford would observe in a profile of Dowling for *Sports Illustrated*: "It made Dowling human, a figure of fun— a typical vain and dim-witted jock who wouldn't even take his helmet off. Worldly-wise Yalies, attending this prestigious institution of learning, preparing to spend the rest of their lives as stockbrokers or C.I.A. operatives, had suddenly found themselves going bananas over a silly football team, just as if they were in the Big Ten—and Trudeau gave them back their sophistication. Once they had laughed at the idiotic football players in 'bull tales'—and certified their Ivy cynicism—they could go out and be hero-worshipers, just like everybody else."

Dowling was leading Yale toward an unbeaten season, but up at Harvard, a splendid team, minus the charisma, was

for 447 yards. He would break every major Ivy career and season record for passing and wind up with 5,345 yards in total offense, fifth highest in the history of major college football at that time. His three-year total of running or passing plays—1,133— was the most ever.

But at Yale, the legend of Brian Dowling was about to glow.

being molded as well. Both squads came into Harvard Stadium on November 23 with 8-0 marks, the first time since 1909 that The Game—now in its 85th encounter—had matched a pair of perfect records.

The Crimson, seeking their first unbeaten season since the 1919 Rose Bowl squad, boasted a defense, led by linebacker John Emery, that had allowed the fewest points of any major college (61). It was known informally as the Boston Stranglers or the Destroyers' Club. Before The Game, optimistic Harvard backers handed out handbills listing the defense as being "wanted for massacring Yale's offensive football team on Saturday, Nov. 23, 1968." And Harvard had the league's leading rusher in Ray Hornblower.

But Yale, averaging 36 points a game (third nationally in total offense) and unbeaten in 16 straight games, had a few talking points of its own. Brian Dowling came in with a 22–0 record in Yale games he had appeared in, including freshman games. He was completing another spectacular season, having thrown for a school-record 17 touchdowns.

The Harvard-Yale matchup of the century unfolded before a capacity crowd of 40,280 on a sunny, 40-degree afternoon, with scalpers getting up to $175 a ticket.

It seemed that Yale's offense was more than a match for Harvard's defense. The Elis held a 22–0 lead in the second quarter on Dowling's 3-yard bootleg run and his touchdown passes to Calvin Hill and Del Marting. (Hill's score gave him the Yale record for most points, 144 to Albie Booth's 138.)

Late in the half, Harvard Coach John Yovicsin removed his starting quarterback, George Lalich, and replaced him with Frank Champi, a 5-foot-11-inch junior from Everett, Massachusetts, with a powerful arm. But Champi's prowess had mostly been confined to the javelin throw. He had little football experience, having thrown only 12 passes all season.

In the final seconds before halftime, Champi tossed a 15-yard touchdown pass to sophomore Bruce Freeman, a second-string end. A bad snap fouled up the extra-point attempt so the gun sounded with Yale leading by 22–6.

Yale appeared to lock up the game early in the fourth quarter when Dowling ran around end from the 5-yard line for a touchdown and a 29–13 lead. Now the traditional flourish of white handkerchiefs and chants of "We're No. 1" or "You're No. 2" arose from the Yale sections.

Dowling and Company were looking for yet another touchdown a little later. But then Bob Levin fumbled on the Harvard 14 after catching a screen pass from Dowling, and the Crimson recovered.

Champi led Harvard downfield, aided by a little luck. A holding penalty against Yale provided a big break. Later, Champi fumbled, but Fritz Reed, a junior tackle, picked the ball up and went from the Yale 32 to the 15.

On the following play, Champi looked for an open receiver. When he couldn't find one, he tried to lateral but was still unable to spot a teammate. Then he dodged some Yale defenders and threw to his right. Freeman grabbed the ball on the 3 and took it

Pete Varney catching the 2-point conversion pass from Frank Champi that climaxed Harvard's "miracle" comeback of 1968 against Yale. (HARVARD UNIVERSITY)

more, Bill Kelly, recovered for the Crimson on the Yale 49.

Harvard took over again. Seemingly trapped on a pass play, Champi ran for 14 yards around left end, and a face-mask penalty put the ball 15 yards closer to the goal line.

Now there were 32 seconds left, the ball on the Yale 20. Champi threw a pair of passes into the end zone, but both were broken up. Then Crim ran up the middle on a draw play, going to the Yale 6. On the next play, Champi was sacked on the 8 trying to pass. Only 3 seconds remained.

Harvard had one last shot. Champi dropped back, seemed trapped again, and once more looked to lateral. He ran around, then spotted the Harvard captain, Vic Gatto, alone in the far left corner of the end zone. Gatto cradled the pass, and now it was Yale 29, Harvard 27. Harvard fans ran onto the field, mobbing Gatto. Then the public address announcer asked "Quiet please" and the field was cleared.

The clock had run out. There would be one remaining play—Harvard's attempt for the tying 2-point conversion. Champi faded back again, scrambled one final time, then found sophomore receiver Pete Varney. He grabbed the pass just inside the goal line. The miracle was complete.

The following Monday, the *Harvard Crimson*'s headline said it all: "Harvard Beats Yale, 29–29."

One former Yale football player did not learn of the final score until a month had passed.

He was John Downey, a lineman on the 1950 team, who had been imprisoned by

in for his second score. Harvard's first bid for a 2-point conversion failed, but Yale was penalized for pass interference. On the second attempt, Gus Crim, a junior fullback, went into the end zone over left guard. Now it was Yale 29, Harvard 21—the Crimson trailed by just a touchdown and another 2-point conversion. There were 42 seconds remaining.

Harvard tried an on-side kickoff. The skidding ball was fumbled, and a sopho-

It's officially a tie, but the *Harvard Crimson* will proclaim: "Harvard Beats Yale, 29–29."
(HARVARD UNIVERSITY)

the Chinese since 1952 when his plane was shot down on a Central Intelligence Agency mission.

"The one thing they always let me get was sports magazines," Downey, who was released in 1973, would recall. He eagerly awaited the results of each year's Harvard-Yale game.

Late in the fourth quarter of the 1968 game, a family friend left Harvard Stadium and sent Downey a postcard: "Jack: Yale undefeated, champions 29–13!"

He received the card two weeks later and "I felt great. Then I waited for the reading material, which got there much slower."

His magazines arrived on Christmas Eve.

"There was a howl of agony. I was probably the last guy on earth who really cared about the game to learn the score. In a way, that was my most memorable Harvard game. I got the sense that in life, nothing is certain. You can't even trust your own eyes."

"TWELVE YARDS AND A CLOUD OF DUST"

BEYOND THE MAGNIFICENT B.D., beyond Harvard's miracle comeback that even Brian Dowling could not avert, the turbulent world of the 1960s reverberated upon the Ivy sports scene.

In the tumultuous year of 1968—the year of the King and Robert Kennedy assassinations, the urban riots, the Tet offensive, and antiwar protests—social and political issues were aired on the fields of play.

The Harvard band targeted Chicago Mayor Richard Daley and his police in the aftermath of clashes with demonstrators outside the 1968 Democratic National Convention. At one game, the band's themes were "Beat the Press" and "Mace the Nation," and it played "Chicago" while lining up to form "Dick," which promptly changed to "Oink."

The band had something to say about the Vietnam War as well. At a Dartmouth game, it formed into a stick figure with a pentagon-shaped head that flew into fragments during a commentary about "not losing our heads."

During halftime of the 1969 Yale-Princeton game, the two bands merged to form a peace symbol.

At Princeton, racial consciousness touched the football team. Late in December 1968, the five black players on the varsity and freshmen squads quit and joined in a letter to university officials accusing the varsity coach, Dick Colman, and the freshman coach, Walter (Pep) McCarthy, of "racist tendencies," saying they were being passed over for starting positions in favor of whites.

Colman, who soon afterward announced he was leaving to become the Middlebury athletic director, responded by saying "they're great boys, but I think they're wrong in their opinions as football players. I'm in complete sympathy with what all blacks are trying to accomplish, but not with these kinds of methods."

A nine-member interracial committee appointed by Princeton's president, Robert F. Goheen, investigated the accusations and concluded that the two coaches "have admirable records of support for the interests of all minority groups over a long period of time."

But the committee cited elements of "impersonality and insensitivity" in the football program that might be hard on blacks who found the institutional structure of a predominately white school alien to them.

There were stirrings of another sort at Princeton in 1969—women were admitted for the first time.

The new football coach, Jake McCandless, a Princeton tailback from 1948 to 1950 and an aide to Colman for 11 seasons, had something to say about that. It would not win him any awards for sensitivity from the women's movement.

"This is going to hurt our football team," McCandless quipped, "because we have a perfectly normal coaching staff and they're anxious to start recruiting pom-pom girls."

Issues of race flared at New Brunswick in the autumn of 1969 when Princeton and Rutgers celebrated the 100th anniversary of their encounter in the first college football game.

The 1869 game was re-enacted in midmorning, and centennial events were to precede the afternoon kickoff of the Princeton-Rutgers season opener. But those ceremonies were delayed when more than 100 black students from Rutgers arose from the south stands and paraded along the sideline with clenched fists raised, demanding financial reparations from the school on grounds they weren't receiving adequate benefits for their tuition. The crowd of 31,000 booed them.

A personality far more emblematic of the 1950s than the 1960s then appeared on the field—Ozzie Nelson, Rutgers Class of 1927, who introduced both teams and presided over the coin toss with an 1869 silver dollar. At halftime, Ozzie was joined by wife Harriet, who presented captains and coaches from Princeton and Rutgers over the past 50 years with commemorative medallions.

(As it had 100 years earlier, Rutgers beat Princeton, this time by 29–0.)

Up at Dartmouth, controversy accompanied the awakening of ethnic pride. During the previous winter, the few Indian students on campus had complained to the Dartmouth Athletic Council that the cheerleader in tribal garb was an insulting caricature. Dartmouth traced its roots to a school founded for Indians, but when the 1969 football season began, the Indian cheerleader had vanished.

Amid all this, the Ivies played some football. Brian Dowling and Calvin Hill had graduated by the time the autumn of 1969 arrived—Hill a first-round draft pick of the Dallas Cowboys—but a star was born at Ithaca.

Cornell's new wonder back out of New Milford, New Jersey, had been coveted by Penn State, Duke, and Army, but looked instead to the Ivy League heroes.

"I read about people like Calvin Hill and Marty Domres and that impressed me," Ed Marinaro would say.

Marinaro did not possess extraordinary speed, but he was blessed with quick feet that enabled him to take deep pitchbacks, spot a hole, and get to it before any defender could. And he had a splendid ability to cut back, leaving would-be tacklers tangled up. At 6 feet 3 inches and 210 pounds, he had good size by Ivy standards.

It didn't take long for Marinaro to be recognized beyond the Ivies. He gained 843 yards in his first four games to emerge as college football's leading rusher. In Game No. 4, a 41–24 upset of Harvard, Marinaro gained 281 yards on 40 carries and scored five touchdowns.

Cornell ran from an I formation that really became Marinaro to the left, Marinaro to the right, Marinaro up the middle. He would rank No. 2 nationally in rushing for 1969, but couldn't do it all—the Big Red finished at 4-5.

Yale had a fine passer in junior quarterback Joe Massey and came into its November 1 game against Dartmouth at New Haven with both teams 3-0 in league play. The Elis took an early lead, but Dartmouth came back for a 42-21 victory, handing Yale its first Ivy loss since the 1966 finale with Harvard.

Led by its all-Ivy junior quarterback Jim Chasey, Dartmouth sailed into its season-ender against Princeton at 8-0 over all and 6-0 in league play. Princeton and Yale were both 5-1 in the conference.

After a woeful beginning against Rutgers, Princeton had mastered a new "pro set" T formation installed in place of the single wing Charlie Caldwell had introduced back in 1945. The Tigers won their first five Ivy games before losing to Yale, 17–14, on a 23-yard field goal by a 5-foot-6-inch soccer-style kicker named Harry Klebanoff.

Princeton recovered at Palmer Stadium with a 35–7 rout of Dartmouth as the sophomore halfback Hank Bjorklund, in only his second start, scored three touchdowns and gained 132 yards. Yale managed a 7–0 victory over Harvard. So Dartmouth, Princeton, and Yale shared first place, the Ivy League's second three-way tie.

Dartmouth and Yale were strong again in 1970, and their game at Yale Bowl on October 31 was the matchup of the season, both coming in with 5-0 records and national rankings. The crowd of 60,820 was the largest there for a non-Harvard game since Army visited in 1954.

Both teams had outstanding quarterbacks returning—Dartmouth's Chasey and Yale's Massey—and the Elis had a terrific sophomore fullback in Dick Jauron, who would set a single-season Yale mark for rushing yardage.

On this day Dartmouth had the edge, getting a 3-yard touchdown run by Brendan O'Neill shortly before halftime en route to a 10–0 victory.

Dartmouth continued on a roll, trouncing Columbia by 55–0 the following weekend and then beating Cornell, 24–0, while holding Marinaro to 60 yards rushing, a rare stumble en route to his No. 1 national ranking as a runner. (He would rack up 1,425 yards, an average of 158.3 per game.)

Cornell's Ed Marinaro, a one-man offense.
(CORNELL UNIVERSITY)

When Dartmouth finished with a 28–0 triumph over Penn, it seemed in line for its second Lambert Trophy—denoting the best in the East—in five seasons. But Joe Paterno, that old Brown quarterback whose Penn State squads had captured the Lambert the previous three seasons, wasn't about to concede anything to an Ivy team. Right after concluding with a 7-3 record, he challenged Dartmouth to a game on December 5 to decide who really was supreme in the East. (Penn State's last game against an Ivy team had been a 43–0 rout of Penn in 1958.)

The Ivies stuck to their ban on postseason play, but Paterno's challenge failed to sway the media vote for the Lambert. The trophy went to Dartmouth, which finished with a No. 14 national ranking in the Associated Press poll of writers and broadcasters, four spots ahead of Penn

Finishing No. 1 nationally in average points allowed—5 per game—and posting six shutouts, Dartmouth romped to a 9-0 record, its third undefeated season in nine years.

State. It would be the last time an Ivy team was ranked in the Top 20.

That was the final year at Dartmouth for Bob Blackman, who took the coaching job at Illinois after 16 seasons in Hanover.

He looked back on three unbeaten teams, seven Ivy titles (outright or shared), and those two Lambert trophies. Blackman was replaced by his former star running back Jake Crouthamel.

The 1970 season was the final one at Harvard for Coach John Yovicsin, who retired with a record of 78-42-5 over 14 years, more victories than any Crimson coach. (Percy Haughton had 71 triumphs in nine seasons.)

Yovicsin was succeeded by Joe Restic, a onetime assistant coach at Brown who arrived from the Canadian Football League's Hamilton Tiger-Cats, whom he had taken to the Grey Cup playoffs three times.

A philosophy major at Villanova, Restic introduced a thinking-man's game at Harvard—the "multiflex" offense.

Standing for "completely multiple and totally flexible," in Restic's words, the system conjured up dozens of formations to keep defenses off balance.

Sometimes the playbook could get too complex even for Harvard. Following a 15–10 victory over Army in 1980, Ron Cuccia, a split end who also played some quarterback, observed how "we confused Army, we confused ourselves and we even confused the officials."

At Cornell, they kept things simple in 1971—just hand off to Marinaro and watch him go.

"Our offense is that old three yards and a cloud of dust," remarked Carmen Piccone, Cornell's backfield coach, looking to the grind-it-out philosophy of Ohio State's Woody Hayes. "But with Ed running the ball, it becomes 5, 6 or even 12 yards and a cloud of dust."

On October 30, Marinaro set an NCAA career rushing record and became the first major-college player to exceed 4,000 yards when Cornell defeated Columbia, 24–21.

Cornell jumped out to a 7-0 record while Dartmouth won its first six games.

Dartmouth went to Baker Field next, coming off that 55–0 trouncing of Columbia the previous season. This time the margin was inches. With 54 seconds to play, the Lions' Paul Kaliades kicked a 34-yard field goal—a tumbler that just cleared the crossbar—for a 31–29 upset that snapped Dartmouth's winning streak at 15 games.

On November 13, a Cornell team ranked second in the East only to undefeated Penn State visited Dartmouth. The night before the game, a traditional Dartmouth bonfire featured a bedsheet inscribed "Happiness Is Getting Marinaro." It went up in flames and burned all evening.

Dartmouth took a 17–0 halftime lead, but early in the third period Cornell scored a pair of touchdowns. The first one came after a blocked punt and nine straight Marinaro carries for 35 yards. The second one was a far swifter strike, a 46-yard run by Marinaro on which he hurdled one tackler and outran two others.

But Dartmouth's Steve Stetson, who had thrown a pair of touchdown passes as a substitute in the loss to Columbia, took his team on a 53-yard touchdown drive that sealed a 24–14 victory and put Dartmouth into a tie with Cornell for the Ivy lead.

The following week, Cornell topped Penn, 41–13, at Franklin Field as Marinaro ran for 230 yards and five touchdowns despite receiving a hard kick in the right calf during the second quarter.

By now, more than a league title was at stake—Marinaro was in the hunt for the Heisman Trophy, and his teammates were doing everything they could to keep things that way.

The starting quarterback, Mark Allen, was injured in the second quarter. His replacement, Cliff Hendry, would later tell how "when I came in I hoped Ed wouldn't think, 'Oh, no, Cliff's going to screw things up.' But he gave me confidence. After the game he hugged me and said he knew I could do it. He tried to kiss me, but our face masks got in the way."

That afternoon, Dartmouth defeated Princeton, 33–7, at Palmer Stadium, propelled by five interceptions and two fumble recoveries. So Cornell and Dartmouth shared the Ivy title.

Marinaro finished with a host of Ivy and major-college records, including 4,715 career rushing yards and a single-season mark of 1,881 yards rushing, set in his

Ed Marinaro showing the form that would break the national collegiate record for career rushing yardage. (CORNELL UNIVERSITY)

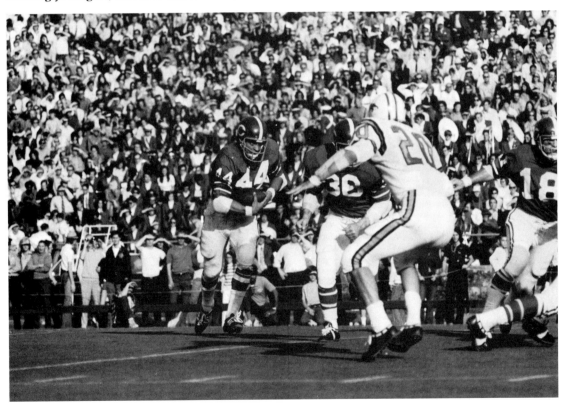

senior year. But he finished second in the Heisman balloting behind Pat Sullivan, the Auburn quarterback.

Marinaro would go on to the Minnesota Vikings as a second-round draft pick and spend six years in pro football. Then he found a new identity. Millions of TV viewers who had never seen Marinaro in a Big Red jersey would know him as Officer Joe Coffey of *Hill Street Blues*.

The 1972 season brought a turnaround for Penn, which had enjoyed just one winning Ivy year since its championship team of 1959. The Quakers, with an outstanding sophomore running back in Adolph (Beep Beep) Bellizeare and a fine receiver in Don Clune, defeated Harvard, Yale, and Princeton, the first time since 1941 that they had beaten all Big Three teams in a single season.

But the race was not decided until the final weekend, when Dartmouth met Penn while Harvard faced Yale, all except the Crimson having a shot at the title.

Playing before 42,422 at Franklin Field, Penn moved to a two-touchdown lead in the first 20 minutes, but Dartmouth came back for a 14–14 tie at halftime. The Quakers took another lead, but a fourth-quarter drive highlighted by Steve Stetson's 45-yard pass play to Jack Thomas brought a 17–17 tie. Dartmouth then forged ahead for a 31–17 victory.

Yale trailed Harvard by 17–0 but rallied for a 28–17 triumph, sparked by Dick Jauron's two touchdowns—one on a 74-yard run—and his 183-yard rushing day. Jauron finished the season with 1,055 yards rushing to go with 28 career touchdowns, both

Yale records, as the Elis won at Harvard for the first time in 12 years.

Dartmouth had come into the final Saturday a half-game in front of Yale so it finished the day with its fourth consecutive Ivy championship. It was another big season for a team that now had a nickname to match—the onetime Indians had become the Big Green.

The Ivy race was even tighter in 1973, four teams going into the finale with a chance—Dartmouth and Harvard at 5-1, Penn and Yale at 4-2.

Harvard featured a terrific passing combination in quarterback Jim Stoeckel and the 6-foot-6-inch junior end Pat McInally. The Crimson had outlasted Penn by 34–30 on a 30-yard pass play in the final two minutes, with McInally making a diving catch, and then had edged a surprisingly decent Brown team by 35–32 as McInally set a Harvard record with 13 receptions.

Harvard-Yale at New Haven figured to be an exciting matchup. The Crimson seemed to have an edge, though, because the Elis' quarterback, Tom Doyle, was sidelined with a shoulder bruise. But Kevin Rogan, a senior promoted from the junior varsity, led a Yale offense that rolled up 523 yards, and the junior halfback Rudy Green ran for a pair of touchdowns. It was a 35–0 romp for Yale.

Dartmouth visited Princeton in a Snickenberger versus Snickenberger duel, pitting the Big Green quarterback, Tom, against his brother, Walt Jr., the Tigers' leading runner. Tom threw a touchdown pass and Walt ran for 124 yards, but the brothers from Ithaca didn't do it all. A couple of Dartmouth players from Illinois—running back Mitch Klupchak, from Olympia Fields, and linebacker Jim Conterato, from Geneva—were the stars of the game.

Klupchak scored three touchdowns and ran for 154 yards on a wet field, finishing his career with 1,788 yards gained, 25 more than the school mark set by his coach, Jake Crouthamel, from 1957 to 1959. Conterato anchored the middle of a formidable defensive line, made an interception, and forced a fumble by Princeton quarterback Ron Beible that led to a touchdown. Dartmouth defeated Princeton, 42–24, for its fifth straight Ivy title.

The 1974 season began on a bizarre note for Princeton. Walt Snickenberger's 1-yard run pulled the Tigers into a 6–6 tie with Rutgers at Palmer Stadium with 22 seconds remaining. But Princeton could not attempt an extra-point kick that would have won the game because Rutgers fans had torn down both goalposts minutes earlier in a premature celebration. As the officials tried to figure out what to do, the Princeton fans yelled "Forfeit." Princeton Coach Bob Casciola then asked Referee Thomas Elliott to allow an extra pair of goalposts to be put up, but he refused. Since Princeton, as the home team, bore responsibility for crowd control, it would have to suffer the consequences of being unable to prevent the visitors' fans from trashing the field. So Princeton had to go for a 2-point conversion. A pass rolled off the receiver's fingertips, leaving the Tigers to settle for a tie.

Dartmouth lost a dozen starters from 1973, including Mitch Klupchak, and suffered through a rare losing year, going 3-6 to end its string of championships.

This time, Yale and Harvard were the class of the league.

Led by Rudy Green, the Ivies' No. 1 ground-gainer in 1973, and a dominant defense anchored by linebacker John Smoot, Yale won its first seven games. Only Penn scored in double digits, losers by 37–12.

After beating Holy Cross in its opener, Harvard was downed by Rutgers, but then swept to five straight victories.

Going into the next-to-last weekend, both Yale and Harvard were unbeaten in league play.

Princeton became the first team all season to take a lead against the Elis, getting a 3–0 edge in the second quarter. But two touchdown runs by Green propelled Yale to a 19–6 victory.

Harvard was not so fortunate. The Crimson were stunned by Brown, 10–7, at Cambridge, a 2-yard leap into the end zone by the Bears' Kevin Slattery bringing the winning touchdown midway in the fourth quarter.

So Yale was 6-0 in Ivy play and Harvard 5-1 going into The Game, played before a sellout of 40,500 at Cambridge.

This one had all the trappings of an old-time Harvard-Yale weekend. Yale students, long accustomed to taking autos or buses to Cambridge, hired a seven-car train from New Haven to Boston's South Street Station, and champagne and screwdrivers flowed freely. Members of the Society of

Orpheus and Bacchus, a Yale singing group, marched through the aisles with choruses of "Daddy Was a Yale Man," a song describing a similar train ride in the 1940s.

Yale moved to a 13–0 lead on a pair of touchdowns by Green and seemed a lock since it came in with the No. 1 defense in the nation, having yielded just 5.7 points per game. But Harvard rallied for a 14–13 halftime edge, its second score set up by Pat McInally's 56-yard "flea-flicker" pass to Jim Curry.

Yale's running game had been stymied, a six-man Harvard line bottling up Green and Tyrell Hennings after the early scoring burst. So quarterback Tom Doyle turned to an air game and would complete 16 passes, 11 of them to a top-notch wide receiver, Gary Fencik. Early in the final quarter, Yale took a 16–14 lead when Randy Carter, a sophomore, kicked a 38-yard field goal soon after a bad snap botched a punt attempt by McInally.

Harvard was still trailing by 2 when it took over on its 10-yard line with just over five minutes remaining. A penalty put the ball back on the 5, but then a left-handed quarterback, Milt Holt of Honolulu—nicknamed "Pineapple"—began to move the team. A 33-yard pass to halfback Steve Dart put the ball on the Yale 42. The next big play came with Harvard on the 12, third down and 4 yards to go. Yale had been keeping Harvard from running up the middle all game, but now fullback Neal Miller did just that, taking the ball to the 1-foot line. On second down, Holt ran to his left looking for a receiver, then carried the ball

around left end and dived into the end zone for the winning touchdown. There were only 15 seconds to play.

The final: Harvard 21, Yale 16.

Just as in the "miracle" tie of 1968, the Crimson pulled off a spectacular finish, spoiled what would have been a perfect Yale season, and gained a share of the Ivy title.

The 1975 season saw a creature unaccustomed to heights fighting for the top of the Ivy standings—the Brown Bear.

Coming off a year in which it had the third-best rushing defense in the nation (yielding 108 yards a game), Brown was looking even better. A 6-foot-6-inch quarterback named Bob Bateman who had passed for more than 1,800 yards at the University of Vermont arrived in Providence after his school dropped football. He would team up with receiver Bob Farnham and running back Kevin Slattery for Brown single-season records in passing, receiving, and rushing yardage. And Jose Violante, an outstanding placekicker, was still in fine form.

At Yale, there was a different look on campus—women were admitted for the first time. To mark the occasion, the new bulldog, Handsome Dan XII, was a female.

Dartmouth, meanwhile, was picking on Columbia again for its football milestones. It had beaten the Lions for the school's 300th victory in 1937 and its 400th in 1960. Now, with a 22–17 comeback triumph, Dartmouth topped Columbia for victory No. 500 since beginning play in 1881.

On the next-to-last weekend, Brown (4-0-1 in league play) had a chance to clinch its first formal Ivy title when it met

Harvard (4-1), drawing a sellout crowd of 18,000 at Brown Stadium for the first time since 1932. But Harvard quarterback Jim Kubacki, coming off an injury to his throwing shoulder, fooled Brown with a series of play-action maneuvers, completed 15 of 18 passes for 289 yards and three touchdowns, and plunged over for a fourth as the Crimson spoiled Brown's hopes, 45–26.

Yale, coming into the weekend at 4-1, defeated Princeton, 24–13, its most spectacular moment coming on the first play of the second period, which began from the Yale 3. Running back Don Gesicki took a pitchout from quarterback Stone Phillips, ran to the left, then tossed a wobbly pass that Gary Fencik gathered in 33 yards downfield. He ran away from two defenders for the longest touchdown play from scrimmage in Yale history.

The league title would be decided by the Harvard-Yale game's centennial matchup. It wasn't the 100th meeting of the teams, but their rivalry dated back to that afternoon of November 13, 1875, when Harvard defeated Yale, 4 goals to 0, at Hamilton Park in New Haven.

At halftime, there was a bit of gamesmanship among the bands. Harvard showed off its immense drum. Yale responded by bringing out a tiny drum on a child's wagon.

The teams went into the fourth quarter at Yale Bowl tied at 7–7. Late in the game, Harvard was driving. On a fourth-and-12 play, Kubacki threw for 21 yards to Bob McDermott, putting the ball on the Yale 14 with two minutes remaining. Four plays later

Harvard had stalled, and now Mike Lynch, a reserve quarterback, was called on to attempt a field goal. He had missed his four previous attempts, had suffered through a miserable game against Princeton two weeks earlier, and had temporarily dropped out of school for scholastic reasons the previous year. But now the junior put all that behind him, kicking a 26-yarder through the uprights with 33 seconds remaining.

The Crimson had a 10–7 victory and their first undisputed championship in 20 years of formal Ivy play.

Brown, winding up its season with a 48–13 victory over Columbia, slipped past Yale for the runner-up spot, the first time the Bears had ever finished higher than fourth.

The 1976 race had a similar shape. Going into the final weekend, Brown and Yale were 5-1 with Harvard at 4-2.

So now Harvard-Yale would have an impact on the Ivy title for the fifth straight season, with Yale overdue for something good to happen. Harvard had scored last-minute victories the two previous seasons, costing Yale an outright title and an undefeated season in 1974 and then a tie for the championship in 1975.

Harvard took a 7–0 lead in the first half when Russ Savage, a defensive end, ran 74 yards with an intercepted pass. But Yale struck back for three touchdowns as halfback John Pagliaro picked up 125 yards to lead a formidable ground game in a 21–7 victory. It was Yale's eighth straight triumph after a loss to Brown.

Brown went into Baker Field a big

Brown's 1977 co-captains, tailback Billy Hill (*left*) and line-backer Lou Cole, admire the Ivy League championship trophy the Bears shared with Yale in 1976. (BROWN UNIVERSITY)

"My father played for Brown around 1950," said Chuck Bryson, a sophomore end. "But when I was growing up in the 1960s, I wouldn't even go to Brown games because they were so bad."

Times had changed.

Yale continued its winning ways in 1977 by opening with victories over Brown and Connecticut, but then came a sentimental matchup. Coach Carm Cozza had arranged a visit from Miami of Ohio, his alma mater. Old-times' sake aside, it wasn't a great idea, as the Elis were beaten, 28–14.

favorite over Columbia, but the prospect of its first Ivy title seemed a bit too daunting. The Bears fumbled at the Lions' 1, had two passes intercepted, and suffered several costly penalties. At halftime, they trailed by 17–7. But they rallied in the final quarter for two touchdowns, both on short runs by junior halfback Billy Hill, and came away with a 28–17 victory and a tie for the championship with Yale.

Cases of beer were hauled into the Brown locker room, one player opened bottles with his teeth, and then the suds were squirted liberally.

"After every other game, all we got was a Pepsi and a box lunch to go home with," said one player.

Bob Blackman returned to the Ivies after six years at Illinois, taking the coaching job at Cornell. The talent at Ithaca was hardly comparable to that on his Dartmouth squads of the 1950s and 1960s, and he would go 1-8 his first season there. Blackman's predecessor at Cornell hadn't done much either, fielding squads that went 1-8 and 2-7. But George Seifert would later find considerably greater success with the San Francisco 49ers.

Entering the final Saturday, Yale led the Ivies with a 6-1 record, Harvard and Brown trailing at 5-2. Once more, The Game would hold the key to the championship.

This time it was a duo from Derby (Connecticut) High School who made the difference—a substitute named Mike Sullivan and the star runner John Pagliaro, whose high school records had been eclipsed by Sullivan.

Harvard came into Yale Bowl as 11-point underdogs, but was trailing by only 10–7 early in the final quarter. Sullivan, the Yale punter and a third-string sophomore running back, was standing on his 21, ready to kick. He took a wobbly pass from center, then got a bright idea.

"I had the opening so I ran," he would say. "Everybody was blocking for me."

Sullivan sped to his right, escaped from four Harvard defenders, then went down the sideline past the Harvard bench on a 79-yard run that broke the game open.

"We worked on the play in practice but he did it on his own," said Cozza.

Later in the game, Pagliaro scored on a 2-yard run and threw the football into the stands. Out came the white handkerchiefs.

Pagliaro had scored the 35th touchdown of his career and would wind up with 1,159 yards rushing for the season, both school records. Yale emerged with a 24–7 victory and sole possession of the Ivy title.

The 1978 season brought a new coach at Dartmouth. Jake Crouthamel, who had succeeded Bob Blackman, departed after winning titles his first three seasons, then finishing around the middle of the pack the next four years. Dartmouth reached outside the Ivy ranks, hiring Joe Yukica, who had been coaching at Boston College for the previous 10 years. Yukica would eventually leave Dartmouth on a sour note, but his debut season proved a huge success. Six of his players would be first-team all-Ivy selec-

tions, among them quarterback Buddy Teevens (who would succeed Yukica in 1987) and split end Dave Shula, the son of Miami Dolphin coach Don Shula.

Brown looked good once again, its fine quarterback Mark Whipple—a future Brown coach—back for his senior season.

The year's big matchup came on the next-to-last weekend when Dartmouth met Brown at Providence, the teams tied with 4-1 records.

Dartmouth took a 21–7 lead early in the third quarter when Jeff Dufresne, a sophomore fullback from White Deer, Minnesota, ran for a 15-yard touchdown, his second score of the game. Dufresne would explain that playing in the Ivies late in the year seemed easy "because back home the ground is always frozen."

But Brown tied the game with a pair of third-quarter scores on Marty Moran's 1-yard run and Whipple's 15-yard pass to Rick Villella.

Dartmouth went ahead again in the final period, Dufresne running 8 yards over left guard for another touchdown. A late field goal clinched matters as Dartmouth emerged with a 31–21 victory.

On the final Saturday Dartmouth spotted Princeton an early touchdown at Palmer Stadium, then came back for a 28–21 triumph as Teevens threw for one score and ran for two others. Dartmouth had its 11th championship since Ivy play had begun (seven outright, four shared).

Up at Ithaca, there was a performance worthy of an Ed Marinaro. Joe Holland, the son of Jerome (Brud) Holland, Cornell's all-America end of the late 1930s, ran for

Dave Shula, the son of Miami Dolphin coach Don Shula and later coach of the Cincinnati Bengals, in action for Dartmouth. (DARTMOUTH COLLEGE)

four touchdowns and 263 yards in a 35–17 victory over Penn. His season total of 1,396 yards had been exceeded only by Marinaro.

For the first time in seven years, Harvard-Yale had no bearing on the Ivy race. But the matchup had its moments nonetheless, winding up as the rivalry's highest-scoring game to date. Yale had a 21-point lead in the final quarter, then held on for a 35–28 victory as Harvard came back for two scores, quarterback Larry Brown passing for 298 yards against the league's top defense.

Brown had become a master at directing Coach Joe Restic's complex schemes, so the following semester he turned professor of sorts, teaching a Sunday night seminar at Harvard in "Fundamentals of Multiflex Offense." Offered under the school's independent study program—providing credits toward a degree and requiring a term paper—the course drew 20 students, seven of them women. Brown would acknowledge, however, that some professors looked askance at the class, and he noted that "the faculty won't give me tenure."

Yale, which had finished strongly in 1978 with two ties and three victories, emerged as a powerhouse in 1979, featuring an outstanding running back in Ken Hill and a defense that would be ranked No. 1 in the nation by early November.

On November 3, Yale won its 700th game, a 23–20 victory over Cornell that brought its record to 7-0, and the following Saturday it clinched the Ivy championship by romping over Princeton. Harvard, meanwhile, was sliding toward the bottom of the Ivies, taking a record of 2-6 into The Game.

A crowd of 72,000 filled Yale Bowl on November 17 on a sunny afternoon for what looked to be a Harvard-Yale mismatch.

But Yale couldn't do anything right. It would fumble six times—three of the fumbles by Hill—have three passes intercepted and suffer eight penalties. Its quarterbacks, Dennis Dunn and John Rogan, were sacked a total of five times.

The Harvard quarterback, Burke St. John, directed an attack that controlled matters with 54 running plays to only 13 passes. Coming in, Yale had allowed fewer rushing yards per game than any other team in the nation. But Jim Callinan, a sophomore fullback for Harvard, wasn't impressed. He ran for a total of 74 yards and scored Harvard's second touchdown on a 62-yard pass play.

Dartmouth's starting quarterback in 1979 and 1980, Jeff Kemp—son of the former Buffalo Bills quarterback and political figure Jack Kemp—scrambles against Penn. (DARTMOUTH COLLEGE)

The Crimson coasted to a 22–7 shocker.

It was the third time in 12 years that Harvard had spoiled a perfect season for Yale—first the 29–29 tie in 1968, then the victory in 1974 when Yale had also come in at 8-0.

The 1980 season brought the finale for college football's oldest rivalry—Princeton versus Rutgers. The Tigers had once toyed with the Scarlet Knights, but then the Ivies de-emphasized football and Rutgers began moving in the other direction. Tired of being pushed around, Princeton had called for an end to a series going back to the afternoon of November 6, 1869, when 50 young men gathered at New Brunswick for what would be known as the first college football game.

The schools were back in New Brunswick for their last matchup on September 27 before a crowd of 26,219, the largest turnout at Rutgers Stadium since the 1969 game with Princeton. Rutgers rolled to a 44–13 victory—its fifth straight triumph over Princeton—as Ed McMichael passed for four touchdowns.

Late in the game, hundreds of fans swarmed onto the field and tore down one of the goalposts, then tried to get the other one, but were foiled by the police.

The series ended with Princeton having won 53 games and Rutgers 17 with one tie—and one set of goalposts still standing.

Yale, defending its Ivy title, figured to be strong again in 1980 with quarterback John Rogan and two fine runners, halfback Rich Diana and fullback John Nitti, among 26 returning lettermen.

The Elis scheduled Air Force for the first time, the October 4 game at Yale Bowl only the second for Yale against a team from west of the Mississippi. (The previous one was the 6–0 loss to Iowa in 1922 when Yale's Tad Jones coached against brother Howard.) Yale was lucky enough to encounter a weak Air Force squad (only 0-3-1) and held a one-touchdown lead in the third quarter. The Falcons drew within a point, at 17–16, on a third-period touchdown, but then went for a 2-point conversion on a run and failed. That ended the scoring. Diana had a big game, scoring on a 25-yard pass play from Rogan in the third quarter and gaining 136 yards rushing.

That Saturday brought a sweep by the Ivies against service academy teams—a flashback of sorts to the 1940s—as Harvard scored a 15–10 victory over Army at West Point.

Columbia had a new coach in Bob Naso, the defensive coordinator at Rutgers for the previous 12 seasons. "We are going to surprise some people, including long-time detractors of Columbia football," Naso promised.

After losing its opener to Harvard, Columbia recorded the 300th victory in school history, edging Lafayette, 6–0. The Lions presented the game ball to the college's new president, Michael Sovern. But the new era for Naso and Sovern brought more of the same—the Lafayette game would be Columbia's lone victory of the season.

The Lions brought joy to Penn in their game the very next Saturday. After trailing

by 13–0 in the first half, the Quakers came back for a 24–13 victory at Franklin Field that ended a 14-game losing streak.

Entering the final weekend, Yale was in first place, a game ahead of Harvard, Dartmouth, and Cornell.

On a brisk afternoon at Cambridge, Yale rebounded from the 1979 defeat that spoiled an unbeaten season. Throwing into the wind, John Rogan tossed a 25-yard scoring pass to Curtis Grieve in the first quarter, and then John Nitti scored from inches away after Harvard fumbled the second-half kickoff. Yale emerged with a 14–0 victory and its second straight Ivy title.

While football teams throughout the country were busy practicing in the spring of 1981, the Ivy League was more concerned with the halftime shows for the coming autumn.

Following growing complaints from alumni and parents, the Council of Ivy Group Presidents asked the deans at the individual schools to suggest that band leaders tone down the infamous exploration of sexual themes.

"You pay money to watch a football game and they don't put 'R' or 'X' whatever on the outside," observed James Litvack, executive director of the council.

Could he have been thinking of that Saturday the previous fall when Princeton's marching band remembered the arrival of women on campus 10 years earlier, when they were housed in Pyne Hall? That halftime show featured a "typical freshwoman" named "Sue Pyne."

Or perhaps he was recalling the time the Yale band members, performing during a televised game, dropped their pants to show off their diapers.

Then there was that game at Holy Cross a few years back when the Brown band demonstrated "how a little Polish boy can grow up to be pope." The script read over the public address system to the heavily Catholic crowd at Fitton Field explained that the papal hopeful simply needed to click the heels of his ruby slippers together and chant "There's no place like Rome."

Of course, Ivy administrators were well aware that the halftime shows were sometimes the highlight of the afternoon.

"It's a game played every year, in a way as interesting a spectacle as Ivy football," remarked Eric Widmer, Brown's dean of undergraduate life. "In some games I can think of, it is more interesting."

Despite the warnings, West Point authorities would be taking no chances in the autumn of 1981—they barred the Princeton band from accompanying the team on its visit to Army. (The Princeton offense was silenced, too, as the Cadets romped by 34–0, their first shutout victory in 11 years.)

As for the action before and after halftime, Yale—seeking its third consecutive Ivy title—seemed the class of the league again. Quarterback John Rogan, running back Rich Diana, and split end Curtis Grieve were all returning.

There was a new coach at Penn in Jerry Berndt, an assistant for eight years at Dart-

Yale's Rich Diana running away from Dartmouth. (YALE UNIVERSITY)

The Princeton marching band puts a customary irreverent face on a halftime show.
(**PRINCETON UNIVERSITY**)

mouth, then head coach for two seasons at DePauw in Greencastle, Indiana. Berndt scrapped the Ivy's only wishbone attack and replaced it with a multiple-set offense. And he extended the new look to uniforms, coming up with a design of his own to replace the familiar jerseys with thick red and blue stripes. "They were completely out of style," linebacker Mike Christiani would remark. "I wore them and I felt old."

In its first game under Berndt, Penn scored a 29–22 victory over Cornell at Franklin Field as Karl Hall caught three touchdown passes from Gary Vura, including a school-record 93-yarder. But the Quakers didn't win another game all season.

Yale scored its biggest victory against a non-Ivy opponent since the advent of formal league play when it defeated Navy, 23–19, at New Haven on Rogan's 24-yard touchdown pass to Grieve with a little over three minutes remaining.

Navy Coach George Welsh, whose team had almost beaten Michigan at Ann Arbor the previous weekend, was bewildered. "I've been coaching major college football for 19 years," he said. "I can't figure it out sometimes."

Yale won its first eight games in 1981 and went into Palmer Stadium with a 5-0 Ivy record. The Elis seemed headed for their 15th straight victory over Princeton, rolling to a 21–0 lead in the first half. But Tiger quarterback Bob Holly began to make it interesting, throwing for four touchdown passes. With 1 minute 39 seconds to play, Princeton got the ball on its 24-yard line, trailing by 31–29. Holly passed his team down to the Yale 20 and then, with a few seconds to go, threw to Derek Graham wide right in the end zone. The pass fell incomplete, but the officials called Yale cornerback Pat Conran for interference. On the next play, Holly rolled left from the 1-yard line for the winning touchdown with 4 seconds remaining.

Holly, a senior from Clifton, New Jersey, wound up with an Ivy League–record 501 yards passing in the 35–31 victory while Graham caught 15 passes for 278 yards.

"It's good that Princeton beats Yale once in a while," remarked Tiger coach Frank Navarro.

Another star quarterback was emerging at Columbia. John Witkowski, out of Lin-denhurst, Long Island, helped the Lions end a 10-game losing streak when he tossed a touchdown pass into a brisk wind in a 20–9 victory over Penn.

The season went into its final weekend with four teams vying for the title: Yale and Dartmouth at 5-1, Harvard and Princeton at 4-1-1.

Yale presumably received some inspiration the day before the Harvard game when Larry Kelley and Clint Frank presented their bronze Heisman statuettes to the school.

"After last week's game against Princeton, I hope they inspire some defensive backs to enroll here," remarked Kelley.

The next day, Yale's defensive backs were just about perfect in a 28–0 victory over Harvard before 75,000 at Yale Bowl, its biggest crowd in three decades. Dartmouth trounced Penn, 33–13, to share the Ivy title with Yale.

Serious celebrating was not, however, confined to New Haven and Hanover. After Princeton capped its season by beating Cornell, the drum major, Stephen Teager, led the band on a traffic-snarling parade down Witherspoon Street. The Princeton police were not amused and charged him with parading without a permit.

In mid-December, New Jersey's governor, Brendan Byrne, who happened to be a Princeton graduate, granted Teager a pardon. "It is impossible to have criminal intent so shortly after a Tiger victory," said Byrne.

"ANOTHER WORLD ALL BY THEIR OWN"

THEY HAD BEEN the founding fathers of college football, their young men doing battle in the sport's very first games. They had drawn up the rules, dominated the all-America teams in football's formative years, supplied the coaches that spread the gospel throughout nineteenth century America.

But now the Ivies were told to take their chairs from the table. There was no room for them in a high-stakes game.

In the winter of 1982, the major football colleges consolidated their control over television revenue by setting standards to reduce their ranks. The new requirements were a bit complex, but essentially decreed that a college must have an average of at least 17,000 in paid home attendance in order to be in Division I-A. Otherwise, the school would be demoted to a newly expanded Division I-AA that, it so happens, would miss out on the big-money TV network broadcasts.

These regulations automatically tossed all the Ivy schools except for Yale out of major college ranks. Yale then voluntarily joined the other Ivies in Division I-AA.

"The Ivy League is in another world all by their own," said Penn State coach Joe Paterno, a onetime Brown quarterback, in defending the cash-hungry power play. "I'm in the real world."

Harvard's coach, Joe Restic, had another view. "I just can't believe what is happening," he said. "I am talking about tradition, philosophy, history, the accomplishments of many great people all the way back to the last century. Do we wipe all that out in one step?"

Cornell's Bob Blackman observed that "the Ivy League really got American football going," but "the almighty dollar sign is the most important thing."

As the 1982 season moved along, Yale—the home of Walter Camp, father of college football—was especially deflated. Having lost Rich Diana, John Rogan, and Curtis Grieve after capturing three straight Ivy titles, the Elis dropped their first three games, the first time in school history that had ever happened.

The big story was Penn, led by Gary Vura, the quarterback; Karl Hall, a 5-foot-7-inch, 155-pound wide receiver; and Steve Ortman, a sophomore running back, and buoyed by an enhanced weight-lifting program instituted by Coach Jerry Berndt when he arrived the previous year.

Penthouse magazine's football preview had rated Penn the third-worst team in the country, ahead of only Northwestern and Colorado, commenting that its program was "like a thoroughbred with four shattered legs; destroying it would be an act of kindness."

But on the opening Saturday, Vura threw for three touchdowns against Dartmouth, the defending co-champion, in a 21–0 upset at Hanover, snapping a 24-game road losing streak. After having won just four games in the previous four seasons, Penn went to 4-0, its best start since 1968, before being beaten at Lafayette.

The Saturday after the first defeat, a crowd of 32,175—erupting in numerous standing ovations—turned out on homecoming day to see Penn beat Yale, 27–14, then shouted for the players to return from the locker rooms for a few bows.

The turnaround took a step backward the following Saturday as Princeton edged Penn, 17–14, at Palmer Stadium on Chris Price's 42-yard field goal that cleared the crossbar by inches with 25 seconds left.

The loss left Penn tied for first place with Harvard.

On November 13, the Crimson visited Franklin Field for the game of the season.

Harvard was trailing by 20–0 with less than nine minutes to play, then rallied for three scores—two on passes by Don Allard—to take a 21–20 lead with 1 minute 24 seconds remaining.

Penn took over at its 20 following the kickoff and rolled downfield behind Vura's passing, setting up a field goal attempt with three seconds left. Dave Shulman tried a 38-yarder, but it was tipped by a Harvard player and wobbled wide left. The Crimson began to celebrate, but then another color came into view—a yellow flag, dropped for a roughing-the-kicker penalty against two Harvard players who had come barreling in from the left side.

The ball was moved to the 11-yard line with no time remaining, and Shulman was given another chance. Penn called timeout, and as the players huddled around Coach Berndt, Shulman stood off by himself, staring at the kicking tee at the 17-yard line. "You've got to get away to keep your composure," he would explain later.

The football was snapped again, and Shulman sailed it through the uprights for a 23–21 victory, sending Penn fans streaming onto the field as the demoralized Harvard players fell to the ground. Penn was again alone in first place, one game ahead of Harvard and Dartmouth.

"It's nice," said tailback Steve Flacco a few days later. "People say 'hi' to you now. Before, they were laughing behind your back."

The great balloon caper—courtesy of an M.I.T. fraternity—at the 1982 Harvard-Yale game.
(BOB BROOKS/M.I.T. MUSEUM)

But on the season's final week, Penn mounted no last-second theatrics. The Quakers were stunned by Cornell, 23–0, at Ithaca as the Big Red's star runner, Derrick Harmon, back from an early-season injury, scored two touchdowns and picked up 179 yards. It was a wonderful finale for Bob Blackman, who was retiring after 34 years as a coach, 22 of them at Dartmouth and Cornell. Holding a bottle of champagne, Blackman was carried off the field by his players.

Dartmouth, meanwhile, beat Princeton, 43–20, while Harvard rolled over Yale, 45–7, at Cambridge. The race wound up in a three-way tie as Penn, Dartmouth, and Harvard finished at 5-2.

The Harvard-Yale game would be remembered not for any play but a wonderful prank.

Midway through the second quarter, just after a Harvard touchdown, a nozzle punched through the turf near the 40-yard line and began to inflate a black balloon in front of the Crimson bench. As the balloon grew larger—approaching six feet in diameter—the legend "MIT" became visible in several spots. Finally, it burst in a cloud of baby powder.

The Harvard coaching staff was taking no chances with this bizarre explosive device. Quarterback Don Allard would recall how "Coach Restic pushed me away from the action and put me behind the linemen on the farthest end of the bench."

John Witkowski broke numerous passing records set by a string of outstanding Columbia quarterbacks. (COLUMBIA UNIVERSITY)

The balloon, inflated and exploded by remote control, was a harmless display of technical wizardry by MIT's Delta Kappa Epsilon fraternity.

But Brent Musberger elevated the caper to a mini-terrorist incident, reporting on the CBS national football roundup that a bomb had floated down from the grandstand and exploded, leaving a three-foot crater.

Harvard's president, Derek Bok, felt that something even more dramatic was occurring. "I thought the phoenix was again rising from the ashes," he said.

Down at Columbia, spectators were consigning parts of Baker Field to the ashes. The final game was being played at the crumbling field, which was to be replaced by a concrete stadium at the same site in 1984.

At halftime of the season-ender against Brown, the Columbia band staged a routine to elicit sympathy for the Baker Field termites, who would be without a home when the dilapidated wooden stands were torn down. When the game ended, several dozen fans from the turnout of 5,775 ripped away or sawed off six-foot-long planks of seating as souvenirs. Stadium security guards helped them.

Columbia's John Witkowski set a host of records in the finale, finishing the 1982 season with 29 touchdown passes and 3,050 yards passing, but had little help from his teammates in a 35–21 loss.

Witkowski had a grand stage on which to show off his talents the following autumn. With construction under way on its new field, Columbia borrowed 76,000-seat Giants Stadium for its meeting with Penn on October 1, a rare Saturday night matchup.

This was the homecoming game, but Witkowski performed before tens of thousands of empty seats. The turnout was 7,221, and the result provided no other happy numbers. Penn won, 35–10, behind Karl Hall's three touchdown receptions. Witkowski suffered a bruised right thumb in the second period and his receivers dropped 10 throws on a rainy night. It was a forgettable evening for the star quarterback and his team, but Columbia had improved some on its two previous appearances at Giants Stadium—47–0 and 69–0 losses to Rutgers, in 1976 and 1978.

Another star quarterback was emerging at Princeton—a sophomore from Orange, California, named Doug Butler. In his first start, Butler threw for 411 yards and a school-record five touchdowns in a 46–28 victory over Bucknell at Palmer Stadium as wide receiver Kevin Guthrie made 16 receptions—also a Princeton record—and scored three touchdowns.

The following Saturday, when Princeton played Navy for the first time in 30 years, Butler set a collegiate record for most passes attempted in a game without an interception, throwing 55 times with 25 completions. (He would go on to break Princeton's single-season record for passing yardage, surpassing the mark set only the year before by Brent Woods.) But Navy's ground game was too strong as tailback Napoleon McCallum gained 222 first-half yards in the Middies' 37–29 victory at Palmer Stadium.

Cornell reached into the pro ranks for a head coach, signing up Maxie Baughan, a former star linebacker with the Philadelphia Eagles and assistant coach with the Detroit Lions. The Big Red still had one of the league's best running backs in Derrick Harmon. But they would win only three games all season.

After losing its first four games, Columbia met another tailender—a Yale team that had also dropped four straight. Breaking a 10-game losing streak, the Lions managed a 21–18 victory at Yale Bowl, and Coach Bob Naso saw good things ahead.

"We've felt all along that once we got the first victory we could put some wins back to back," he said.

It was not one of history's more accurate projections. Columbia would play two ties later in the season but would not win another game until October 9, 1988.

But Witkowski continued to set records and would finish his career with 56 touchdown passes and 7,849 passing yards, becoming the seventh quarterback in college football history to exceed the 7,000-yard mark. He would then go on to another Lion team—in Detroit.

Early in November, the Brown Bears got a taste of "the real world," as defined by Joe Paterno in his defense of the Ivies' demotion to Divison I-AA. In a bizarre matchup, Paterno's alma mater visited State College to play his Penn State team. The Bears went into the game a five-touchdown underdog but did not exactly get sand kicked in their faces. Brown outgained Penn State in total offense for the first half, 229 yards to 205, before being worn down in a 38–21 loss.

Going into the season's final week, Harvard, Penn, and Dartmouth were tied for first place with records of 4-1-1.

The Harvard-Yale game at New Haven would have a bearing on the Ivy title, but it didn't need that extra flourish. For this was the 100th edition of The Game.

Commerce mixed with conviviality, a logo with an intertwined crimson *H* and blue *Y* over the number 100 having been designed for handkerchiefs ($2), T-shirts ($6), Lucite paperweights ($30), and 14-karat gold stickpins ($65). Game programs were jacked up from their usual $1 to $5.

Yale's Football Y Association was host to a luncheon at Woolsey Hall for old grads, and the two oldest were on hand: for Harvard, former Congressman Hamilton Fish Jr., age 96, the 1909 captain and star tackle, and for Yale, Henry Ketcham, age 92, the 1913 captain.

During the morning, there was a bid to rekindle the 29–29 "miracle" tie of 1968, the players having been invited back for a touch-football encounter. The 1968 Harvard team that staged a comeback for the ages got an outright victory this time—by default. Only Brian Dowling showed up for Yale.

Before the kickoff, a spectacle more suited to the Super Bowl than Ivy sophistication unfolded—members of the United States Navy Chute Stars, a freefall team, dropped by.

Thirty-two captains from previous Harvard teams and an equal number from Yale took part in the coin toss on a field decorated with a crimson *H* and a blue *Y* with 100 written in white across crimson and blue diamonds in the end zones.

Yale, which had won only one game all season, held Harvard to a 7–7 tie in the first half. But Harvard pulled away on a 2-yard run by fullback Steve Ernst and a field goal by Rob Steinberg for a 16–7 victory. Harvard quarterback Greg Grizzi, who had been so discouraged earlier in the year that he wanted to switch to running back, led the way with 104 yards running and 94 yards passing.

There was one unhappy note amid the revelry and reminiscences. A Harvard freshman named Margaret Cimino was struck in the head when fans tore down a goalpost and required several months' hospitalization. She later sued Yale and the city of New Haven and in 1986 obtained what her lawyer said was a $925,000 settlement.

Harvard shared the Ivy championship with Penn, which knocked Dartmouth out of the title race with a 38–14 victory at Franklin Field. Fullback Chuck Nolan, normally a blocker, ran for 130 yards and two touchdowns. "It was just one of those days where I couldn't do anything wrong," Nolan said. "Maybe I should have played the horses."

Television arrived on the Ivy scene in the autumn of 1984 as a network of 11 Public Broadcasting System stations in the Northeast aired a game each Saturday. The packager, Barry Frank of Trans World International, said the telecasts would be "for people who are fed up with the powerhouses."

What better way to draw a contrast with football's powers than to have the debut telecast feature Columbia.

The cameras rolled on a special Saturday for the Lions—the opening of Lawrence A. Wien Stadium, built on the site of the old Baker Field. The stadium cost $7 million in its first phase with $3 million donated by Wien, a Columbia Law School graduate, Class of 1927, and real-estate investor. The stands, all behind the Columbia bench, had a capacity of 10,500—benches for 8,500 spectators along with 1,000 armchair seats and 1,000 contoured seats, Columbia's version of luxury boxes. (A 6,500-seat visitors' grandstand was erected in 1986 thanks to another donation from Wien.)

Among the spectators at the opener with Harvard was Julius Witmark, Class of 1925, who had been a regular at shabby old Baker Field. "I've been getting splinters in my backside for too many years," said Witmark, who recalled how he used to tell Columbia athletic officials "they should include a pair of tweezers with a season ticket."

Mayor Ed Koch, participating in the pregame ceremonies at Columbia's first sellout since the 1954 Navy game, managed to overlook 12 straight losing seasons and five consecutive losses to Harvard.

"We're going to beat the hell out of them," puffed the mayor. "We did it when the stands were wooden. Imagine what we can do now."

The New York television audience was, however, spared the hyperbole—a technical glitch botched the audio feed.

Columbia stayed in the game most of the way and even had a chance to win. But with the Lions trailing by 6 points, Harvard linebacker Brent Wilkinson intercepted a pass by Henry Santos and ran it back 45 yards for the clinching score. The final: Harvard 35, Columbia 21.

It would be all downhill for the Lions, who finished the season at 0-9, their worst record ever.

Brown had a new coach in 1984 when John Rosenberg, a Harvard graduate and longtime assistant to Joe Paterno, replaced John Anderson, who announced his resignation late the previous season.

The Ivy League may not have been the "real world" in Paterno's eyes, but there were pressures nonetheless on coaches. Anderson had produced eight consecutive winning seasons but then, after three poor-to-mediocre years, the stress of having to recruit good players caught up with him. "Everyone expects you to win all the time and we just can't do it," he said. "It's been getting to me, like a monkey on my back."

The new coach had an instant star in the season-opener when Keiron Bigby, a sophomore defensive back, scored on 91- and 102-yard interception returns as Brown defeated Yale, 27–14. But soon the Bears began to fade.

Penn, having tied for the Ivy title the previous two years, opened with a 55–24 victory at Dartmouth, the most points scored by a visitor to Hanover since Yale's 113–0 squeaker 100 years earlier.

By late October, Penn and Harvard, the previous year's co-champions, were both 4-0 in league play.

Princeton's Doug Butler was once again the league's top passer, and he almost knocked off Harvard when he threw for 325 yards and two touchdowns. Only a junior, Butler broke Dick Kazmaier's school mark for career total offense—4,354 yards—but the Crimson hung on for a 17–15 victory at Palmer Stadium.

The Ivy race was essentially decided on November 10 when Penn romped over Harvard, 38–7, before 38,810 at Franklin Field as tailbacks Steve Ortman and Rich Comizio combined for 156 yards.

The following Saturday, Penn routed

Cornell, 24–0, at Ithaca for its first outright Ivy title since 1959 as John McGeehan threw for two touchdowns. Finishing at 8-1, their only loss coming against Army, the Quakers became the first Ivy team to go through a league schedule undefeated since Dartmouth in 1970.

The first year of Ivy telecasts—with four corporate sponsors—proved a modest success. They reached 700,000 viewers each Saturday while surmounting a few mini-crises: in the Harvard-Brown game a power failure kept the picture off the air for 28 minutes and at Yale-Dartmouth workers spent three hours before the kickoff attempting to lure a skunk from electrical cables.

The week after the season ended, two coaches were gone. Frank Navarro, at Princeton for seven seasons, stepped down after his third straight losing year. And Columbia's Bob Naso resigned, leaving behind a record of 4-43-2 over five years.

Columbia reached into the pro ranks in 1985 and came up with Jim Garrett, an emotional man with an incident in his distant past to live down.

Back in 1966, while coaching at Susquehanna College in Pennsylvania, Garrett had rammed the side of a player's helmet with the heel of his hand. Although the school president said he wanted Garrett to stay on, the uproar over the incident brought his resignation. (The president, Gus Weber, coached the team in its final two games, completing an 0-10 season.)

That had ended Garrett's college coaching career. Now, after 20 years in the National Football League working for the Cowboys, Giants, and Browns as a scout, assistant coach, and executive, he arrived at Morningside Heights with every indication that his intensity had not dimmed. He put the team through what he called 33 "hideous" preseason practices in 12 days and proclaimed: "I'm insulting and demanding, and I'll put a spotlight on a player who's erred and make it clear that he's let us down."

The spotlight shone very brightly on Garrett himself when Columbia opened its season against Harvard at Wien Stadium. The Lions got off to a 17–0 lead, then saw the Crimson score seven touchdowns for a 49–17 trouncing.

Afterward came the magic words.

"They are drug-addicted losers," Garrett told reporters in the locker room. "One adversity comes"—now he smashed a fist into his palm— "and bang! They're right back in the sewer again."

True to his word, he singled out a particular miscreant—in this case Peter Murphy, the punter, an all-Ivy honorable-mention selection as a kicker the previous season. Murphy had punted eight times for an average of 38.5 yards—3 yards more than his average over the two previous seasons—but Garrett was incensed over three punts that did not, in his view, have sufficient hang time.

"The punting killed us," he said. "The punts didn't go 15 yards in the air. I just told the squad he'll never kick for me again."

"We're in this game to win," Garrett went on. "Don't tell me it's a college atmosphere. This is an atmosphere that creates people for the future. I want to see him when he graduates and goes to work down-town on Wall Street and does three things that he did today. See how long he is gonna work for that company, how long Merrill Lynch or Smith Barney is gonna have him around."

It was not exactly a manner in which Ivy coaches customarily referred to their student-athletes.

For every punt that Murphy supposedly fouled up, there was a Columbia adminis-trator rushing to condemn Garrett's rebukes. The coach drew fire from Robert Pollock, the dean of Columbia College; Norman Mintz, Columbia's vice president for academic affairs; and Al Paul, the athlet-ic director. A *New York Times* editorial said that Garrett "seems determined to make even George Steinbrenner look good."

After meeting with Columbia officials the following Monday, Garrett character-ized his remarks as "a gross error." The only "drug" the Columbia players were addicted to was "losing," the coach explained. Mur-phy nevertheless quit the team.

The next Saturday, Columbia lost at Lafayette, 20–0, but Garrett seemed chas-tened. He praised the Lions for their "resiliency."

"They're not addicted losers, because addicted losers would not have resiliency," he said.

Elsewhere around the league, Penn, Princeton, and Harvard emerged as con-tenders.

On November 3, Penn, at 4-0, and with a pair of outstanding running backs in Rich Comizio and Chris Flynn, took on a Prince-ton team one game behind in the stand-ings.

The new Princeton coach, Ron Roger-son, had put in a wing T, a formation geared to the running game, but Doug But-ler was still showing off his arm. Butler would break every Princeton passing record except for Bob Holly's single-game yardage mark of 501, and his 7,291 passing yards would double the Princeton career record.

Led by Butler's two touchdown passes, Princeton took a stunning 21–0 first-half lead at Franklin Field only to see Penn rally for a 31–21 victory, the go-ahead points coming on a 29-yard field goal by Ray Saunders in the fourth quarter.

But on the next-to-last weekend of the season, Penn's Ivy League winning streak ended at 13 games with a 17–6 loss to Har-vard at Cambridge. The Crimson quarter-back, Brian White, ran for 91 yards and passed for 92 more. When it was over, the teams were tied for the league lead at 5-1.

On the final Saturday, Harvard went up against a Yale team that had been a presea-son favorite for the title but came into the game at Cambridge with a 2-3-1 Ivy mark and the worst defense in the league. That, of course, meant nothing. Yale knocked Harvard out of a chance for a league cham-pionship, scoring a 17–6 victory.

Penn played Dartmouth at Franklin Field, going for the title without much of its offensive power. Coach Jerry Berndt benched quarterback Jim Crocicchia for missing team meetings, and halfback Rich Comizio left the game with a sprained ankle. But the Quakers, with a stout defen-sive effort, hung on for a 19–14 victory.

Dartmouth coach Joe Yukica did not go quietly when the school tried to say good-bye.
(DARTMOUTH COLLEGE)

Penn students chanted "Four, four, four," tore down the goalposts, and dumped them into the Schuylkill to celebrate Penn's fourth straight Ivy title, outright or shared.

Jim Garrett, who had called upon his Columbia team to go 10-0, found the numbers reversed when the stormy 1985 season had ended. The Lions went 0-10 and extended a losing streak to 21 games. Three days after the final debacle, a 34–0 drubbing by Brown, Garrett resigned. He was replaced by Larry McElreavy, who had revitalized the football program at the University of New Haven over the previous three years.

The new coach had personally sampled the dreary Columbia football environment. In 1980, while an assistant with Yale, he fell through a rotting plank in the Baker Field seats while climbing to the press box.

McElreavy set out to restore school spirit by having his players sing "Roar, Lion, Roar" at preseason camp. How had they done? "They're better football players than singers," he told a reporter. But even that would be debatable.

Columbia had to make do without a Jim Garrett legacy it was counting on for the 1986 season and beyond. The departed coach had three sons envisioned as a force that could make the Lions at least respectable. John Garrett, a wide receiver, was on the varsity roster in 1985 but suffered a broken collarbone and missed the entire season. Jason, a quarterback who was the most valuable player on the Princeton freshman team in 1984, had transferred and was expected to be a starter. Judd, a fullback, had run for 11 touchdowns on Columbia's 1985 freshman team.

But all three defected to Princeton when their father left Columbia.

While the controversy over Jim Garrett faded away, another dispute was brewing at Dartmouth. The school's athletic director, Ted Leland, had dismissed Coach Joe Yukica after the Big Green went 2-7-1 in 1985, their third straight losing season. But Yukica, who had won three Ivy titles in eight years at Dartmouth, went to court, arguing he had the right to continue as coach until his contract expired in June 1987. (Dartmouth was willing to continue paying Yukica but wanted to assign him to other duties.)

"This has to do with more than the game of football," said Yukica, who insisted he was fighting for a principle. "It's the game of life."

Yukica called three coaches as witnesses—Penn State's Joe Paterno, Boston College's Jack Bicknell, and the former Ivy coach Bob Blackman. They all testified that Yukica's future would be damaged if he were fired.

In December 1985, a judge barred Dartmouth from dismissing Yukica, and the following month he reached a settlement. He would be allowed to finish out his contract but the school could start searching for a successor the following fall.

There was a coaching change at the top of the Ivies in 1986. After leading Penn to four straight titles, Jerry Berndt went to Rice and was replaced by 34-year-old Ed Zubrow, who became the league's youngest coach.

On the opening Saturday, an old coach on the way out faced a new coach when Dartmouth took on Penn at Hanover. Joe Yukica's team kept things close into the third quarter, but there would be no instant vindication for him. Penn won, 21–7.

Up at Ithaca, a coach coming off some rough years enjoyed a turnaround. Maxie Baughan had been through three losing seasons since arriving at Cornell, but now the Big Red went on a point spree in the opener against Princeton. After Cornell scored its fifth touchdown late in the final quarter, Baughan and his assistants threw away their earphones and clipboards and led the entire bench in charging onto the field. Marty Stallone's three touchdown passes brought a 39–8 romp, Cornell's first opening-game victory since 1980.

The following Saturday, Princeton was host for the first game between Ivy League and Big Ten teams since Penn was beaten by Ohio State and Michigan in 1953.

At least Princeton had enough sense to schedule the Big Ten's closest equivalent to the Ivies in Northwestern, an academic power but perennial football patsy.

"It's not like they're playing the Chicago Bears," observed Northwestern's athletic director, Doug Single.

"We scheduled this game back when they were 0-22," said Princeton's associate athletic director, Sam Howell. "Then they got better." (Northwestern had won only 3 of 75 games from mid-1957 to mid-1982, but was 3-8 the previous season.)

The Tigers were gutsy enough. A Princeton defensive end, Edwin Elton, had his helmet knocked off, but chased the runner for 50 yards.

Nevertheless, if anyone had envisioned another "Team of Destiny"—a latter-day version of the 1922 Princeton team that upset the Big Ten's University of Chicago—those notions disappeared when the Tigers' Sean Welsh threw an interception on his first play. Minutes afterward, Northwestern had its first touchdown, and six Princeton turnovers later, the Wildcats went home with a 37–0 victory.

Penn and Cornell were the class of the Ivies in 1986 and were both unbeaten in the league when they met on the final Saturday at Ithaca. It was the first time since 1968—when Harvard and Yale staged their memorable 29–29 tie—that a pair of undefeated teams played for the title.

This time there was little drama. Penn's running game, led by Rich Comizio's 162-yard effort, overwhelmed Cornell by 31–21 for the Quakers' fifth straight championship.

"It was a nightmarish end to a dream season," said Maxie Baughan.

Down at Palmer Stadium, Joe Yukica—coaching his final Dartmouth game—received a rousing sendoff as quarterback David Gabianelli threw four touchdown passes in a 28–6 triumph over Princeton.

At Wien Stadium, as the players walked off the field the scoreboard read: "Brown 45, Columbia 46." But it was somebody's joke, a slight adjustment to the real score of Brown 45, Columbia 7, closing out another 0-10 season for the Lions.

As the opening Saturday of the 1987 season neared, Coach Larry McElreavy had a prediction: "We will not break the record."

He was hoping that the Columbia football guide had not provided a regrettable omen when it showed the coach posing with his captain, Mike Bissinger, who wore No. 35.

Columbia was four losses away from running up 35 straight defeats and breaking Northwestern's record—set between 1979 and 1982—for most consecutive defeats by a major-college team. (The all-time record was 50 straight suffered by Macalester College of St. Paul, Minnesota, a Division III team, from 1974 to 1980.)

The Columbia recruiters were certainly trying their best. Amid much publicity, the team reached out to Texas for a player, signing up John Robinson, a 6-foot-4-inch, 240-pound linebacker from Southern Methodist, whose football program had been suspended for repeated violations of NCAA rules. Robinson had his eye on a graduate degree in business from Columbia. But he arrived in New York a bit apprehensive, never having been further north than Oklahoma.

"I heard someone talking about the subways in New York, about how dirty it is

Judd Garrett helping Princeton send Columbia to a record 35th straight defeat.
(**PRINCETON UNIVERSITY**)

and the people on there, a lot of gangs," Robinson said. "I'd like to ride the subway—maybe once anyway."

Robinson was at right defensive end when Columbia opened at home against Harvard, and he made six tackles and had a sack, but the non-Texans didn't do so well. The Lions lost, 35–0.

Columbia then fell to Lafayette and Penn to tie the Northwestern streak for futility, inspiring the *People* magazine headline: "Hail, Columbia, Where Losing Isn't Everything, It's the Only Thing."

A record-breaking 35th straight loss loomed on October 10 when Columbia vis-

ited Princeton where it would be greeted by the three sons of Jim Garrett. Jason, a junior quarterback; Judd, a sophomore halfback; and John, a senior wide receiver, were all starring for Princeton after having sat out a season upon transferring from Columbia.

Columbia's crack at the record was now a national story. More than 120 press credentials—100 over the usual figure—were issued at Palmer Stadium.

A nine-year-old boy paraded with a placard reading: "Please win before I grow up."

The signs were not good for Columbia. The van carrying the Lion cheerleaders broke down. They switched to a taxi that got a flat tire. Then they took another van whose driver got lost, arriving at the stadium around the end of the third quarter.

By then things were already decided, the Garrett brothers having wasted no time. Judd scored on a 58-yard run in the opening minute, Jason threw a 76-yard touchdown pass to John on Princeton's second possession, and Judd scored on a 1-yard run late in the first quarter.

Princeton had a 38–8 rout and Columbia had the record losing streak.

"I'd be lying if I didn't say this game meant a lot," said Jason Garrett afterward. But he added: "We knew a lot of guys on the other side of the ball. I feel kind of sorry for them."

Princeton had a new coach that autumn in Steve Tosches, the successor to Ron Rogerson, who died of a heart attack the previous summer. At Dartmouth, the former star quarterback Buddy Teevens took over for Joe Yukica. Both Tosches and Teevens were only 30 years old.

Yale and Harvard, meanwhile, were relying on outstanding quarterbacks in Kelly Ryan and Tom Yohe.

Despite a knee injury the previous season, Ryan had become the leading passer in Yale history. But the Elis had to forget about a debacle early in October, a 12,000-mile round trip for a game with the University of Hawaii. The visit to Honolulu, orchestrated by Frank Ryan, a former Yale athletic director, was supposed to be the centerpiece for an alumni shindig. But only 400 old grads signed up for the package tours, and Yale was trounced, 62–0—its most decisive

defeat ever—while losing two starting tackles for the season with blown-out knees.

Penn and Cornell figured to be the best teams in the league. They had faced each other on many a Thanksgiving Day, but this time met on the opening Saturday at Franklin Field.

Penn's "Barking Dog Defense" growled away in an effort to intimidate Cornell's junior quarterback, Aaron Sumida, but the Big Red unleashed some invective of their own.

"Every time we shut them down, I growled like a rottweiler," Cornell's strong safety, Brent Felitto, said afterward. "Deep and scratchy, not soft or squeaky. I didn't want to sound like a poodle."

The Big Red Rottweilers prevailed, 17–13, and Penn would sink to a 3-4 league mark after five titles. But Cornell wouldn't be in the running either.

Harvard and Yale moved to the top behind their quarterbacks. On the next-to-last Saturday, Tom Yohe threw his 16th touchdown pass of the season—tying a school mark—as Harvard beat Penn, 31–14, while Kelly Ryan, passing for 329 yards and three touchdowns, led Yale past Princeton, 34–19.

The Harvard-Yale game would decide the title for the first time since 1975 and the third time since formal Ivy play had begun in 1956.

It turned up 19 degrees in Yale Bowl with winds gusting to 40 miles an hour, numbing the players' hands and causing the football to sail. Harvard fumbled four times, Yale three.

With the foresight to bring along Crimson overcoats for the sidelines, Harvard emerged with the title, beating Yale by 14–10. Running back Tony Hinz scored on a 57-yard run late in the first half, then got the clinching touchdown when Yohe, working with the wind at his back, tossed a 19-yard pass to him in the third quarter.

"My senior year in high school, I had six games in the snow," noted Hinz, who happened to be from Great Falls, Montana. "I learned how to block out cold weather."

It was a disappointing finale for Yale, but Coach Carm Cozza would be nicely honored before the 1988 season began.

Cozza, in his 24th year at Yale, became the first occupant of the "Joel E. Smilow 1954 Coach of Football" endowed chair. Smilow, Class of 1954, a former touch football player at Yale who had become chairman of Playtex, donated $1 million to establish the first endowed coaching position at his alma mater.

Although endowed professorships often carried tenure along with high salaries, Cozza did not gain job protection if, say, Yale were to post an 0-10 season or two. And he wasn't becoming an instant millionaire—much of the $1 million could be used toward upgrading Yale's overall athletic program.

Cozza was not the first Ivy coach so honored—the Princeton and Cornell football coaches were already occupying endowed positions—but the publicity surrounding the announcement led to a raised editorial eyebrow or two.

While saying that "the idea is not as silly as it sounds," the *New York Times* couldn't resist a chortle.

"What next, a tenured tuba player?"

asked the *Times*. "A lifetime annuity for Handsome Dan, the ineffably ugly bulldog who serves as Yale's mascot?"

When the 1988 season got under way, Cozza and his fellow Ivy coaches would be scrutinized by far more alumni than usual. The Ivy League obtained a national television contract for the first time, ESPN agreeing to cover six games.

With Jason and Judd Garrett returning, Princeton was favored to take the title, and the Tigers lived up to expectations with victories in their first two league games. Then they went up to Columbia on October 9.

Having surpassed Northwestern's record losing streak for a major college with its loss to Princeton the year before, Columbia was taking aim on the all-time mark of 50 straight defeats set by Macalaster. The Lions had lost their first three games in 1988—to Harvard, Lafayette, and Penn—bringing their slide to 44.

It was homecoming day at Wien Stadium, but not too many old grads were finding the weekly carnage appealing—the crowd was an underwhelming 5,420.

Columbia seemed headed for its customary drubbing when Princeton took a 10–0 lead. But late in the fourth quarter the Lions were within 4 points, at 13–9, as Greg Abbruzzese rolled along en route to a 182-yard rushing performance. Then they drove into Princeton territory, and with 5 minutes 13 seconds remaining Solomon Johnson scored on a 2-yard run. Columbia had a 16–13 lead.

A stunned Princeton team got within hailing distance, and on the final play the Tigers attempted a 48-yard field goal for a

After 44 consecutive losses, Columbia stuns Princeton. (COLUMBIA UNIVERSITY)

tie. Finally, the Lions had a little luck—the kick fell short.

The puny crowd had grown toward the end as students began rushing up from Morningside Heights upon hearing the fantastic news that Columbia was leading. Now they swarmed onto the field, tore down the goalposts, took them five miles downtown to the campus, and paraded with the trophies on fraternity row. Strands of toilet paper were strewn through trees along Broadway and students pranced with bottles of champagne.

Afterward, someone asked Coach Larry McElreavy when he thought his team had the game won. "About four minutes after the game was over," he said.

The following Saturday Columbia came back to earth, fumbling seven times in a 24–10 loss to Yale.

On the final weekend, Penn and Cornell faced each other at Ithaca for the Ivy championship. Penn was 9-0 over all and 6-0 in league play, Cornell 5-1 in the conference.

Cornell's Maxie Baughan got ready for Penn's "barking dog" intimidation by having his second-stringers shove and curse the regulars in practice.

"We knew we weren't preparing for the Little Sisters of the Poor," linebacker Mike McGrann would note.

And a motivational poster was plastered in the Cornell locker room.

Circled in red at the top were head shots of Penn's key offensive players—quarterback Malcolm Glover and tailback Bryan Keys. Underneath, it read: "Dear Census Bureau: Please add these players to the list of deceased players of the week." Below that was written: "Spill Your Guts and They Will Lose Theirs."

Not very Ivy-like but presumably effective, as events would prove.

The Penn defensive players ran onto the field carrying a 15-pound sledgehammer with a red and blue handle—the Big Stick—awarded each week to the defender making the hardest hit.

The game was indeed a rough one, marked by five personal-foul penalties against Penn and four against Cornell.

"Their guys were grabbing us in the pile, spitting in our faces whenever they could, and mouthing off," Cornell quarterback Aaron Sumida would complain afterward.

The costliest personal foul, called on Penn at its 9-yard line in the fourth quarter, led to a 1-yard run by Scott Malaga that gave Cornell a 16–6 lead.

Cornell came away with a 19–6 victory and a tie with Penn for the Ivy title, its first time at the top since 1971, when it shared the championship with Dartmouth in Ed Marinaro's senior season.

"It was pandemonium—the Super Bowl and World Series all wrapped up in one," said Malaga. "I screamed for 15 minutes straight."

The following autumn brought several coaching changes, a couple of them enmeshed in most unusual circumstances.

Cornell's Maxie Baughan and Penn's

It's time to "Roar, Lion, Roar."
(COLUMBIA UNIVERSITY)

Ed Zubrow both resigned despite championship seasons. Citing "personal tensions" that had "engulfed the program," Baughan departed after the *Ithaca Journal* reported he had been involved romantically with the estranged wife of his chief assistant coach, Pete Noyes. Baughan was replaced by another aide, Jack Fouts. Zubrow was succeeded by his defensive assistant, Gary Steele.

Columbia's Larry McElreavy quit soon after taking his team to a 2-8 season, which happened to be the Lions' "best" year since 1978. McElreavy's offensive coordinator, Doug Jackson (the Ivy player of the year as a Columbia running back in 1975), had accused him of excessive drinking and of having an extramarital affair with a member of the athletic department. McElreavy, the Columbia administration, and the woman all denied the accusations, but the coach stepped down nonetheless, saying, "I cannot subject those I love and admire to further public abuse." McElreavy was replaced by Ray Tellier, a highly successful coach at the University of Rochester, a Division III school.

Princeton got off to a good start with a familiar face leading the offense. Judd Garrett, the only remaining brother of the three Princeton offensive stars, ran for 167 yards and a touchdown as the Tigers opened with a 20–14 victory over Dartmouth.

There was a new look at Yale. Coach Carm Cozza, beginning his 25th season, had an outstanding runner in quarterback Darin Kehler, so he turned to a wishbone offense—keyed to quarterback option plays

and fullback dives—for the first time since 1972. Kehler ran for 112 yards as the Elis opened with a 12–3 victory over Brown.

Penn had a strong running game as well, led by Bryan Keys, who picked up a school-record 249 yards on 37 carries and scored four touchdowns in a 32–30 triumph against Brown in mid-October.

The season's first big game came on the last Saturday of October when Penn visited Yale, both unbeaten in league play. With 10 seconds remaining, Yale's Ed Perks kicked a line-drive 27-yard field goal that barely went over the crossbar for a 23–22 victory.

Two weeks later, Yale and Princeton, each with Ivy marks of 5-0, met at Palmer Stadium before 37,762, the biggest crowd there in 24 years. The Elis, who had blocked four punts in previous games (three of them thwarted by cornerback Rich Huff), came close to blocking one by Princeton's Brad Remig five times in the first half. Then, with the score tied at 7–7 in the third quarter, Huff finally blocked a punt, and Yale took over at Princeton's 17. Four plays later, fullback Chris Kouri scored from the 1. Yale emerged with a 14–7 victory.

Yale could finish alone in first place by beating Harvard at home. But that prospect quickly unraveled as the Crimson (4-2 in league play) took a 21–0 lead early in the third quarter. Yale then struck for three touchdowns, but the conversion kick on the third one was partly blocked, so Harvard clung to a 21–20 edge going into the fourth period. The Crimson then pulled away for a 37–20 victory.

Down at Palmer Stadium, Judd Garrett

ran for two touchdowns as Princeton beat Cornell, 21–7.

So Yale had to settle for a tie at the top with Princeton, which got a share of the championship for the first time since finishing in a three-way tie back in 1969.

It was the fifth time since 1974 that a Harvard victory had deprived Yale of an outright or shared Ivy title.

"Everything was ours for the taking," said Kehler. "We just didn't play a very good game."

Having lost Judd Garrett to graduation, Princeton stumbled in its 1990 opener, falling by 17–14 to Cornell, which had its third coach in three seasons. Jim Hofher, a Cornell quarterback in the 1970s and most recently an assistant at Tennessee, became the first Big Red alumnus to coach the squad since Dan Reed back in 1911. He had 13 returning starters, including a fine running back in John McNiff.

Dartmouth, which won its last four games of 1989, had 14 starters returning, but Dave Johnson, who had set school passing records, was not among them. His replacement, Kevin Peck, came down with mononucleosis three days before the season began. So it looked as if another disappointing year was in store when the Big Green lost their opener to Penn, 16–6.

But Dartmouth had a fine runner in Shon Page, who led the way in a 27–17 victory over Yale. Next for Dartmouth was the Cornell game at Schoellkopf Field, which was preceded by a little ceremony marking the 50th anniversary of the schools' infamous "Fifth Down Game." This time Dartmouth prevailed without having to wait a couple of days for an official's gaffe to be confirmed, scoring an 11–6 victory behind Dennis Durkin's three field goals.

By the end of October, Page, a 5-foot-8-inch, 200-pound senior from Oakland, California, had propelled Dartmouth to a spot among the Ivy leaders, running for a school-record 222 yards and two touchdowns in a 17–0 victory over Harvard.

The following Saturday saw an even more impressive running performance—from a second-stringer. Cornell's McNiff went out with a bruised thigh returning the opening kickoff against Yale. His backup, Scott Oliaro, raced into the huddle even before his coach had formally summoned him. On the first play from scrimmage, he ran 69 yards for a touchdown. By the time the afternoon was over, Oliaro, a junior from Williston, Vermont, had carried for 288 yards and three touchdowns, breaking the Ivy single-game rushing mark set by Ed Marinaro (281 yards) against Harvard in 1969. And he added a pair of scoring catches.

The next weekend, Oliaro was rewarded with a seat on a very wet bench when Cornell met Columbia before 860 rain-soaked fans at Wien Stadium. McNiff, the league's leading rusher, was back in fine style, running 95 yards for a touchdown in a 41–0 romp. (Oliaro did manage to score on a 2-yard run and 33-yard screen pass.)

Cornell had yielded 115 points in its first three games, but going into the final Saturday the Big Red were tied for the league lead with Dartmouth, both at 5-1. They would share the championship as Cornell defeated Penn and Dartmouth topped Princeton. It was Dartmouth's first time atop the Ivies since 1982 and the first winning team for Coach Buddy Teevens, in his fourth season. Dartmouth added a flourish in individual honors, Shon Page edging John McNiff for the Ivy rushing championship, 754 yards to 749.

In December, the Ivy League embarked on postseason play for the first time since Columbia's Rose Bowl stunner over Stanford in 1934. An all-star team of seniors traveled to Yokohama to face players from Japanese universities in the first Ivy Bowl.

The Japanese would prove cooperative hosts each winter in what became an annual event, losing every time while their countrymen cheered the Ivies. At the inaugural game, half the 28,000 fans in Yokohama Stadium were given blue pom-poms and directed to root for the visitors. But the Ivy team didn't need any encouragement, its edge in experience and a hefty weight advantage bringing a 47–10 victory as Penn's Steve Hooper ran for four touchdowns.

Play-calling would be especially easy for the Ivy quarterbacks, thanks to the language gap. In the event a change in strategy was needed just before the ball was snapped, the quarterback wouldn't have to worry about disguising his intentions with arcane code words. As Kevin Callahan, an all-Ivy halfback for Yale who played in the 1991 Ivy Bowl, noted: "If our offense had really bogged down, I suppose our quarterback could have called an audible, something like 'Receiver. Run 15 yards, turn around, and I'll throw you the ball.'"

The Ivy League hadn't been a heavyweight in college football for decades, but when the 1991 season arrived it shared a distinction with heavyweight title fights— Ivy games were now offered on pay-per-view. Cable subscribers in the Northeast and Mid-Atlantic regions were given a five-game schedule, concluding with Harvard-Yale, at $9.95 per game in a production effort by TVOne, an Atlanta company.

Dartmouth seemed ready to roll again, opening its 1991 season with a 21–15 victory over Penn as quarterback Matt Brzica threw for one touchdown and ran for another.

But Brzica, the Ivy League sophomore of the year in 1990, was soon moved to wide receiver as a new sophomore, Jay Fiedler, took over the quarterbacking. Fiedler, 6 feet 3 inches and 213 pounds, had good size but had not been highly recruited because of a knee injury incurred while playing for Oceanside High School on Long Island. It didn't take long for other schools to realize what they had missed out on.

In mid-October, with Dartmouth trailing Yale by 3 points, Fiedler took his team 79 yards to a score in the final two minutes. He completed six straight passes and then, after two incompletions, threw a 10-yard touchdown pass to Mike Bobo with 23 seconds remaining to give Dartmouth a 28–24 victory. Two weeks later, Fiedler threw four touchdown passes against Harvard in a 31–31 tie at Cambridge. The Crimson had a chance to win it, lining up for a 27-yard field goal with 30 seconds remaining. But another sophomore quarterback, Harvard's Mike Giardi, dropped the center snap and was late in setting up the ball. The kick by the barefooted Scott

Johnson went directly into the scrimmage line.

Though unable to match Fiedler's passing skills, Giardi also emerged as a standout quarterback and would score 13 touchdowns that season, a Harvard record.

Harvard closed out an Ivy tradition when it traveled to West Point in September. It was the final game between an Ivy League team and Army, which had won 14 of 16 games against the Ivies in the 1980s, including a 56–28 trouncing of Harvard in 1989.

Playing before a crowd of 35,881 at Michie Stadium, the 30-point underdog Crimson stunned the Cadets by taking a 20–7 lead in the third quarter as Giardi threw a 72-yard touchdown pass to fullback Matt Johnson. Army rallied, however, for a pair of touchdowns, the final one with 1 minute 6 seconds left, for a 21–20 victory.

Johnson would have a more spectacular day in November when he ran for 323 yards on 30 carries in a 35–29 victory over Brown, breaking the Ivy League single-game rushing record set the previous year by Cornell's Scott Oliaro.

Cornell booked a strange matchup for mid-October, visiting Stanford. Though the Pacific-10 team's record was only 1-3 going in, its talent pool hailed from a world unfamiliar to Cornell. Stanford frolicked, 56–6.

Princeton had a big name in its lineup that autumn—a Tarkenton. When the Tigers played at Brown in October, father Fran was on hand to watch his son, Matt, a wide receiver. But a couple of other Tigers were dazzling that day.

Michael Lerch tied a college football record for most receiving yardage in a game when he racked up 370 yards on only nine passes, scoring on throws of 45, 64, 79, and 90 yards from quarterback Chad Roghair in a 59–37 rout. And a sophomore from Lacey Township, New Jersey, named Keith Elias displayed speed and elusiveness, running for 110 yards at the outset of a remarkable college career.

The Ivy race came down to the final Saturday when Dartmouth (5-0-1) faced Princeton (5-1) at Hanover. Dartmouth dominated on a muddy field as Al Rosier, the school's career rushing leader, ran for 190 yards on 35 carries in a 31–13 victory.

It was the first outright title for Dartmouth since 1978, when Coach Buddy Teevens was the co-captain and star quarterback.

After the game, the Ivy League championship bowl was presented to Teevens in the Alumni Gym. "It's great," he said, "because we don't have to share it with anyone." Teevens himself would no longer be sharing football wisdom with Dartmouth players. Ten days later he rode his success out of the Ivy League, taking the coaching job at Tulane.

Dartmouth's Fiedler and Princeton's Elias would dominate again in 1992.

The new Dartmouth coach, John Lyons, got off to a good start as Fiedler threw five touchdown passes in the second half of a 36–17 victory over Penn. Fiedler fired four more in a 39–27 triumph over Yale and by then had set a Dartmouth career record with 28 scoring passes.

Though slowed by an ankle injury early in the season, Elias was rolling up the

Princeton's Keith Elias in action against Yale in 1992 en route to setting a school single-season rushing mark. (PRINCETON UNIVERSITY)

yardage. By mid-November, when he ran for 140 yards in Princeton's 36–7 victory over Yale, he had achieved a single-year school rushing mark of 1,368 yards.

Princeton also had a throwback to the days of one-platoon football in Lerch, the 5-foot-7-inch, 160-pound receiver who also played defensive end in passing situations. In Princeton's 21–6 victory over Harvard, Lerch recorded two and a half sacks and blocked an extra point. Two weeks later, in a 20–14 triumph over Penn, he caught a 70-yard touchdown pass, gained 21 yards on a reverse run, and ran back four punts for 41 yards. But that wasn't all. In the final seconds, he nailed Penn quarterback Jim McGeehan as he sought to throw for a winning touchdown from the Princeton 23.

Columbia had an iron man of sorts in 5-foot-11-inch, 230-pound Des Werthman, who was listed as an inside linebacker but also ran from an I formation.

Werthman scored all three Columbia touchdowns and had 22 tackles, 17 of them solo, in a 38–19 loss to Dartmouth. In mid-November, he played a huge role in smashing Cornell's bid for an Ivy title. The Big Red had broken Dartmouth's 15-game Ivy unbeaten streak late in October and came to Wien Stadium with only one loss in league play and a seven-game winning streak. Werthman was hardly intimidated. He made 16 tackles, had two fumble recoveries, returned a blocked punt 24 yards to the Cornell 4, and on the next play carried the ball in for a score. He later had another touchdown, scored a 2-point conversion on a reception, and kicked two extra points. With quarterback Chad Andrzejewski, the Ivies' leader in passage yardage for the season, throwing for 294 yards and Mike Sardo tying a school record with 13 receptions, Columbia emerged with a 35–30 victory.

The following Saturday, Werthman tacked on three more rushing touchdowns—gaining 114 yards—in a 34–28 victory over Brown to give the Lions their first two-game winning streak since 1978.

It was all very simple to Werthman—just different shades of power football.

"As a linebacker, I'd rather hit than be hit," he said. "It's the same thing running with the ball. You try to hit them first."

For the second straight season, the Ivy race came down to the final Saturday's Dartmouth-Princeton game. Dartmouth tied Princeton for the title with a 34–20 victory as Jay Fiedler passed for 272 yards and two touchdowns and carried the ball himself for another score. Keith Elias ran for two touchdowns and 207 yards, finish-

ing the season as college football's leading rusher with an average of 157 yards per game.

The football season's social highlight was celebrated at Yale Bowl during halftime of the Yale-Fordham game. Rori Myers, Class of 1992, and Jim Lockman, Class of 1989—former members of the Yale band—were married in a ceremony on the 50-yard line with the band providing accompaniment.

"It's not the craziest thing the band has ever done," said Myers. "Blowing up a drum on the field—that, I'd say, was crazier."

Before the 1993 season got under way, the Ivy League struck a blow at such cute nicknames as Dartmouth's Pea Green squad, Yale's Bull Pups, and Harvard's Yardlings. The Ivies decided to forgo their freshman football programs and allow first-year players to join the varsity teams.

But in emulating the rest of the college football world, the league was not seeking to go big time again. This was actually an economy move. The Ivy presidents agreed to cut the number of annually recruited freshmen players from 50 to 35 per team. That was considered too few to field freshmen squads for six-game schedules.

Dartmouth, seeking a fourth straight Ivy title, figured to fight it out once again with Princeton as Jay Fiedler and Keith Elias entered their senior seasons.

But Penn had an outstanding junior tailback in Terrance Stokes—the one-man gang in its single-back offense—a good quarterback in Jim McGeehan (his brother John helped Penn win Ivy titles in 1983 and

1984), and four all-Ivy choices returning on a defense led by linebackers Pat Goodwillie and Andy Berlin.

Penn was at home to Dartmouth on the first Saturday in what what was expected to be one of the season's biggest games. But a complication arose—the sort of snafu that could occur only in the Ivy League. The new rule allowing freshmen to play stated that they couldn't see action if their orientation programs were still going on. Dartmouth's was, so none of its first-year players were in uniform. Penn was also forbidden to play any freshmen lest it gain an unfair edge.

Operating from a no-huddle offense, McGeehan connected seven times with the 6-foot-4-inch sophomore receiver Miles Macik while the 156-pound Stokes ran for 129 yards. Fiedler, operating on a wet field, was pressured by the Penn defenders, slipped a few times, fumbled two snaps, and hit only one scoring pass. Penn emerged with a 10–6 victory and seemed ready for a formidable season.

On the first Saturday of November,

Dartmouth quarterback Jay Fiedler, having tormented Princeton in the game deciding the 1992 Ivy title, was voted the league's outstanding player. He won the Asa S. Bushnell Cup—named for a longtime college sports official who happened to be a Princeton grad. (DARTMOUTH COLLEGE)

Penn met Princeton in a matchup of unbeaten teams.

Princeton had warmed up for that game with a 14–3 victory over Columbia on a rainy afternoon at Palmer Stadium as Elias ran for 226 yards—his 12th consecutive 100-yard-plus game. During halftime, as what passed for the Columbia band—a dozen alleged musicians—went through its routine, an announcement over the public address system stated that Elias had suffered an ankle injury in the second quarter and might not return. But soon there was another message from the press box—by a Princeton spokesman. It had been a Columbia prank.

Elias was indeed healthy and looking forward to facing Penn. "It's the battle of the undefeateds—it doesn't get any better than this," he said. "It's like Wrestlemania."

That wasn't all he had to say. In an interview a few days later, trash-talking Ivy style, Elias claimed that Penn had an unfair advantage over his team—it had recruited many players who didn't have the grades to get into Princeton.

Scores of Penn alumni sent faxes of the interview to Penn Coach Al Bagnoli, expressing outrage at Elias, and the sports editor of the *Daily Pennsylvanian* called the Princeton star "a loudmouth."

At halftime of the game, Penn's marching band retaliated with a routine that spelled out telephone procedures for admission to Princeton:

Penn's Terrance Stokes leaves a Dartmouth defender behind. (UNIVERSITY OF PENNSYLVANIA)

Press 1 if your father went to Princeton.

Press 2 if your grandfather went to Princeton.

Press 3 if you were a bad child actress [à la Brooke Shields, Princeton 1987].

Press 4 if you're a white Anglo-Saxon Protestant.

The Penn players also answered back.

Elias had been given a Mohawk haircut by his quarterback, Joel Foote (he'd never lost a game after seven previous Mohawks), but was not so ferocious on the field. He had been averaging 184 yards a game, but was held to 59 yards on 15 carries. He was outshone by Stokes, Division I-AA's leading rusher, who ran for a Penn single-game record of 272 yards on 42 carries.

Penn outmaneuvered Princeton by sending its talented wide receivers, Macik and Chris Brassell, downfield and then giving the football to Stokes for big-yardage draw plays. Princeton sabotaged itself by fumbling eight times and couldn't even get the center snap right—Foote and center John Nied fouled it up four times.

The Quakers came away with a 30–14 victory before a Franklin Field crowd of 35,810.

Stokes, a product of a single-parent home, from the inner-city Trenton Central High School (hardly the image popularly associated with Princeton men), was asked afterward if he felt badly for Elias. "I don't feel any sympathy for Keith Elias," he said. "He flapped his mouth and he didn't back it up."

The following weekend, Penn was almost knocked off by Harvard in Coach Joe Restic's last home game. Retiring after 23 years at Cambridge, Restic was saluted at halftime when players from every team he had coached gathered at midfield and passed a ceremonial football along to him. Harvard was leading by 10 points in the third quarter and was driving for another touchdown. But fullback David Sprinkle fumbled on a play that began at the 4-yard line, and two plays later McGeehan combined with Stokes on an 80-yard touchdown pass. Penn went on to a 27–20 victory in what Restic called "a bittersweet" home finale. (He came close again against Yale at New Haven, but a Crimson rally fell short in a 33–31 loss.)

Penn went into the final Saturday against Cornell—their centennial matchup—with a 6-0 Ivy mark. Dartmouth and Princeton, facing each other, were at 5-1.

Penn was trailing by 14–0 midway through the third quarter, but struck back for a pair of touchdowns. With less than six minutes remaining, the Quakers' Marc Horowitz kicked a 31-yard field goal for a 17–14 victory. Penn emerged with a 10-0 season and the Ivy title.

Dartmouth beat Princeton for the fourth straight season in the final college encounter between Fiedler and Elias. (They would go on to pro teams who were long-standing rivals, the Eagles and Giants.) The Dartmouth quarterback passed for two touchdowns, the Princeton running back went in for two more, but with Penn finishing off a perfect season,

Dartmouth's 28–22 victory meant nothing in the Ivy title race.

Springtime 1994 brought some unusual sightings on Ivy football fields—players in pads hitting blocking sleds. For the first time since 1952, spring practice was permitted.

The preparation paid off on the first Saturday of October when seven Ivy teams won against nonleague opponents (Penn was idle). Five victories came against Patriot League squads—not especially strong teams—but Yale's 28–17 triumph over Connecticut, a member of the more competitive Yankee Conference, was its first in the rivalry since 1987.

There was even cautious optimism at Columbia when the season opened. The Lions had two good quarterbacks—Jamie Schwalbe for the passing game and Mike Cavanaugh as a running threat—along with an outstanding two-way player in Marcus Wiley, a 245-pound defensive end and running back.

But Columbia had lost its previous 15 openers, all to Harvard, so when the Crimson came to Wien Stadium to start the season, Coach Ray Tellier was apprehensive.

"You don't fall into that same trap of 'here we go again,'" he said.

It seemed Columbia would break the slide when the Lions battled back from an 18-point deficit to take a 32–31 lead with just under five minutes remaining on Wiley's 1-yard plunge. (Wiley was so excited that he went into an exuberant victory celebration, costing Columbia a 15-yard penalty. Joe Aldrich put the Lions ahead with a 35-yard extra point.)

But Harvard went on an 82-yard drive and, with 21 seconds remaining, quarterback Vin Ferrara scored on a 4-yard run. The Crimson emerged with a 39–32 victory in the Harvard coaching debut of Tim Murphy, recruited from the University of Cincinnati to succeed Joe Restic.

The following Saturday, there was more frustration for Columbia. Schwalbe completed a 26-yard, fourth-down touchdown pass to Justin Fossbender with 12 seconds left to put the Lions into a 28–28 tie with Lehigh. But then disaster struck again. Aldrich may have been good from 35 yards out the week before, but this time Lehigh's Rich Owens blocked the extra-point attempt. A sure victory turned into a disappointing tie.

But the Lions beat Lafayette and Fordham the next two Saturdays, then played well against a Penn team carrying a 15-game winning streak before losing to the Quakers by 12–3.

After that, Columbia went up to New Haven and routed Yale by 30–9 as Schwalbe threw for 265 yards and completed nine passes to his 6-foot-4-inch, 230-pound tight end Brian Bassett, the Ivies' leading receiver.

The season would end on an exasperating down note as Columbia took a 24-point lead against Brown into the third quarter, only to see the visiting Bears score eight straight touchdowns for a 59–27 romp.

But Columbia finished at 5-4-1 for its first winning season since 1971.

It was an even better year for Brown, which went 7-3 under a new coach, the former Bears' quarterback Mark Whipple, following six straight losing seasons.

The Bears' 59-point spree against Columbia tied an Ivy record set by Princeton in 1991. And the offensive deluge, with four touchdowns coming from the junior tailback Paul Fichiera, represented the most points scored by Brown since a 62–3 laugher against the Camp Kilmer, New Jersey, army base back in 1943.

Penn, led by running back Terrance Stokes and wide receiver Miles Macik, figured to be the class of the league once more and had a fine beginning despite a fashion disaster.

A laundry fire a few days before the season-opener destroyed the team's road uniforms. So when Penn faced Dartmouth at Hanover, the squads made a switch, the Quakers wearing their blue home jerseys while Dartmouth dressed in road white.

This promised to be the game of the season since Penn was the defending, unbeaten champion and Dartmouth the runner-up. It was a good one, coming down to the final minute. Trailing by 4 points, Dartmouth was poised to go ahead, but its top runner, Pete Oberle, was stopped a yard short of the Penn goal line on fourth down by Pat Goodwillie, the Quakers' all-Ivy linebacker. Penn then took a safety and came away with a 13–11 victory.

Cornell, not Dartmouth, emerged as the main challenger to Penn. Led by an outstanding running back in sophomore Chad Levitt, the Big Red went to 6-0. But then quarterback Per Larson hurt his knee early in the Brown game and Cornell was

upset, 16–3. The next week Cornell lost to Yale, and the race was essentially over.

Penn finished at 9-0, running its winning streak to 21 games and breaking the Division I-AA consecutive-game streak of 20 set by Holy Cross in 1990 and 1991. But the record-breaker didn't come easily. Trailing Cornell by 11 points going into the fourth quarter of the season-ender, Penn needed a 1-yard scoring run by Stokes with less than two minutes left to emerge with an 18–14 victory at Ithaca.

The Quakers won their first three games in 1995, then came into Wien Stadium to face a Columbia team that had gotten off to an exhilarating start. For the first time since 1979, the Lions had beaten Harvard in their customary season-opener.

Penn outgained Columbia by 441 yards to 292 on a drizzly afternoon, but Joe Cormier, the Lions' free safety, picked off a couple of passes, his first interception leading to a 34-yard touchdown run by quarterback Mike Cavanaugh. Columbia took the lead for good on Roy Hanks's 39-yard punt return in the third quarter and emerged with a 24–14 victory that ended Penn's winning streak at 24 games.

Princeton, meanwhile, was rolling along with a terrific defense led by tackle Dave Patterson and an offense featuring tailback Marc Washington, receiver Kevin Duffy, and alternating quarterbacks, Harry Nakielny for drop-back passing and Brock Harvey for option plays.

Three weeks after knocking off Penn, Columbia faced Princeton at Palmer Stadium, each team 3-0 in Ivy play. This time

Columbia looked like the Lions of old, throwing seven interceptions and fumbling the ball away twice, as Princeton romped, 44–14.

"Midterms were this week, but we had as good a week of practice as we've had all year," observed the Tigers' coach, Steve Tosches. "They were very attentive, full of energy. Probably flunked all of their tests."

The following weekend, playing before 34,504 at Franklin Field, Princeton sacked Penn quarterback Mark DeRosa five times and came away with a 22–9 victory.

The Tigers went into their game with Yale at 8-0 while the Elis were stumbling at 2-6.

The weekend started off on a spectacular note for Princeton when Gordon Y. S. Wu, a Princeton-trained engineer who was one of Hong Kong's wealthiest men, donated $100 million to the School of Engineering and Applied Sciences, the largest cash gift ever by a foreigner to an American university.

It seemed that Princeton, playing at home, would enjoy a superb football Saturday as well. On the Tigers' first play from scrimmage, Brock Harvey ran 92 yards for a score. But Yale stayed in the game and trailed by 6 points in the fourth quarter. Then the Elis mounted a drive climaxed by Kena Heffernan's 4-yard touchdown run with 3:35 left. The extra point gave Yale a 14–13 edge. With 57 seconds left, Yale linebacker Matt Sisosky recovered a fumble by Harvey in the Tiger end zone to cap a huge 21–13 upset.

Now Princeton's visions of an outright title were clouded. Cornell, led as usual by the running of Chad Levitt and passing of Steve Joyce, beat Columbia, 35–14, for its fifth consecutive league triumph after a loss to Princeton. Dartmouth defeated Brown while Penn was beating Harvard, keeping them in the race as well.

Going into the final Saturday, a deadlock at the top involving half the Ivy League was in sight. Princeton and Cornell each had one defeat, Dartmouth and Penn two losses apiece. If Dartmouth beat Princeton and Penn topped Cornell, there would be an unprecedented four-way tie for the championship.

Penn jumped off to a 21–0 lead over Cornell and rolled to a 37–18 victory in Philadelphia. Dartmouth was within seconds of creating that four-way deadlock, holding a 3-point edge over Princeton at Hanover as their game wound down. But the Tigers staged a 15-play drive ending with Alex Sierk's 18-yard field goal on the final snap to manage a 10–10 tie.

Finishing its Ivy season at 5-1-1, Princeton staggered to its first outright championship since the undefeated squad of 1964, winding up a half-game ahead of Cornell and Penn.

But the biggest crowd of the Ivy season turned out at Yale Bowl where 35,103 weathered a cold rain to watch the 112th renewal of The Game.

Harvard had beaten only Colgate and seemed headed for its lone season without a single Ivy victory since formal play had begun in 1956. Yale was coming off its upset of unbeaten Princeton.

But the Crimson prevailed, 22–21, as tailback Eion Hu—having become the first Harvard player to exceed 1,000 rushing yards two years in a row—scored the winning touchdown on a 3-yard run with 29 seconds remaining.

After Yale's upset victory over Princeton, Carm Cozza had made a remark that he—or any other Ivy coach—could have repeated on this final Saturday of the Ivies' 40th league season.

The coach was now in his 31st autumn at Yale. He had surveyed dozens of encounters among evenly matched teams of young men whose horizons extended far beyond the Heisman Trophy.

As Cozza put it: "This is the Ivy League—nothing surprises you."

APPENDIX
IVY LEAGUE CHAMPIONS:
THE FIRST 40 YEARS

Year	Team	IVY RECORD	Year	Team	IVY RECORD
1956	Yale	7-0-0	1976	Brown	6-1-0
				Yale	6-1-0
1957	Princeton	6-1-0	1977	Yale	6-1-0
1958	Dartmouth	6-1-0	1978	Dartmouth	6-1-0
1959	Pennsylvania	6-1-0	1979	Yale	6-1-0
1960	Yale	7-0-0	1980	Yale	6-1-0
1961	Columbia	6-1-0	1981	Dartmouth	6-1-0
	Harvard	6-1-0		Yale	6-1-0
1962	Dartmouth	7-0-0	1982	Dartmouth	5-2-0
1963	Dartmouth	5-2-0		Harvard	5-2-0
	Princeton	5-2-0		Pennsylvania	5-2-0
1964	Princeton	7-0-0	1983	Harvard	5-1-1
1965	Dartmouth	7-0-0		Pennsylvania	5-1-1
1966	Dartmouth	6-1-0	1984	Pennsylvania	7-0-0
	Harvard	6-1-0	1985	Pennsylvania	6-1-0
	Princeton	6-1-0	1986	Pennsylvania	7-0-0
1967	Yale	7-0-0	1987	Harvard	6-1-0
1968	Harvard	6-0-1	1988	Cornell	6-1-0
	Yale	6-0-1		Pennsylvania	6-1-0
1969	Dartmouth	6-1-0	1989	Princeton	6-1-0
	Princeton	6-1-0		Yale	6-1-0
	Yale	6-1-0	1990	Cornell	6-1-0
1970	Dartmouth	7-0-0		Dartmouth	6-1-0
1971	Cornell	6-1-0	1991	Dartmouth	6-0-1
	Dartmouth	6-1-0	1992	Dartmouth	6-1-0
1972	Dartmouth	5-1-1		Princeton	6-1-0
1973	Dartmouth	6-1-0	1993	Pennsylvania	7-0-0
1974	Harvard	6-1-0	1994	Pennsylvania	7-0-0
	Yale	6-1-0	1995	Princeton	5-1-1
1975	Harvard	6-1-0			

COMPOSITE IVY STANDINGS, 1956–1995

| | RECORD IN LEAGUE PLAY | | | CHAMPIONSHIPS | |
	Wins	Losses	Ties	Outright	Tied
Dartmouth	186	85	9	8	8
Yale	168	104	8	6	6
Princeton	162	113	5	3	5
Harvard	156	115	9	2	6
Pennsylvania	132	144	4	6	3
Cornell	129	146	5	0	3
Brown	100	173	7	0	1
Columbia	61	214	5	0	1

BIBLIOGRAPHY

Back when Harvard, Princeton, and Yale were truly the Big Three of college football, their matchups inspired press coverage on a scale approaching the World Series and Super Bowl outpourings of today. In looking to newspaper accounts of Ivy Saturdays, I found the *New York Times* to be especially helpful.

BOOKS

Beale, Morris A. *The History of Football at Harvard, 1874–1948*. Washington: Columbia Publishing, 1948.

Bergin, Thomas G. *The Game: The Harvard-Yale Football Rivalry, 1875–1983*. New Haven: Yale University Press, 1984.

Bishop, Morris. *A History of Cornell*. Ithaca: Cornell University Press, 1962.

Boyle, Robert H. *Sport: Mirror of American Life*. Boston: Little, Brown, 1963.

Brady, John T. *The Heisman: A Symbol of Excellence*. New York: Atheneum, 1984.

Brondfield, Jerome. *Rockne: The Coach, the Man, the Legend*. New York: Random House, 1976.

Bynum, Mike, editor. *Pop Warner: Football's Greatest Teacher*. Gridiron Football Properties, 1993.

Cohane, Tim. *Great College Football Coaches of the Twenties and Thirties*. New Rochelle, N.Y.: Arlington House, 1973.

———. *The Yale Football Story*. New York: G. P. Putnam's Sons, 1951.

College Football's Twenty-five Greatest Teams. St. Louis: The Sporting News Publishing Co., 1988.

Danzig, Allison. *Oh, How They Played the Game*. New York: Macmillan, 1971.

Dubois, Diana, editor. *My Harvard, My Yale*. New York: Random House, 1982.

Eisenhammer, Fred and Eric B. Sondheimer. *College Football's Most Memorable Games, 1913 Through 1990*. Jefferson, N.C.: McFarland, 1992.

Ford, Gerald R. *A Time to Heal*. New York: Harper & Row, 1979.

Grange, Harold E., as told to Ira Morton. *The Red Grange Story*. New York: G. P. Putnam's Sons, 1953.

Hill, Dean. *Football Through the Years*. New York: Gridiron Publishing, 1940.

Kane, Robert J. *Good Sports: A History of Cornell Athletics*. Ithaca: Cornell University, 1992.

Martin, Ralph G. *Seeds of Destruction: Joe Kennedy and His Sons.* New York: G.P. Putnam's Sons, 1995.

McCallum, John. *Ivy League Football Since 1872.* New York: Stein and Day, 1977.

McCallum, John and Charles H. Pearson. *College Football U.S.A., 1869–1973.* New York: Hall of Fame Publishing, 1973.

Newhouse, Dave. *After the Glory: Heisman.* St. Louis: The Sporting News Publishing Co., 1985.

Rice, Grantland. *The Tumult and the Shouting.* New York: A. S. Barnes, 1954.

Robinson, Ray. *Iron Horse: Lou Gehrig in His Time.* New York: W. W. Norton, 1990.

Rottenberg, Dan. *Fight on Pennsylvania: A Century of Red and Blue Football.* Philadelphia: The Trustees of the University of Pennsylvania, 1985.

Schreiner, Samuel A., Jr. *A Place Called Princeton.* New York: Arbor House, 1984.

Schwartz, Charles. *Cole Porter: A Biography.* New York: The Dial Press, 1977.

Sperber, Murray. *Shake Down the Thunder: The Creation of Notre Dame Football.* New York: Henry Holt, 1993.

Stiles, Maxwell. *The Rose Bowl.* Los Angeles: Sportsmaster Publications.

Turnbull, Andrew. *Scott Fitzgerald.* New York: Charles Scribner's Sons, 1962.

Weyand, Alexander M. *Football Immortals.* New York: Macmillan, 1962.

Whittingham, Richard. *Saturday Afternoon.* New York: Workman, 1985.

ARTICLES AND BOOKLETS

"Albie Booth—Yale's Bare-Legged Jumping Bean." *The Literary Digest,* Nov. 23, 1929.

Baltzell, E. Digby. "Goodbye to All That." *Society,* January/February 1994.

Barry, Jay. "Heisman." *Brown Alumni Monthly,* December 1972.

"Barry Wood—Harvard's Football Meteor." *The Literary Digest,* Nov. 14, 1931.

"Cambridge to Pasadena and Return." Author unknown. Privately printed in 1920; reprinted by Harvard Varsity Club, 1994.

Crichton, Kyle. "Quick, Harlow, the Needle." *Collier's,* Oct. 12, 1935.

Daley, Arthur. "The Fabulous Herman Hickman." *The New York Times Magazine,* Oct. 28, 1951.

Deford, Frank. "B.D." *Sports Illustrated,* Sept. 5, 1988.

Drake, Ross. "On Harvard-Yale." *People,* Nov. 25, 1983.

Fimrite, Ron. "Hobey Baker: A Flame That Burned Too Brightly." *Sports Illustrated,* March 18, 1991.

Frank, Stanley. "He Doesn't Have to Win." *The Saturday Evening Post,* Nov. 16, 1946.

———. "The Man Who Saved the Day for Yale." *The Saturday Evening Post,* September/October 1953.

"Fritz." *Brown Alumni Monthly,* October 1970.

Green, Theodore Francis. "How the Brown Bear Came to Brown." *Brown Alumni Monthly,* 1923.

Hall, Robert A., with Arnold Nicholson. "Cornell Goes to the Movies." *The Saturday Evening Post,* Oct. 26, 1940.

"Harvard-Oregon Football Game in Pasadena." *The Literary Digest,* Jan. 17, 1920.

"Haughton Deserts Harvard for Columbia." *The Literary Digest,* May 29, 1923.

Heffelfinger, W. W. (Pudge), with George Trevor. "Nobody Put Me on My Back." *The Saturday Evening Post,* Oct. 15, 1938, and "Football's Golden Age." *The Saturday Evening Post,* Oct. 29, 1938.

Hickman, Herman. "The Coach's 90-Day Headache." *The New York Times Magazine,* Nov. 1, 1953.

"Ivy League Directory and Record Book—1995–96." Council of Ivy Group Presidents, Princeton, New Jersey.

Kelley, Larry, with George Trevor. "Everybody

There Saw Kelley." *The Saturday Evening Post,* Oct. 16, 1937, and Oct. 23, 1937.

Lambert, Craig. "The Greatest College Prank of All Time." *Harvard Magazine,* November/December 1990.

Lewis, Lincoln. "Ivy League Mascots."

Lieber, Jill. "A Big Win for the Big Red." *Sports Illustrated,* Nov. 28, 1988.

Lippmann, Walter. "Legendary John Reed." *The New Republic,* Dec. 16, 1914.

Mano, D. Keith. "Don't Laugh..." *TV Guide,* Oct. 22–28, 1988.

Martin, John Stuart. "Walter Camp and His Gridiron Game." *American Heritage,* October 1961.

Montgomery, Cliff. "Recalling Columbia's Startling Trip to the Rose Bowl." *The New York Times,* Dec. 27, 1981.

Montville, Leigh. "Penn and Needles." *Sports Illustrated,* Nov. 15, 1993.

Norris, Edwin M. "Some Recollections of John Prentiss Poe Jr." *Princeton Alumni Weekly.*

Olderman, Murray. "Ivy League Revolutionary." *The Saturday Evening Post,* Nov. 8, 1958.

"Palmer's Princely Present." *Princeton Alumni Weekly,* Oct. 8, 1954.

Peabody, Endicott. "On the Road to All-American." *Harvard Gazette,* June 7, 1990.

Reynolds, Quentin. "Bewildering Lou." *Collier's,* Oct. 12, 1934.

Riordan, Leo. "The Football Blues Hit Penn." *The Saturday Evening Post,* Nov. 7, 1953.

Rudolph, Jack W. "Rutgers Muzzles the Tigers." *American History Illustrated,* October 1980.

Schwed, Peter. "The 1889 Super Bowl." *Esquire,* October 1980.

Siler, Tom. "The Prayin' Colonels." *Sports Illustrated,* Nov. 8, 1954.

Smith, Red. "They Weep No More at Princeton." *The Saturday Evening Post,* Oct. 11, 1947.

Sunness, Sheldon. "Ivy Leaguers in the N.F.L." *The New York Times Magazine,* Dec. 7, 1986.

Watkins, T. H. "Remington and the Eli Eleven." *American Heritage,* October/November 1981.

Watterson, John S. "Inventing Modern Football." *American Heritage,* September/October 1988.

Wetherbee, Sedgwick. "How Harvard (With the Help of McGill) Saved Football for America." *Harvard Magazine,* October 1973.

Wind, Herbert Warren. "Harvard Never Loses at Halftime." *Collier's,* November 1951.

INDEX